BLACK DAHLIA AVENGER III

BLACK DAHLIA AVENGER III

STEVE HODEL

A VIREO BOOK | RARE BIRD BOOKS

LOS ANGELES, CALIF.

THIS IS A GENUINE VIREO BOOK

A Vireo Book | Rare Bird Books
453 South Spring Street, Suite 302
Los Angeles, CA 90013
rarebirdbooks.com

FIRST TRADE PAPERBACK ORIGINAL EDITION

Set in Dante
Printed in the United States

10 9 8 7 6 5 4 3 2 1

Publisher's Cataloging-in-Publication data available upon request.

Publisher's Cataloging-in-Publication data
Names: Hodel, Steve, 1941–, author.
Title: Black Dahlia Avenger III / Steve Hodel.
Series: Black Dahlia Avenger
Description: Includes bibliographical references. | First Trade Paperback Original
Edition | A Vireo Book | New York, NY; Los Angeles, CA: Rare Bird Books, 2018.
Identifiers: ISBN 9781945572975
Subjects: LCSH Short, Elizabeth, 1924–1947. | Hodel, George. | Murder—
California—Los Angeles—Case studies. | Murder—Investigation—California—
Los Angeles—Case studies. | BISAC TRUE CRIME / Murder / General
Classification: LCC HV6534.L7 H63 2018 | DDC 364.152/3/0979494—dc23

Contents

PREFACE

DURING MY ACTIVE YEARS as an LAPD detective III homicide supervisor, I was required to review and approve what the department referred to as "Homicide Progress Reports."

The department manual required that these reports be submitted by the assigned homicide detectives *every six months on any active and unsolved murder investigation.*

Additionally, if the case were solved and a filing obtained with the LADA's office, any "new evidence" that the detectives may have developed, post-arrest, would be required to be extensively detailed in a follow-up report.

I would ask that my readers consider this publication of *Black Dahlia Avenger III* just that.

It is my newest follow-up report to you on my ongoing investigation, which now spans some nineteen years (1999-2018).

During those years I have presented four books: *Black Dahlia Avenger* (2003), *Most Evil* (2009), *Black Dahlia Avenger II* (2014), and *Most Evil II* (2015).

Four separate books, which include twenty-five crimes, committed in a dozen separate police jurisdictions, but yet they remain—*one suspect. One investigation.*

In effect, the publications are really my ongoing "progress reports."

Consequently, to understand the big picture and how George Hodel's crime signatures all interlink, ideally one needs to read all four (now five) books.

We discover that each of his crimes builds on the previous and George Hodel's MO and signatures from the distant past become "variations on a theme" in his later ones.

By example, his taunts and mailings as the Chicago Lipstick Killer morphed into his mailings as "Black Dahlia Avenger," which then two decades later became entwined in his letters to the press as "Zodiac."

In *Black Dahlia Avenger III*, I present dramatic new evidence and new exhibits further linking my father, Dr. George Hill Hodel, to the Black Dahlia and other LA Lone Women Murder crimes of the 1940s.

Also, I present additional new linkage further connecting him to the Chicago Lipstick Murders and to the San Francisco Bay Area crimes where he reinvented himself using the pseudonym, "Zodiac."

Separate from the actual crime investigation, I have also included new chapters taking a deeper dive into the Hodel personal family connections.

Included in these are George Hodel's "Cast of Characters" listing his direct personal acquaintance with many hitherto unnamed Hollywood personalities.

There is a full chapter on my half sister, Tamar Nais Hodel, and her remarkable life, along with a never-before-published ninety-minute interview, transcribed in full, from a video interview she did at my request back in 2004.

Her first-person description of our father, her sexual victimization by him and others, and her ongoing love and fear of him are both heartbreaking and riveting.

Because of the historical importance of my father and his serial crimes and their direct connection to the City of Los Angeles in the 1940s, I have examined his influence on Hollywood and classic films in a chapter entitled "Reel Life Crimes."

We then follow Dr. George Hodel to Hawaii and "A New Life and New Wife" after he fled Los Angeles to avoid arrest and prosecution for several of his LA crimes.

I close this follow-up investigation with a short summary and review of each of the (to date) twenty-five crimes George Hodel committed as Chicago's "Lipstick Murderer, Los Angeles's "Black Dahlia Avenger," and San Francisco's "Zodiac."

As of this writing, I am actively continuing my ongoing investigation of "The Early Years" which will examine and present my father's serial murders in the 1920s and 1930s.

1

A New Man Ray Nexus: "Les Invendables" (The Unsalables) 1969

I N LATE DECEMBER 2016, while I was conducting some internet research in preparation for an interview scheduled for the seventieth anniversary of the Black Dahlia murder, I chanced upon a Man Ray lithograph that I had never seen before.

It was a poster announcing a Man Ray exhibition, "Les Invendables" (The Unsalables), to be held at the Galerie Alphonse Chave in Vence, France.

The Man Ray drawings would be on exhibit at the gallery in April and May 1969.

Further searches led me to the discovery of an online 1969 original brochure/catalog announcing the exhibit, which included an introduction by Man Ray written in French.

1969 Man Ray "Les Invendables" Alphonse Chave gallery catalog with introduction by Man Ray

On December 27, 2016, I sent the below short email to my good friend Yves Person in Paris, asking if he might translate Man Ray's words. Yves is the high school teacher who "cracked the Zodiac cipher" after discovering that George Hodel used the ancient Celtic "tree alphabet," OGHAM, to sign his name "HODEL" in an authenticated cipher Zodiac mailed to the *San Francisco Chronicle* in 1970. (See *Most Evil II*, Rare Bird Books 2015, Chapter 10 for complete details of Mssr. Person's decryption and solving of the Zodiac cipher.)

Paris high school teacher, Mssr. Yves Person 2015

My email to YP:

Dear Yves,

Between gradings could you take a peek at the attached text which Man Ray wrote for the 1969 catalog *Les Invendables*? Anything there of interest? How do you interpret the name he uses? The unsellables? Meaning works that he would not or could not sell? Or works that did not sell? Any clue in his written text? (attached)

Best, Steve

YP's response with translation:

Steve,

As I translated it in a previous message, "les invendables" means: "things that couldn't be sold." One says: "C'est invendable!" to speak of something too ugly or too damaged for someone to sell it.

Yves then provided me with his translation of Man Ray's words as written in the catalog:

"The unsalable. Why? Because the name is the only thing which is for sale. Without a signature, the picture is worthless. You must buy (take) them both (away) (at the same time).

Some people turn the painting backward to see if it's made out of a good and fine linen canvas. The painter handles his hairy stick as the barber does with his shaving brush, as the musician does with his bow, and as the soldier does with his machine gun; and so they handle their sex to pee or to make love. Truth? Nothing more subversive than truth."

—MAN RAY

The Homage Puzzle—The Fourth Piece

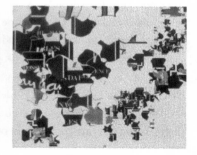

Left to Right: William Copley, Juliet and Man Ray, Gloria De Herrera (Copley's girlfriend at that time), and Marcel Duchamp aboard the SS De Grasse, before departure for Paris, March 12, 1951. Lifelong friends, I refer to these surrealists as "The Three Amigos."

BEFORE THIS DISCOVERY OF Man Ray's 1969 Minotaur poster, we only had three large pieces of the homage puzzle in place. Let's review them.

First, we had George Hodel's 1947 thrice-paid homage to Man Ray—where, as a crime signature, he used the body of his murder victim Elizabeth "Black Dahlia" Short as his canvas and posed her to mimic Man Ray's *Minotaur* (1933) and included the surgical incisions to her body meant to reproduce Man Ray's paintings of *L'Equivoque* (1943) and *The Lovers Lips* (1932–34).

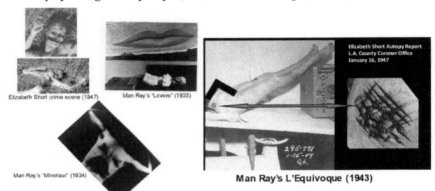

Puzzle Piece No. 1: *Elizabeth Short body posed at crime scene compared to Man Ray's* Minotaur *and* Lover's Lips (Les Amoureux) *and* L'Equivoque.

The second homage (puzzle piece No. 2) came from the surreal artist, William Copley (Amigo No. 1) in his 1961 painting, *It is Midnight Dr. _____*. A wink and a nod *back to* Dr. George Hill Hodel, revealing publicly, albeit in secret, that Copley KNEW the name of the Black Dahlia's surgeon killer and literally spelled the name represented by a surgeon's tools in his *"Alphabet-for-Adults–like"* cipher hidden within the artwork.

Alphabet for Adults was a book published in 1948 by Man Ray and Bill Copley in Los Angeles, while they were actively socializing and remained close friends with Dr. George Hodel.

Much like a child's book or abecedarium, it represented each letter of the alphabet and incorporated them as illustrations, only "for adults."

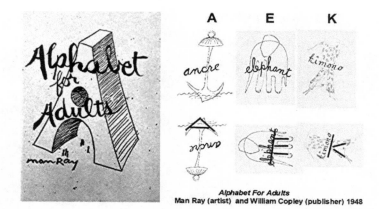

A   E   K

Alphabet For Adults
Man Ray (artist) and William Copley (publisher) 1948

In that publication (a limited edition of five hundred printings), the two surreal artists included a drawing of Dr. George Hodel's magnificent residence, the Sowden/Franklin House. The illustration was drawn to depict a man likely George Hodel and an unidentifiable woman arguing in the inner courtyard and had them represent the letter "Q" for Quarrel.

Exhibit left shows an original page from Alphabet for Adults *representing the letter Q for "querelle" (quarrel). (This exhibit is from the later republished French edition.) The Hodel Sowden House and its inner courtyard (a familiar party location for Man Ray and his fellow artists) are easily architecturally recognizable. Man Ray has included the overhead stone roofline leading directly to the large partitioned sliding glass doors. The object that appears as an "all-seeing eye" is a Man Ray sculpture,* L'Occuliste, *which Man Ray gifted to George Hodel in 1948, the same year as the book was published.*

Bill Copley, Man Ray, and Marcel Duchamp were the closest of friends. In 1951, Copley shut down his Beverly Hills art gallery and traveled with Man Ray and Juliet to Europe to start a new life.

Il est minuit Dr. _____
(It is Midnight Dr._____)
Oil Painting by William Copley, 1961

Note: Copley uses 6 surgical tools (Panel 1) to imply, and from which we infer, the spelling of a doctor's name with which to fill-in the blank. In order to further subtly disguise his naming-meme Copley leaves out the 'arm' between the two 'legs' of the visually perceived 'H' & reverses the 'E's' 'arms' (made visible in Panel 2 &3). The artist's use of these surgical instruments leaves no doubt the 'doctor' in question is a surgeon named **HODEL, MD.**

Panel 1   Panel 2   Panel 3

It is Midnight Dr. **H∘D∃I** ～∘.
HODEL MD

Puzzle Piece No. 2: *Copley's homage to Dr. _____. (Dr. George Hill Hodel)*
(Graphic by Robert J. Sadler)

In addition to the surgical tools cipher, I would also suggest that Copley is giving a second secret homage to his mentor by incorporating Man Ray's *Les Amoureux* (*The Lovers*) lips to form the doctor's mouth. A double entendre both to Man Ray and to suggest his personal knowledge of Dr. Hodel's use of them as part of his Black Dahlia crime signature.

Is it possible?
In this blown-up section of Wm. Copley's "*Il est minuit Dr. ___*" that the full lips of the 'Dr. figure' is an homage to Man Ray's: *A l'heure de l'observatoire, les Amoureux*

The English title: Observatory Time, the Lovers
Man Ray's 1934 painting, oil on canvas depicts full red lips floating in the sky

Man Ray's Les Amoureux, "The Lovers" lips used to shape the doctor's mouth.
(Graphic by Robert .J. Sadler)

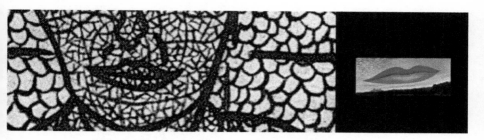

Copley's doctor's lips enlarged and compared to Man Ray's lips in Les Amoureux

Another Copley Cryptogram?

ON MAY 18, 2017, I received the following email and new graphic from my good friend, Robert "Dr. Watson" Sadler, the retired Dallas police officer and private investigator. Robert had previously assisted me by providing many valuable insights during my follow-up investigations, including his addendum chapter, *Essay and Analysis of Zodiac Cryptogram: Scratching the Surface of the Zodiac Ciphers* published in *Most Evil II* (Rare Bird Books 2015).

Steve,

In the 1961 William Copley painting titled: *It is Midnight Dr. _____*, an enigma is portrayed. On a tile-like background covered with scalloped lines, like fish scales, are two figures and six medical instruments. The standing male figure is drawn wearing a herringbone suit, a shirt, and tie, and carrying what one takes (because of the painting's title and the instruments) to be a medical bag in his right hand. The recumbent female figure is nude and lying in the classic *Odalisque*-type pose. The heavily outlined figures and the instruments are filled with crisscrossed curving lines mimicking a cloisonné effect that renders the images darker than the tile-like background.

As previously noted, the upper five instruments to the viewer's right of the "Dr." figure are easily anthropomorphized as emblematic of the letters H O D E L and the lower instrument as M D.

In the same vein as the modern-day hidden digital "Easter Egg," made popular in the 1979 Atari 2600 video game *Adventure*, hidden messages have long been a staple in art expression. Sometimes the "Easter Egg," is only an inside joke, a disguised "trick" of the artist that may or may not be seen or discovered. One example is the recently revealed and previously indecipherable swirls of light in a famous Man Ray photograph *Space Writing* (self-portrait, 1935) to be his backward left-to-right signature that when viewed in a mirror appears a proper right-to-left signature.

(SKH Note: I referenced this photograph earlier in BDA II *in the* George Hill Hodel: A Surrealist Serial Killer *chapter. See below screen grab where I have highlighted Copley's lifelong friend Man Ray's hidden signature in white.)*

Journalist Abby Callard's November 10, 2009, article in Smithsonian Mag.com revealing photographer Ellen Carey's decryption of Man Ray's 1935 ciphered signature.

Robert Sadler's email continues:

> Wondering if there could be any other hidden
> 'letters' in the two thus far unexplored figures of *It
> is Midnight Dr. _____*. I looked closely at the doctor. I was
> struck by the variety of lines used to create the figure.
> Though the "shirt" and "tie" have opposing straight
> lines (the tie 'design' has a brick-like effect), I was drawn
> to the more widely spaced vertical and horizontal lines
> that make up the Dr.'s hatband. I almost immediately
> noticed the lines looked like a series of connected H's.
>
> As I looked closer, I could visualize block letters
> forming the name H O D E L. I thought, "Oh my." I was
> almost satisfied that I might have discovered something
> significant, something definitive. However, that didn't
> cover the entire band. Then I realized I could trace
> enough lines to see two names!
>
> I grabbed a screen capture of Copley's painting and
> opened the image in Photoshop. I was mindful that I did
> not want to "create" anything, add anything to the actual
> image that would distort or change it. I decided to fill
> the hat band with a separate layer of white. I turned the
> opacity down until I could see the vertical, horizontal,
> and edge lines of the hatband. I then took the eraser
> tool and erased the "white" overlaying the individual
> lines that created the two names: GEORGE HODEL.

Right or wrong, this is what I observed in Copley's Dr.'s hatband.

> To demonstrate, I put three equal-sized images of
> the Dr.'s hat, head, and shoulders side by side and then
> put the same three images (only larger) on top of one
> another. The first image (on the left and top) shows the
> hatband as is. In the second image (or middle blow-up)
> you have the same image with the lines making up the
> two names exposed by erasing the white overlay. This
> results in the areas around the specific lines that make
> up GEORGE HODEL shaded white. No lines were

created, just the white overlay was removed that makes the area around the name appear "whited over." In the third image (right side or bottom blow-up) you have the same hatband with the white area now opaque or solid white with only the 'erased' areas or lines that make up GEORGE HODEL left visible.

Again, no lines were added or removed. I only revealed what had been hidden, in plain sight, on the hatband by the series of horizontal and vertical lines in the band.

Robert J. Sadler's "Hat Trick" exhibit as described above.
Are the letters there? Again, I quote my old friend Master Detective Charlie

Chan, "I'd say yes, but facts say maybe." Or, to paraphrase OJ's defense attorney Johnny Cochran, "If the hat's on tight, you must indict."

The third homage, *Etant Donnes*, was presented to us by Marcel Duchamp (Amigo No. 2). Duchamp's friend and fellow surrealist Bill Copley had purchased *Etant Donnes* and gifted it to the Philadelphia Museum of Art after his good friends death.

Duchamp died in France in October 1968, and the public first viewed his *Etant Donnes* in Philadelphia on July 7, 1969.

Duchamp's postmortem secretly pays homage to Dr. George Hodel by revealing his twenty-year project as a duplication and knowledge of Hodel's 1947 crime.

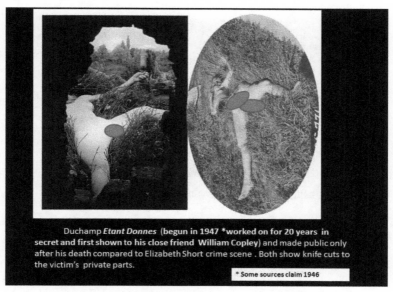

Duchamp *Etant Donnes* (begun in 1947 *worked on for 20 years in secret and first shown to his close friend William Copley) and made public only after his death compared to Elizabeth Short crime scene . Both show knife cuts to the victim's private parts.

* Some sources claim 1946

Puzzle Piece No. 3: Etant Donnes *in imitation of victim Elizabeth Short's body posed at the vacant lot in 1947 Los Angeles.*

The three pieces fit perfectly into place: Hodel's surreal/real masterpiece as homage and a one-upmanship to his fellow surrealists and their later homage as "back at you" from two of the three amigos, Copley and Duchamp.

But why had Dr. Hodel's closest surrealist friend and family photographer, Man Ray, remained silent?

The answer is, he didn't. Man Ray's homage to Hodel was there. I merely had not discovered it. Another purloined letter hiding in plain sight, waiting to be found.

The timing of Man Ray's *Minotaur* public presentation was perfect and obviously planned.

Copley revealed his knowledge of Hodel's crime in his cryptic painting *It is midnight Dr. _____* in 1961.

Duchamp's knowledge of the Hodel crime was revealed nine months after his death in July 1969 in his *Etant Donnes*.

Man Ray's (Amigo No.3) new *Minotaur* as an "unsalable" had its first public viewing in April 1969, just three months before the pending opening of Duchamp exhibit of *Etant Donnes* in the US.

Puzzle Piece No. 4: *First public display April 1969 in Vence, France.*

Man Ray's 1969 *Minotaur* poster is visual proof of what, before its discovery, was what some readers considered simply my own theoretical suppositions.

Man Ray, in this drawing, presents direct evidence of his knowledge that Elizabeth Short was slain by George Hodel and then posed at the vacant lot in imitation of his photograph, *Minotaur*.

What are we seeing in this Man Ray poster?

First, the female model is clearly meant to replicate his earlier 1943 painting, *L'Equivoque*. (Based on and detailed in our earlier investigation, Elizabeth Short was Man Ray's 1943 living model for *L'Equivoque*. See BDA II, Chapter 26.)

Man Ray identifies the 1969 *Minotaur* female as being the same as drawn in his earlier *L'Equivoque*. How? We see her identical breasts, placed in the same position, and they are the same shape and size. He again paints her unique curly hairstyle and, as in the earlier version, makes her face blank sans features. He then applies the same original reddish-brown color (burnt sienna) to the new painting, using it to portray blood flowing from her upper torso outward to create the bull's body. He positions her hands above her head to create the monster's horns, the surrealist's universally recognized gesture for their adopted pet, *Minotaur.*

Inarguably, Man Ray's lithograph, the fourth and final piece of the homage puzzle, is a visual confirmation (along with the Copley and Duchamp artworks) that Man Ray recognized the posing of Elizabeth "Black Dahlia" Short's body was a signature work, a masterpiece, by the artist, George Hodel, the living embodiment of—*Minotaur.*

2

New Clue Further Links Dr. George Hodel to 1947 Dahlia and Red Lipstick Murders

IN LATE SEPTEMBER 2016, I discovered a new "taunting clue" left by my father at the scene of the crime of former actress and aviatrix, Jeanne French (LA's 1947 "Red Lipstick Murder").

Again, the clue had remained in plain sight and readily discoverable all along; I had simply missed it for the past fifteen years.

Before revealing it, let's take a short refresher course of George Hodel's crime-signature MOs as presented earlier in both *Black Dahlia Avenger I & II*.

Chicago Lipstick Murder
January 6, 1946, Chicago, Illinois

> **Chicago Daily Tribune** · · FINAL
> # KIDNAPED GIRL FOUND SLAIN; DISMEMBERED, HID IN SEWER

Suzanne Degnan, age 6

IN THE HORRIFIC KIDNAP-MURDER of little Suzanne Degnan, age six, the child was taken from her home and slain in the basement of a nearby apartment building which detectives determined was "The Murder Room."

A surgical procedure known as a hemicorpectomy was performed (body bisected between the second and third lumbar vertebrae) and her body parts were then placed in various storm drain sewers in the neighborhood. After a tip from an anonymous caller (most likely her killer) advising police to "check the sewers," most of the child's body parts were found, but not all.

Six weeks later, the victim's arms, posed and "bent at the elbows," were discovered, again hidden in a sewer, half a mile from the Murder

Room. As shown in the below *Chicago Daily Tribune* article, the arms had been posed and placed just off Hollywood Street. I quote from that follow-up article, dated February 20, 1946:

> Gruesome discovery of victim Suzanne Degnan's severed arms came six weeks later. On February 19, 1946, a city electrician found them in a sewer three blocks from the Degnan house in an alley just off Hollywood St. As shown above, they were "bent at the elbows, resting palms down."
>
> Dr. Jerry Kearns, the coroner's physician, identified the arms as belonging to the Degnan child and said, "they bore additional evidence of the skill with which the dismemberment of her body was accomplished."

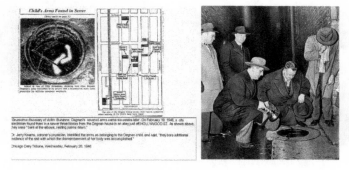

(Left) 1946 Chicago Daily Tribune sketch (Right) Chicago detectives' gruesome discovery off Hollywood St.

Black Dahlia Murder
January 15, 1947, Los Angeles

Elizabeth Short, age 22

ELIZABETH SHORT'S BODY WAS surgically bisected at George Hodel's Hollywood residence. A surgical procedure known as a hemicorporectomy was performed (body bisected between the second and third lumbar vertebrae, identical to the bisection of Suzanne Degnan one year earlier). The two body parts were then transported from the residence to a vacant lot in the Liemert Park district of Los Angeles, some seven miles south of Hollywood.

On January 15, 1947, her body, "arms bent at the elbows," was found posed in public view, just off the sidewalk.

George Hodel, as a taunting clue, placed the body on what he thought was Degnan Blvd. This was a subtle "catch me if you can" clue to his earlier Chicago Suzanne Degnan "Lipstick Murder." Unbeknownst to George Hodel, the street mysteriously transitions mid-block from Degnan Blvd. and becomes Norton Avenue, just south of where he posed her body.

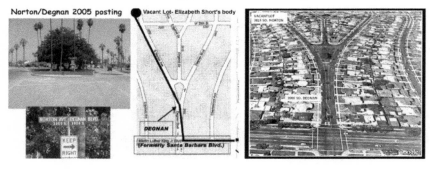

Map and aerial view of "Degnan/Norton" transition. Center divider did not exist back in 1947.

Elizabeth Short, Norton/Degnan vacant lot 1947.
LAPD crime photo showing posed body Jan 15, 1947.

The secret DA Hodel/Black Dahlia files discovered in 2003 document that victim Elizabeth Short *was in Chicago and actively investigating the Degnan and other "Lipstick Murders" in June 1946.*

She became fearful for her life and fled to San Diego in November after George Hodel's unexpected return from China and just six weeks later was abducted and brutally tortured and murdered on January 15, 1947.

The Jigsaw Murder
May 28, 1967, Manila, Philippines

Lucila Lalu, age 28

LUCILA LALU WAS KIDNAPPED from her place of business (a beauty salon) in Metropolitan Manila, Philippines, on May 28, 1967. Her body was surgically bisected by a skilled surgeon and placed on a vacant lot in the Makati District of Manila, adjacent to a street named Zodiac.

Six months earlier, Riverside, California murder victim Cheri Jo Bates (George Hodel's first known "Zodiac" victim) was slain. In a typewritten note, sent one month later, her killer promised he would commit a kidnap/murder and "I shall cut off her female parts and deposit them for the whole city to see."

The following May, Dr. Hodel fulfilled that promise in his then resident city, Manila, where he posed Lalu's body parts on the vacant lot, adjacent to Zodiac Street. This location was just one mile from his private residence in the exclusive residential district known as Forbes Park. The Manila Coroner publicly announced his belief that the bisection "had to have been performed by a skilled physician."

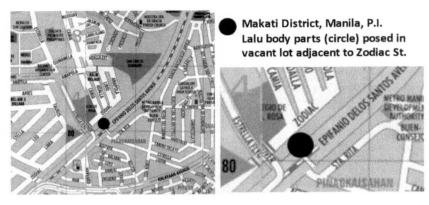

Makati District, Manila, P.I.
Lalu body parts (circle) posed in
vacant lot adjacent to Zodiac St.

Manila's 1967 "Jigsaw Murder" circle marks position of body of victim Lucila Lalu

The Red Lipstick Murder: The New Clue
February 10, 1947, Los Angeles

Jeanne French, age 40

MRS. JEANNE FRENCH WAS last seen having dinner with "a dark-haired man with a mustache" at the Picadilly Restaurant, 3932 Sepulveda Blvd., in West Los Angeles on February 10, 1947. Mrs. French left her vehicle, a 1928 Ford Roadster, in the restaurant parking lot and was seen leaving with the suspect at 2:00 a.m. in what a restaurant witness described as a "1937 black sedan." (George Hodel drove a 1937 black Packard.)

The coroner estimated Mrs. French was slain at approximately 4:00 a.m., just two hours after leaving the restaurant. Her body was found posed in a vacant lot near the intersection of Indianapolis and Grand View St.

Written on her nude torso were the words, "FUCK YOU BD." (Killer's taunt to the press and police meant to inform them that he was the Black Dahlia Avenger, and the same man who had slain Elizabeth Short just three weeks earlier.)

Jeanne French "Red Lipstick Murder"
February 10 1947

LAPD and press at the Jeanne French crime scene. Nude body was posed with fur coat initially covering the lipstick message, "Fuck You, BD."

The New Clue

IT WAS NOT UNTIL September 25, 2016, some fifteen years after initiating my investigation and viewing photographs of the Jeanne French crime scene, that I realized I had missed an obvious clue that had been in plain sight now for some seventy years.

Just two weeks before the Jeanne French "Red Lipstick Murder," funeral services were held for Elizabeth "Black Dahlia" Short.

The Short family decided to have her buried near one of her sisters' homes in Oakland, California.

Body of "Black Dahlia" Is Buried at Oakland

OAKLAND, Calif. (INS)— The body of Elizabeth Short, Los Angeles torso murder victim, was laid to rest in Oakland's Mountain View cemetery Saturday after a simple ceremony.

Funeral chapel and graveside prayers for the "Black Dahlia" were said by the Rev. G. Raymond White of Oakland.

Photograph shows the funeral, held on January 25, 1947. (Ten days after her body was found on the vacant lot in Los Angeles.)

The article in the *Oakland Tribune* reads:

Body of "Black Dahlia" Is Buried at Oakland

OAKLAND, Calif. (INS)—The body of Elizabeth Short, Los Angeles torso murder victim was laid to rest in *Oakland's Mountain View Cemetery* Saturday after a simple ceremony.

Funeral chapel and graveside prayers for the "Black Dahlia" were said by the Rev. G. Raymond White of Oakland.

Two weeks after those services, Dr. George Hill Hodel kidnapped and brutally murdered Mrs. Jeanne French.

The cause of death was "blunt force trauma to the head." (The coroner suspected a possible tire iron was used.) The victim was then dragged from the vehicle, stripped of her clothing, and stomped on, causing her ribs to puncture her heart.

The profane lipstick message was then written on her torso, and her fur coat placed over the letters to make it a dramatic "surprise taunt" for the police to discover.

As seen in the map and photo exhibit below, in 1947, the location chosen to pose the body was another isolated vacant lot.

Jeanne French body posed off Mountain View Ave.

The name of the street directly adjacent to where the body was placed?

MOUNTAIN VIEW AVENUE

We know from our earlier investigations that the reason for George Hodel's murder of Jeanne French was his response to the press's attempt to have him turn himself in by their using a ruse.

Recall that just a few days prior, on February 3, 1947, then popular mystery screenwriter Steve Fisher—*Dead Reckoning* (1947), *Lady in the Lake* (1947), *Song of the Thin Man* (1947)—had written an article published in the *Herald Express* newspaper. Fisher not only claimed that he believed he and the police knew the name of her killer but went on to suggest a way to flush him out.

Excerpt from Fisher's *Herald Express* article, entitled, "Noted Film Scenarist Predicts 'Dahlia' Killer Will Soon Be in Toils":

> ...
>
> If a legitimate suspect made a confession and the police announced the case solved? The real killer would be so frustrated and upset that he would "be driven at some point to come in and give the lie to the phony suspect's confession. But, I believe the police right now have a definite 'line' on the real killer, and that kind of 'staging' won't be necessary. Look for a thriller finish to this case."

Incredibly, five days later, on February 8, 1947, the *Herald Express* put the mystery writer's plan into action and came out with four-inch headlines that read:

CORPORAL DUMAIS IS BLACK DAHLIA KILLER
IDENTIFIES MARKS ON GIRL'S BODY IN LONG CONFESSION

The *Herald Express* at the time of publication knew that Corporal Dumais had provided a false confession, and that LAPD had established that the soldier was on his military base on the East Coast at the time of the murder. However, the paper apparently saw this as their opportunity to do as Fisher had suggested: "flush the killer out and have him turn himself in."

The result? Did the Dahlia killer turn himself in? Did he confess?

On the following night, February 9, 1947. Dr. George Hodel did take action. He did respond.

Moreover, he did confess. But, not by turning himself in—no, rather by killing again and signing his response to their ruse by writing in lipstick on the dead victim's body:

FUCK YOU

BD

Not only did he announce himself to be BD, the Black Dahlia Avenger, but he added still another, new street name to his body-posing MO: Hollywood, Degnan, and now—Mountain View.

George Hodel would save his fourth street clue for another twenty years, to begin an all-new crime spree by posing the Manila Dahlia copycat murder victim, Lucila Lalu, on Zodiac St.

This crime was followed shortly by more murders in the San Francisco Bay Area, where in 1968 he would introduce himself to the police and press and the world by way of his new self-appointed pseudonym—Zodiac.

George Hodel's four victims posed at their street name taunts showing original newspaper headlines.

The discovery of this newest latent Mountain View Street clue came to me as if by happenstance.

Completely unanticipated, it jumped out at me as I was simply making a casual review of an online Google map.

The next "newest clue" came just nine months later.

This time it came to me "secondhand" thanks to a comment and recommendation from one of my astute readers.

"One More for the Ripper"

IN LATE JUNE 2017, I wrote and posted a blog on my website stevehodel. com/blog entitled, *"Former South Pasadena High School Spelling Champion George Hodel Feigns Illiteracy as Part of his Black Dahlia Avenger, Lipstick, Zodiac Crime Signatures."*

I received about a dozen comments back from readers, including the below from one of my regulars, a Mr. Luigi Warren, who has contributed many important investigative insights and observations over the years.

As we are about to discover, this one from "LW" proved to be invaluable in advancing the further understanding of my father's "clews"[1] as his unique crime signatures.

Here is Luigi Warren's original comment relating to that specific blog as received on June 24, 2017.

> Steve,
>
> You have pointed out that the idea for the misspellings appears to have been appropriated from JtR case, along with certain other crime signatures (the dripping pen, the severed ear). I see the first book-length treatment of the case came out in 1929—Leonard Matters' *The Mystery of Jack the Ripper: The World's Greatest Crime Problem*. Alfred Hitchcock's *The Lodger*, featuring a JtR-like murderer who calls himself the "Avenger," was

---

1   The spelling of the word "clews" was used by Zodiac in some of his 1970s mailings to the San Francisco newspapers and is significant as it was the preferred spelling by journalists both in Jack the Ripper articles from 1888 as well as US crime reportage in the 1920s–1940s. George Hodel, as a young crime beat reporter for the *LA Record*, would have been familiar with and regularly used this unique spelling in his own articles from that day.

released in the US in 1928. Matters' book apparently covers the case including the purported Ripper letters in some depth and detail. Matters claimed JtR was a physician on a revenge trip. Today his story of an obscure deathbed confession to this effect is generally dismissed as a fabrication. I'm wondering if you've had a chance to read Matters' book. Might there be a giveaway in there that it was an inspiration? —Luigi Warren

I had not previously heard of Leonard Matters nor was I familiar with his 1929 book, *The Mystery of Jack the Ripper.*

A quick online check revealed a copy was available at a bookstore in the UK, I ordered, received, and began reading it in early July.

Leonard Matters, The First Ripperologist—

Leonard Matters in South Africa during the Boer War.

Here is a short bio on author/journalist Leonard Matters from Wikipedia:

Leonard Warburton Matters (26 June 1881–31 October 1951) was an Australian journalist who became a Labor Party politician in the United Kingdom.

He was born a British subject in Adelaide, Australia, and fought in the Second Boer War in South Africa. He worked as a journalist in Argentina and was managing editor of the *Buenos Aires Herald*.

In 1926, Matters proposed in a magazine article that the notorious serial killer Jack the Ripper was an eminent doctor, whose son had died from syphilis caught from a prostitute. According to Matters, the doctor, given the pseudonym "Dr. Stanley," committed the murders in revenge and then fled to Argentina. Matters claimed he had discovered an account of Stanley's deathbed confession in a South American newspaper. He expanded his ideas into a book, *The Mystery of Jack the Ripper*, in 1929. The book was marketed as a serious study, but it contains obvious factual errors and the documents it supposedly used as references have never been found.

—WIKIPEDIA

Leonard Matters' The Mystery of Jack the Ripper *originally published in 1929. Above edition republished by Arrow (London, 1964)*

Author/journalist, Leonard Matters, some forty years after the fact, conducted his own in-person crime scene investigation into the various JtR murder locations.

Here is Matters' description of his search related to the Mary Ann "Polly" Nichols Ripper murder from his 1929 book, *The Mystery of Jack the Ripper*, page 37:

> …Not without some difficulty did I find Bucks Row.
>
> Apparently, the civic authorities decided after the murder to change the nomenclature of most of the streets in the immediate neighbourhood. To Bucks Row, they gave the rather imposing name of Durward Street. It is a narrow, cobbled mean street, with shabby, dirty little houses of two storeys, and only a three-feet pavement separates them from the road, which is no more than twenty-five feet wide from wall to wall.
>
> …Going still further east, an abandoned London County Council school building breaks the wide and open Durward Street into two narrow lanes or alleys. The left-hand lane retains the name of Durward Street, "late Bucks Row" and the other is Winthrop Street. Both are equally dirty and seemingly disreputable, but the left-hand lane claims the distinction of having been the scene of a "Ripper" murder.

Entering the words "Jack the Ripper and Winthrop Street" in my search engine, I got 144,000 returns. Obviously, Winthrop Street figured prominently in the Ripper lore.

Henry Tomkins was a witness who testified at the Nichols inquest on 3 September 1888.

Tomkins was employed at Barber's Yard, *a horse slaughtering house on Winthrop St.* [emphasis mine]

The slaughter yard location was approximately 150 yards from where the body of Mary Nichols was found at Buck's Row, which was directly behind Winthrop Street and running in the same direction.

An article in *The Star* newspaper of 3 September 1888 reported the following account of Tomkins' testimony at the inquest:

Henry Tompkins said he lived at 12 Coventry Street, Bethnal Green. He was a horse slaughterer in the employment of Mr. Barber. He spent Thursday night and Friday morning in the slaughterhouse in Winthrop Street. He started at between eight and nine p.m., his usual time. His time for leaving was four in the morning. He left off work at twenty minutes past four on Friday morning. He went for a walk. They generally went home when they left work, but didn't that morning. He went to see "that woman that was murdered." Police Constable Pain was passing, at a quarter past four, the slaughterhouse, and told them a woman had been murdered in Buck's Row. There were three men at work in the slaughterhouse—himself, James Mumford, and Charles Britten. At twenty minutes past twelve, witness and Britten left the slaughterhouse and went back at one. "We didn't go far away, only down the court there."

Winthrop Street

QUESTION: WHY WOULD CHICAGO'S 1946 Lipstick Murderer select a seemingly random basement washroom located on a street just three blocks from the kidnap residence of little six-year-old Suzanne Degnan as the location for his slaughterhouse? Or, as the Chicago press dubbed it, "The Murder Room."

Answer: Because it was not random. The murder room was preselected and deliberate. Very likely "cased" and chosen in the days immediately preceding his crime.

The killer needed a large tub or basin to perform his surgery, check. He needed running water, check. He needed an isolated room with relative privacy, check.

But, most importantly he needed to choose a location that would prove him to be a master criminal.

After all, following December 10, 1945, the second Chicago Lipstick killing of thirty-three-year-old Frances Brown, found stabbed and posed kneeling by her bathtub, the newspapers were describing him as another "Jack the Ripper."

JACK THE RIPPER TYPE SOUGHT AS WAVE'S SLAYER

Police disclosed last night that a Jack the Ripper type of slayer is being sought in the murder of Miss Frances Brown, 33, attractive secretary and former WAVE, who was found shot and stabbed Monday in

December 1945, Chicago press is describing Lipstick Killer as "Jack the Ripper."

Perfect. George Hodel being highly versed in Ripper Lore would make it so.

Based on our recent review of what *we know* to be George Hodel's later crime signature (using street names as taunts: Hollywood, Degnan, Mountain View, and Zodiac) we can now assert with high confidence that he chose the Chicago address of 5901 Winthrop St—because *he knew that it figured prominently in the original Jack the Ripper serial crimes.*

Winthrop was frequently mentioned as the street immediately adjacent to Saucy Jack's first murder, that of Mary Ann "Polly" Nichols.

An inquest witness, Tomkins, who worked at the horse slaughterhouse down the alley on Winthrop, testified, "it was just 150 yards away."

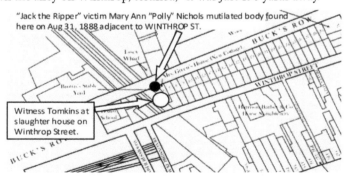

Jack the Ripper, Winthrop Street, London, England 1888

The map shows JtR victim Polly Nichols's 1888 attack location adjacent to Winthrop St.

Witness Henry Tomkins worked at the Winthrop St. slaughterhouse and went to the crime scene but arrived after police, and he saw and heard nothing.

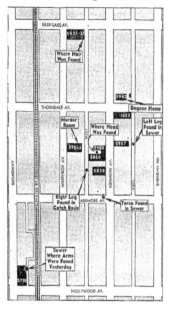

Lipstick Murderer, Winthrop Street, Chicago, Illinois 1946
Map from Chicago Tribune shows Lipstick Murderer's route from Suzanne
Degnan's abduction residence to the "Murder Room" at 5901-3 Winthrop St.,
where he performed the surgical dissection of body parts and distributed them
in the nearby sewers. (Locations are shown in black)

Exterior of "Murder Room" 5901-3 Winthrop St., Chicago, Illinois.

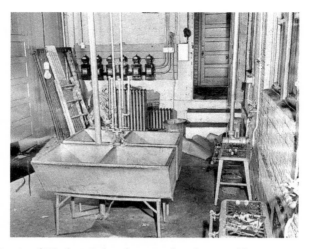

Interior of Winthrop St. laundry room where the surgical hemicorpectomy bisection and dissection of body parts were performed. Body parts were then washed, wrapped in paper, and distributed to five separate sewer basins north, south, east, and west of the crime scene, all within a three-block radius.

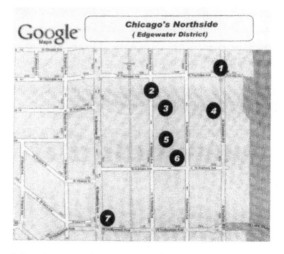

Locations of distribution of Suzanne Degnan's body parts:

1. Degnan home. (Location of abduction/kidnap)
2. Murder Room, 5901-3 Winthrop St.
3. Head found in sewer
4. Left leg found in sewer

5. Right leg found in catch basin
6. Torso found in sewer
7. Arms found posed above head in sewer
8. (The arms were not located by authorities until February 19, 1946, *some forty-three days after the murder.* Discovered in an alley sewer off Hollywood St.)

Chicago Winter Horror—February 19, 1946, Degnan arms found just off Hollywood St. (press photo)

Chicago PD Detectives recovering Suzanne Degnan's arms found six weeks after the murder in an alley off Hollywood St., three blocks southwest of the Murder Room on Winthrop Street.

From Foggy London of 1888 to the Windy City of Chicago of 1946

George Hodel's introducing JtR's Winthrop Street, and choosing it as the location of his "Murder Room" in his savage Lipstick Killer killing of little Suzanne Degnan, has now become the fifth deliberate street clew taunt. (Winthrop, Hollywood, Degnan, Mountain View, and Zodiac.)

Though the last street name to be discovered, Winthrop appears to be the first one he used. (I say "appears" because I am only partially into my ongoing investigations of his "Early Years" [1920–1940] crimes, so must reserve judgment, as more may yet be discovered.)

OUT-RIPPING "THE RIPPER"

DR. GEORGE HODEL, THOUGH highly pleased with his subtle Winthrop Street message which demonstrated his arcane and masterful knowledge of all things Ripper, may have had some second thoughts. "Too subtle." "The dumb cops will never make the link." "Only one in a million will get it."

So, George decided to give them another JtR clew. This one, not so subtle. This one he would make even bolder and take it right out of Saucy Jack's bag of tricks. He would out-rip the Ripper *by actually doing what his predecessor had only promised.*

JtR never followed through on his threat, so, "Let George Do It."

And what exactly was it that JtR promised in his 1888 letter to the police? Oh yes, he wrote:

> The next job I do I shall clip the ladys [sic] ears off and send to the police officers just for jolly. PS—They say I'm a doctor now. Ha ha.
>
> Jack the Ripper-1888

On January 29, 1946, just over three weeks after the child murder, a package addressed to the mother, "Mrs. Degnan, 5942 Kenmore Ave, Chicago, Illinois" was received at the Degnan home through the public mails.

The item, wrapped in tissue paper and placed inside a small cardboard box contained *a human ear*. A handwritten note was also enclosed that read, "Will cut off your ear next."

Follow-up revealed that the human ear had been stolen from a local medical clinic or laboratory, but no additional information was provided.

Chicago Daily Tribune
Wed. Jan 30, 1946

Human Ear Sent Degnan

Elimination of Campbell and Costello left police without immediately promising leads. Storms said they planned to start all over again.

A macabre note during the day was the delivery of a severed human ear to the Degnan home by mail. The ear, wrapped in tissue paper, was contained in a small cardboard box addressed to James E. Degnan, Suzanne's father. It was turned over to police.

Suzanne's ears had not been severed from her head, which was recovered from a sewer near her home.

Chicago Tribune *photo of package containing human ear mailed to Degnan home*

George Hodel/Jack the Ripper Identical Crime Signatures/MOs

- Showed extreme savagery and overkill toward his female victims
- Left victims in public places so bodies would be readily discovered
- Carefully posed victims' bodies and their personal effects at crime scene
- Sent numerous handwritten, cut-and-paste taunting notes to press and police
- Feigned illiteracy
- Drew crude knife dripping blood and mailed to press
- Taunted police with "catch me if you can"
- Mailed human body part to victims' relatives and/or police
- Used red ink and/or iodine in letter to authorities to imitate blood
- Signed mailings to police and press as, "a friend."
- Terrorized cities (London, Los Angeles, Chicago, Riverside, and San Francisco Bay Area) by promising to commit additional killings—"there will be more"—and also threatened to include "boys and girls" in his future murders.

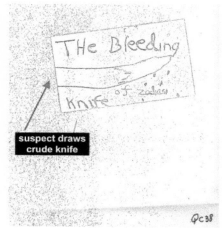

(Top) Jack the Ripper original "Boss Letter" showing killer's "bleeding knife" sent to London police. (Lower Left) Black Dahlia Avenger article indicating killer sent in, "a crude drawing of a dagger dripping blood." (Newspaper did not provide a reproduction of the actual drawing.) (Lower Right) FBI file showing a crude drawing of "the bleeding knife of Zodiac" believed to be mailed by Zodiac to press in the "Fairfield Letter." George Hodel as both "Black Dahlia Avenger" and "Zodiac" is taunting press and police with another "Jack the Ripper"–inspired "Bleeding Knife," further demonstrating his knowledge and familiarity with JtR's MO

From *Most Evil* (Dutton 2009) page 267:

> Some people develop their natural-born abilities to achieve greatness in music, science, and fine art. Dr. George Hodel used his cunning and intelligence to become a very successful and lethal serial killer. He

created a hysterical terror from Manila to Chicago and left behind a legacy that includes not just one series of high-profile crimes, but at least three.

He did this by studying fictional and real criminal masterminds including the infamous Jack the Ripper. He then planned his own crimes meticulously to outwit the police. He left his own unique signature by positioning his victims' bodies to create an intricate map of his ghastly work. As a self-proclaimed member of De Quincey's "Society of Connoisseurs in Murder," Dr. George Hodel elevated murder to a fine art.

One final observation needs to be made as to journalist-author, Leonard Matters' 1929 book, *The Mystery of Jack the Ripper.*

In my opinion, it is what I have previously termed "faction." Half fact and half fiction.

Three-quarters of the book deals with the author's objective on-scene reinvestigation of the various crimes scene locations as well as the coroner's findings and eyewitness accounts as written and recorded in the 1888 separate inquest hearings.

All good and well and "by the book."

However, in the ending chapters, I believe Matters' imagination takes flight and presents us with what he claims was a "confession and solution" to the who and why of Whitechapel's most infamous serial killer.

The who? He identifies JtR as a medical doctor, one "Dr. Stanley" (not his real name) from London's West Side. Wealthy and respected in that day for his unparalleled skill as a surgeon.

The why? Revenge! "Dr. Stanley" became an *avenger* who searched the East Side of London for the prostitute who had supposedly infected his son with syphilis and whom the avenging father blamed for his sudden and early death.

Matters writes that "Dr. Stanley" identified his son's girlfriend as the young and attractive "Marie Jeanette Kelly," a twenty-five-year-old prostitute living and working on the East Side of London.

After his son's death, "Dr. Stanley" supposedly searched for Mary Kelly for months and that he killed the other Ripper victims (Mary Ann

Nichols, Annie Chapman, Elizabeth Stride, and Catherine Eddowes) after questioning them on separate nights and months as to the whereabouts of Marie Jeannette Kelly. The stated reason for their murders was to prevent them from identifying and/or informing on him and his mission.

Matters writes that the doctor finally located Mary Kelly on the early morning of November 8, 1888, alone in her apartment. He cut her throat, then spent several hours removing body organs and placing them on the bed, then left.

His "mission accomplished," he stopped killing and left the country for Argentina.

There, after many decades, he contracted cancer and made a "death bed confession" as to the murders, and claimed he was the one true "Jack the Ripper."

Leonard Matters' source on the "confession" was from a local Argentinean newspaper article, which he later presented in his book as "the solution."

Whether his story is fact or fiction is not important to our investigation.

What is important is that it was written in 1929, and very likely read by the highly impressionable young genius.

George Hodel, just twenty-two, had just entered medical school at UC Berkley. He would become a highly skilled surgeon, as well as a "master criminal" and an "avenger" slaying women in various cities as he performed copycat crime signatures that have been directly sourced back to the acts and crimes of Jack the Ripper.

Without question, we have to consider author Leonard Matters' book as additional "source material" for the young and impressionable George Hodel, who, as you will soon learn from my ongoing investigations into "The Early Years," had by 1929 already become an accomplished killer.

GHH Uses Degnan Lipstick Murder to Pay Homage to a Second Infamous "Crime of the Century"—The 1932 Lindbergh Kidnapping

CONVINCED OF HIS INVINCIBILITY and driven to demonstrate his encyclopedic knowledge of infamous crimes, George Hodel, the Master Criminal, in my opinion, doubled down on the Degnan Lipstick murder.

He would not limit this crime simply by using "Ripper Clues" from the past century (1888) as crime signatures. No. That was the salt, but he decided that this horrific child murder also needed more pepper, so he added taunting clues from a more recent "Crime of the Century"— The 1932 Baby Lindbergh Murder.

Below I list just a few crime signatures, but enough to make his intent clear—his MO would copy the New Jersey crime that had headlined across the nation just fourteen years earlier. Only this time George Hodel— unlike his predecessor, the Lindbergh kidnapper/murderer, Richard Hauptmann—would be sure to avoid detection and arrest and thus demonstrate his superior skills after committing an identical crime.

> Degnan: The kidnap-murder of a child from a wealthy family.

> Lindberg: The kidnap-murder of a child from a wealthy family.

> Degnan: A ladder was used to access the child's second-story nursery window late at night on the side of the expensive private residence.

> Lindberg: A ladder was used to access the child's second-story nursery window late at night on the side of the expensive private residence.

> Degnan: A handwritten note was left inside the nursery demanding a ransom as follows: "Get $20,000 Reddy & waite for word. Do not notify FBI or Police. Bills in 5's & 10's. Burn this for her safty."

> Lindberg: A handwritten note was left inside the nursery demanding a ransom as follows: "Dear Sir- Have 50000$ redy. 25000$ in 20$ bills 15000$ in 10$ bills and 10000$ in 5$ bills. After 2-4 days we will inform you were to deliver the mony We warn you for making anyding public or for notify Police the child is in gut care."

Indications for all letters are signature and three holes.

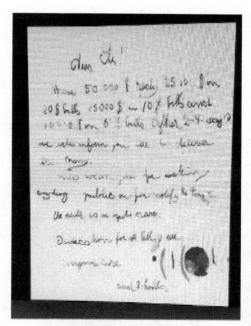

1932 Lindbergh Nursery Ransom Note

NOTE—Here is one side of note found in victim's room. It reads: "Get $20,-000 reddy & waite for word do not notify F B I or police Bills in 5's & 10's."
—Associated Press wirephoto.

1946 Degnan Nursery Ransom Note

SKH Note: Interesting that George Hodel, in feigning illiteracy in his Degnan Note, not only mirrored the identical Lindbergh instructions but also mimicked the unusual wording, ordering the parents to "get the money ready" and deliberately misspelling that very word as had the Lindbergh suspect. (Reddy vs. Redy). As we know, George Hodel had a perfect photographic memory, and again I say, at least in his copying of crime signatures, "there is no such thing as coincidences."

3

Paul Veglia Interview: A Walk Through the Willows

INVESTIGATIVE "TIPS" COME TO me these days usually as an email or phone call. In late February 2017, it was the latter.

An afternoon call from my brother Kelvin and his wife, Angel.

"Hi, Bro. Had a strange thing happen the other day. I was doing one of my harmonica gigs for some Seniors, and this guy walks up to me, looks at the name printed on my fatigues (Kelly was a Navy Corpsman like me) and he says, 'Hodel, that's strange. I was just reading this book last night by a guy named Steve Hodel.'"

Kelly responded, "Yes, that's my brother. He's written several books about the Black Dahlia."

Kelly went on to inform me that the man claimed to have met and spent time with Elizabeth Short back during the war years.

I explained to my brother that I get a lot of those kinds of claims. Most are psychos who are obsessed with the Dahlia story who email me and want to give me clues and tell me what she "was really like."

My brother, backed up by his wife, Angel, persisted.

"I don't think that is the case with this guy, Steve. I think he's the real deal. He gave me his name and phone number. Maybe just call and talk to him. See what you think? Guy's name is Paul Veglia." He gave me Paul's phone number and told me he lived in Santa Monica.

Angel backed him up. "I also got the impression he was telling the truth, Steve."

I thanked my brother and Angel for the call, took the name and phone number, and threw it into the "To Do" box on my desk.

An hour later, my curiosity got the best of me. Though confident this was just another delusional crank; I knew that I would be able to ferret out the truth within five or ten minutes of conversation. I made the call.

"Yes, this is Paul Veglia. Oh, hello Mr. Hodel, yes thank you for calling."

He talked, I listened. Twenty minutes later, convinced that he and his story claiming personal contact with Elizabeth Short was, as my brother had said, "the real deal," I agreed to meet with Paul at Art's Delicatessen, in Studio City, the following morning.

The Interview

Former Met Opera singer Paul Veglia, age eighty-four, describes his connections and personal contact with Elizabeth "Black Dahlia" Short when he was a young farm boy of twelve growing up in Casmalia, California in 1943. (Photo taken by author at Art's Deli, Studio City, February 2017.)

WE FOUND A QUIET back table and Paul politely corrected me on my mispronunciation of his name. "The g is silent. It's Paul Velia, rhymes with Casmalia."

Paul Veglia was a handsome, gregarious man of eighty-four. Physically fit, intelligent, and extroverted. He was a man who knew the world and its streets. He opened our conversation by saying:

"Now please bear with me. I have ADD (Attention Deficit Disorder). It has affected my life since I was a boy, so if I lose my train of thought or repeat myself, just understand it's the ADD. However, it doesn't "add"; it subtracts and has been the cause of missed opportunities for most of my life."

Author Note: Here is the Merriam-Webster Medical definition for Attention Deficit Disorder. 1. A developmental disorder that is marked especially by persistent symptoms of inattention (such as distractibility, forgetfulness or disorganization) or by symptoms of hyperactivity and impulsivity (such as fidgeting, speaking out of turn, or restlessness) or by symptoms of all three, and that is not caused by any serious underlying physical or mental disorder.

My interview with Paul lasted three hours.

He talked about his remarkable life, his career as an opera singer (he performed twice at the NY Met) and in national tours of *Kismet* (1962) and *Candide* (1971) and *La Bohème* at the Santa Monica Civic Opera. Paul also performed the role of "Elder Hayes" in *Susannah* at the Dorothy Chandler Pavilion in 1966.

Los Angeles Times Aug 15, 1974

'La Bohème' to Note Birthday of 'Opera Assn.

SANTA MONICA — In celebration of its 30th anniversary, the Santa Monica Civic Opera Assn. will present three performances of Puccini's "La Bohème" on Saturdays, Aug. 24 and 31, at 8:15 p.m. and Sunday, Sept. 1, at 2:30 p.m. All performances will be in the auditorium at Santa Monica High School.

Featured in the role of Mimi on Aug. 24, will be Natalie Garretto. Other cast members will be tenor Paul Veglia and baritones Mario Farrar and Lanny French.

Leads on Aug. 31, are Joan Shattuck as Mimi, with Nicolas Semachjahyn as Rodolfo.

For the matinee Sept. 1, the soprano role will be sung by Younghee Cavanogh with Paul Veglia as tenor.

All performances will be presented in Italian, with chorus, scenery and orchestra conducted by Mario Lanza. The production will be staged by Mario Farrar.

PUCCINI OPERA—Paul Veglia, tenor, and Younghee Cavanogh, soprano, rehearse scene from 'La Bohème' which will be presented by the Santa Monica Civic Opera on Saturday, Aug. 24-31, at 8:15 p.m.; Sunday, Sept. 1, 2:30 p.m.

Paul Veglia age forty-two, rehearsing for a role in La Bohème *in 1974*

Paul was married to Monika Henreid, the daughter of famed actor, Paul Henreid, who was an A-List star in Hollywood, perhaps best remembered for his role as "Victor Lazlo" in the 1942 film classic, *Casablanca*.

Paul Henreid, Ingrid Bergman, and Humphrey Bogart in scene from
Casablanca *(1942)*

While it was fascinating to hear about Paul's life and personal anecdotes, I am going to focus on and present his verbatim memories of a two-month period in the summer of 1943, when he was a farm boy of twelve.

During those two months, he came into daily contact with the then nineteen-year-old, Elizabeth Short, who four years later would become Los Angeles's most infamous murder victim, know as "The Black Dahlia."

Those familiar with the crime will recall that the victim was initially listed as "Jane Doe No.1" and just a day later was identified through fingerprints from an arrest for "Minor Possession" (being present in a bar in Santa Barbara under age). Her work records showed Elizabeth was employed at Camp Cook (later renamed Vandenberg Air Force Base) at the PX (Post Exchange) as a salesgirl just eight miles from the small town of Casmalia. This narrative takes place during those months in 1943.

Here is Paul's verbatim recounting of those two months:

> In 1943, I was twelve years old. I was a farm boy growing up in Casmalia, California.
>
> Casmalia is a small town about seven miles north of Camp Cook.
>
> I met Elizabeth Short, is it OK if I call her Beth, it's shorter to say? I met Beth when she was staying at a cabin at the Ranch House in Casmalia. Dave Thompkins was a twenty-four-year-old farm boy, and he had met Beth somewhere, and he said to her (I'm assuming this) said, "Why don't you stay at the guest house at my ranch?
>
> That cabin where Beth stayed was about a quarter mile from my bedroom. At that time I was living in the back of the Hitching Post, which is now a world-famous restaurant. Back then it was a ten-room hotel. Later, in 1948, after the war, Boyd Wyse came and offered my dad, Mario, a deal and they became partners and opened it up as a restaurant. It became famous and still is for "The Best Bar B Que in the world."

Google Map showing Casmalia and the Hitching Post Bar B Que restaurant, as it appears today. (Basically, unchanged from how it looked in the 1940s.)

Paul continued his narrative:

> For two months in the summer of '43, I saw Beth every
> day. We never really spoke other than for her to say,
> "Good morning, Paulie." I was just a kid of twelve, and
> she was about nineteen or so.
>
> Physically, she had black hair. It was almost touching
> her shoulders. She usually wore black slacks and a white
> short-sleeved blouse. She would come out from her
> cabin when I was sweeping her porch. She would come
> out and say to me, "Good morning" or I would say it to
> her too. Then she would thank me for sweeping off her
> porch, and she would walk barefoot across the pasture
> and through a clump of willow trees to the post office
> and store. The water would collect on the ground, and
> she was barefoot and would walk through the water to
> the Post Office.
>
> Beth had Post Office Box 66, which was right next to
> our box which was 65. My mother later told me, or
> somebody told me, that Beth would come to pick up
> her letters every day.

This Elizabeth Short Santa Barbara Police Department Booking Photo was
taken on September 23, 1943, just two months after she resided and had contact
with Paul Veglia at the ranch cabin in Casmalia

I would get up during school vacation sometimes at 4:00 a.m., and Johnny Tyler, my schoolmate, would drive and come and pick me up in his car. We would drive back to Camp Cook, and we'd sell a hundred newspapers each for five cents apiece. I'd make two cents per paper, so I made $2.00 every morning during the summer.

I'd be back home at 7:00 a.m., go to the ranch, pick up my shovel, feed the cows some hay, the horses alfalfa, and the chickens some grain. Then I'd sweep Beth's porch and sweep all the chicken manure off it.

My father owned the Hitching Post, and I am one of three sons. I started working for my dad peeling potatoes when I was seven. My mother was the bartender at the Hitching Post. I remember one time when I saw Beth with David Tompkins there at the bar. My mother served them drinks. I think I remember that Beth had a cherry in her drink. Beth was pretty, but she wasn't Elizabeth Taylor beauty.

I was born in Santa Maria, California about eight miles from Casmalia. My mother gave birth to me at sixteen. I was the first born, named after my grandfather who was a deputy sheriff up there.

Beth and I really had no conversations, just, "Good morning, Paulie." No, I never saw her with guys. We never even shook hands.

In 1952 or 1953, I came in to California for four to five days, in uniform on furlough. I was in the Air Force. My mother came up to me and said, "Paulie, remember Elizabeth?" I said, "Elizabeth? Oh, you mean Dave Tompkins' girlfriend?" That's when my mom said, "She was murdered." My mom didn't even know about the body being divided, just that she had been murdered.

(At this point I inform Paul that the murder occurred back in 1947.)

Oh, I thought she was murdered in '52 or so? 1947? I was still in high school in Santa Maria then. My mother didn't hear about it until 1953.

Beth went to Camp Cooke AFB every day, just like me. I have no idea how she got there? Maybe her boyfriend, David Tompkins took her? He was six or seven years older than me.

(Paul draws a map on restaurant paper.)

Beth's guest house was here. A corral was here. Dave Tompkins lived here with his brothers and sisters. Here's the store, where I worked. I stacked vegetables for twenty-five cents for Boyd Wyse, who became partners with my dad and later on, they opened the Hitching Post Bar B Que.

My three-hour interview with Paul came to an end. I thanked him for sharing his memories of Elizabeth Short and the stories of his life with its trials, tribulations, and successes.

It wasn't until I returned home and transcribed the taped interview that I became aware of how powerful an impression Paul's story and description of Elizabeth had made on me.

It was not Paul's conversation with her that had impressed me. In truth, there were no conversations between them, just a regular morning "Hello" and "Thank you, Paulie."

However, the picture Paul has shared with us, as seen through the eyes of a twelve-year-old farm boy, *is very real and very powerful.*

After hearing his story, I find myself haunted by his personal description of Elizabeth Short more than any other "witness" I have interviewed over the past fifteen years. Why?

Because he confirmed and had made real what I have always felt and suspected was the essence of Elizabeth Short—*her loneliness.*

A young woman alone, with few or no real friends. Living in a rural broken-down cabin with a porch covered with chicken manure that needs to be swept away each morning.

She walks barefoot out her front door, through the wet pastureland, passing through the clump of standing willow trees, walking the quarter mile to the Post Office. On her slow walk, she has hope in her heart. Hope that a soldier or sailor that she dated has written her to say, "I love you. Come join me." But, it was not to be.

Thank you, Paul Veglia, for lending us your twelve-year-old eyes that saw more of the truth in those two short months than all those that have come forward since to claim "they knew her well."

These three sketches, depicting Elizabeth Short's summer of '43 were drawn by my good friend, Mssr. Yves Person, the high school teacher from Paris, France who "cracked" the Zodiac cipher by recognizing the five hidden Ogham letters (H O D E L) as detailed in Most Evil II *(Rare Bird Books 2015).*

Thank you, Yves, for your beautiful drawings that help us to capture a brief "through the willows" moment in the young life of Elizabeth Short. Merci!

4

The Black Dahlia in La La Land

I know the name of the killer [Black Dahlia Avenger] and the psychology of his deed. ...There is only one form of hatred that can equal in violence the symbolizing rage of the lunatic—and what that hatred is I will leave unsaid.

Ben Hecht, Hollywood Screenwriter,
Los Angeles Herald Express, *February 1, 1947*

I think I know who the killer is and think the police do also, and in a very short time will have his name. When the killer's name is published, I think a lot of his friends will be very surprised and terrified. ...Look for a thriller finish to this case.

Steve Fisher, Hollywood Screenwriter,
Los Angeles Herald Express, *February 3, 1947*

THE ABOVE QUOTES ARE extracts from two separate back-to-back articles that appeared in the *Los Angeles Herald Express* two weeks after the Elizabeth Short "Black Dahlia" torture-murder had occurred.

All six LA newspapers were covering the sensational murder, and the *Herald Express* was out-scooping its competition by keeping the story "above the fold."

In 1947, Ben Hecht and Steve Fisher were two of Hollywood's highest paid screenwriters, and both had recently finished noir mysteries for the big screen.

Hecht had written the screenplays for *Spellbound* (1945) and *Notorious* (1946) and Fisher had just adapted Raymond Chandler's *Lady in the Lake*, which MGM released on January 23, 1947, *only eight days after the Dahlia murder* and just ten days before Fisher's lengthy article, entitled, "Noted Film Scenarist Predicts 'Dahlia' Killer Will Soon Be in Toils" appeared in the newspaper.

In a chapter in *BDA II*, I detailed the linkage between many of these 1940s "Hollywood Insiders" both as personal friends to George and Dorothy Hodel and as partygoers to the Franklin/Sowden house.

Before proceeding deeper into the La La Land linkage, let's take a quick look at some of the names that would have been on the Hodels' Guest List back in the 1940s—Dr. George Hill Hodel's special "Cast of Characters."

"The Cast"

1. **John Huston:** Lifelong friend of GHH beginning in their teens—ex-husband to Dorothy Huston Hodel (married seven years). Famed A-List Hollywood actor, screenwriter, director, credited with making forty-seven films. To name a few: *The Maltese Falcon* (1941), *The Treasure of the Sierra Madre* (1948)—Dorothy Huston Hodel was an uncredited script doctor—, *Key Largo* (1948), *We Were Strangers* (1949), *The Asphalt Jungle* (1950), *Moulin Rouge* (1952), and forty-one additional director credits. Huston hired his good friend and GHH accomplice Fred Sexton to sculpt the "Black Bird" for his early film, *The Maltese Falcon*. John was a regular partygoer to the Franklin House. His role as Noah Cross in *Chinatown* (1974) is believed to be based on and inspired by his intimate knowledge of and close friendship to Dr. George Hill Hodel.

John Huston was still married to Dorothy in 1933 when this photo was taken at the LA Coroner's Inquest. Huston was driving a vehicle that struck and killed Mrs. Tosca Roulien while she was crossing Sunset Blvd. A shaken Huston looks on while the jury absolves him of any blame. Tosca Roulien was the twenty-five-year-old wife of Brazilian actor Raul Roulien, known as "the South American Valentino."

2. **Walter Huston**: Famed stage and screen A-List actor. Father of John Huston, father-in-law to Dorothy Huston Hodel. A close friend of screenwriters Gene Fowler and Ben Hecht and starred in numerous Hecht screenplays such as *The Beast of the City* (1932), *The Outlaw* (1943), *Duel in the Sun* (1946).

Walter Huston greeting newlyweds John and Dorothy Huston at LA train station in 1926

3. **Gene Fowler:** Top Hollywood screenwriter with thirty film credits. Close friend and cowriter with Rowland Brown on *State's Attorney* (1932) and *What Price Hollywood?* (1932). Friend and cowriter with Ben Hecht on *Shoot the Works* (1934) and *Some Like It Hot* (1939). Cowrote screenplay *The Mighty Barnum* (1934) with friend John Huston who was at that time married to Dorothy Huston (Hodel). His son Will Fowler was a news reporter and one of the first to arrive at the 1947 Black Dahlia crime scene and obtain photographs depicting position, trauma, and torture to the victim's face and body. Will was the likely source of circulating untouched crime photos to his father and friends, many of whom were acquainted with GHH.

3825 S. Norton Ave, Los Angeles. Gene Fowler's son, news reporter Will Fowler (light hat) seen kneeling next to the body of Elizabeth "Black Dahlia" Short on the morning of January 15, 1947. LAPD Detective Harry Hansen (dark hat) and LAPD criminalist also seen examining the body. Will Fowler in his memoirs maintained he and his press photographer, Felix Paegel, were the first to arrive at the scene and claimed he had obtained numerous photographs before the police arrived. These original photographs would certainly have been shown to his screenwriter father and Gene's inner circle of friends such as Ben Hecht, Steve Fisher, Rowland Brown, and others.

4. **Ben Hecht**: Novelist and during Hollywood's Golden Years was its highest paid screenwriter. Began writing in the 1920s up until his death in 1964 with 165 credits. Best known for *The Front Page* (1931), *Scarface* (1932), *Stagecoach* (1939), *It's a Wonderful World* (1939), *The Outlaw* (1943), *Spellbound* (1945), *Gilda* (1946), *Notorious* (1946), and many more. In 1922 Hecht wrote his first novel, *Fantazius Mallare: A Mysterious Oath*, illustrations by Wallace Smith. That novel was followed in 1924 with its sequel, *The Kingdom of Evil*. Hecht and Smith were charged with obscenity after the publication of *Fantazius Mallare* and ultimately pled "no contest" and paid a $1,000 fine. Smith "passed" on doing the illustrations for Hecht's sequel, and his replacement artist was Anthony Angarola. Below, a sample of Hecht's writing and Smith's drawings from the first book. In both books, Hecht conjures in Mallare a tortured soul, a misogynist and misanthrope acting out his hallucinatory madness.

...

Rising from his chair, Mallare attacked one by one the canvases and statues. Goliath watched him in silence as he moved from pedestal to pedestal from which, like a company of inert monsters, arose figures in clay and bronze. The first of them was a man four feet in height but massive-seeming beyond its dimensions. Mallare had entitled it "The Lover."

Its legs were planted obliquely on the pedestal top; their ligaments wrenched into bizarre muscular patterns. Its body rose in an anatomical spiral. From its flattened pelvis, that seemed like some evil bat stretched in flight, protruded a huge phallus. The head of the phallus was enlivened with the face of a saint. The eyes of this face were raised in pensive adoration. At the lower end of the phallus, the testicles were fashioned in the form of a short-necked pendulum arrested at the height of its swing. The hands of the figure clutched talon-like at the face, and the head was thrown back as if broken at the neck. Its features were obliterated by the hands except for the mouth which was flung open in a skull-like laugh.

Several of Wallace Smith's erotic sketches included in Ben Hecht's Fantazius Mallare: A Mysterious Oath *(1922)*

Here is an excerpt by Hecht's *The Kingdom of Evil: A Continuation of the Journal of Fantazius Mallare:*

Luminous and strange, its roofs careening like wing-stretched bats it lay encircled by hills—a Satanic toy, a

thing of unearthly marvels. Its painted streets beckoned
to Mallare. Its demons, horrors, and lusts waited for him.

As referenced in *BDA II*, the Hecht-Hodel connection began back in
1925 with George Hodel choosing Hecht's just-published *The Kingdom of
Evil* as his first book review as editor for his self-published elitist magazine,
Fantasia.

Over the years, some readers have requested I publish my father's full
Ben Hecht 1925 book review. Here then is a scanned reproduction of those
pages from the original *Fantasia* magazine. I also include the cover, front
matter, and dedication.

As you read George Hodel's editorial review of Hecht's novel, keep in
mind that the year is 1925, and at the time of that writing, George has just
turned eighteen and had been expelled two years earlier from Pasadena's
prestigious CalTech University for sexual improprieties with a professor's
wife. Further, in 1925 George was employed and actively involved in ride-
alongs with LAPD Vice and homicide detectives as a crime reporter for one
of Los Angeles's largest newspapers, *The Los Angeles Record*.

Original cover of the first edition of Fantasia
—George Hill Hodel, editor

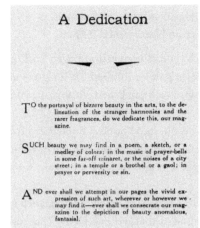

A Dedication

TO the portrayal of bizarre beauty in the arts, to the delineation of the stranger harmonies and the rarer fragrances, do we dedicate this, our magazine.

SUCH beauty we may find in a poem, a sketch, or a medley of colors; in the music of prayer-bells in some far-off minaret, or the noises of a city street; in a temple or a brothel or a gaol; in prayer or perversity or sin.

AND ever shall we attempt in our pages the vivid expression of such art, wherever or however we may find it—ever shall we consecrate our magazine to the depiction of beauty anomalous, fantasial.

The Kingdom of Evil   *By Anthony Angarola*

George Hill Hodel's Fantasia *"Dedication." Author, Ben Hecht, Illustrations by Anthony Angarola*

In Review

"THE KINGDOM OF EVIL." By Ben Hecht. Pascal Covici, publisher.

Macabre forms, more dank and putrescently phantasmal than any of Hecht's former imagining, grope blindly and crazedly in the poisonous fog out of which loom the rotting fancies that people his "Kingdom of Evil."

This, Ben Hecht's latest book, is a continuation of the journal of Fantazius Mallare, the uncouth figure that stalks darkly across the varicolored vistas of the author's conjuring. Here the sonorous note of his former work is replaced in a measure by a frailer, yet a more poignant, strain of a most strange and lyrical nature.

Hecht has, perhaps unwittingly, resorted at times to the devices of the sensationalist, the dauber, the splurger in colors too blazing for his understanding, but through it all there seems a basic sincerity too often notoriously lacking in his writings.

Mounting in its pellucid and rounded mellifluence in passages to a poetry in prose to be likened only, perhaps, to the more artificial tales of Edgar Allan Poe, his fancies take on richly and darkly tinted hues. Most notably toward the end, where is pictured the debacle, the decay of the Kingdom, is the tempo powerful and the imagery colossal. A passage:

"As the tremendous stalk wilts, toppling into an ever deeper and more sinister arc, its walls blaze with a continual sunset. Phosphorescent seas appear to run down its broken sides. The flames and banners of decay creep out of its roots and spread in slow and ghostly conflagrations toward its summit. Daily the spectacle of its dissolution increases. Alkaline pinks and excremental yellows, purples and lavenders like tumerous shadows; browns that float like colossal postules through seas of lemon; reds that ferment into wavering islands of cerise and salmon, that erupt into ulcerous hills of scarlets and magentas—these revolve about the walls, mounting into vast patterns and dissolving one into the other. Slowly death postures in its coquettish shrouds."

Recurring in persistent refrain throughout "The Kingdom of Evil" is seen Ben Mecht's phallic symbolism—sometimes exhausting the sexual vocabulary in lecherous blatancy, sometimes shrouded in veils of obscure yonic characterization.

The black-and-white illustrations by Anthony Angarola, which accompany the text, are massive and gauntly superb, though they are obviously forced in order to harmonize with the grotesque theme of the fantasy.

With almost animate pigments has Hecht painted this monstrous dream of Mallare's, and with delicate and meticulous craftsmanship has he fashioned its cadaverous and perverse beauty.

George Hill Hodel.

Let us now return to our running list of "The Cast." Those individuals that were in close association with George Hodel and for the most part would have been considered part of his "inner circle" of friends.

5. **Tim Holt:** A-List actor costar of Huston film, *Treasure of Sierra Madre*. Credited with making seventy-four films. Primarily a Western film star. Boyfriend to actress Carol Forman, who at that time (1948–1950) was renting a room and living at the Hodel Franklin House. Holt, a regular visitor to our home, made several cowboy films with Forman, such as *Under the Tonto Rim* (1947) and *Brothers in the Saddle* (1949). Holt appeared in a comic book series as cowboy hero, "Red Mask" as did Carol Forman as "Spider Woman." Two decades later, GHH as "Zodiac" would include Holt's "Red Mask" character in the taunting "clews" he mailed to the press.

Photo upper left clip from John Huston's The Treasure of Sierra Madre *(1948) Left to Right: Humphrey Bogart, Tim Holt, and Walter Huston. Photo lower left is also from the same film and shows Bogie with then child actor Robert Blake in the "lottery ticket" scene. (The dialogue for this scene was rewritten by my mother, Dorothy Huston Hodel, at John's request.) Photo right is from 1950 comic book series of Tim Holt as "Red Mask," and Holt as that cowboy hero will play a significant role in later "clews" mailed to the* San Francisco Chronicle *by Zodiac in 1970.*

6. **Carol Forman:** Actress. Twenty-six film credits. *Nocturne* (1946), story by Rowland Brown, who was at that time having an affair with Dorothy Huston Hodel. Carol Forman was given a bit part, playing a secretary in Brown's noir film. In 1948 she would move into the Hodel Franklin House as a tenant and continue dating cowboy star Tim Holt, remaining in residence until the arrest of GHH in October 1949. Best known as one of Hollywood's first screen villainesses in serials starring as Sombra in *The Black Widow* (1947) and Spider Lady in *Superman* (1948).

Forman played a receptionist in Nocturne, a noir film, story by Rowland Brown set in 1940s Los Angeles. It was released in November 1946, just two months before the Black Dahlia Murder. (Right) Poster showing Carol as "Sombra," aka The Black Widow in 1947 release.

7. **Rowland Brown:** Screenwriter, film director. A top film director in the 1930s: *The Doorway to Hell* (1930), *Quick Millions* (1931) (with Ben Hecht cowriter), engaged in an active ongoing love affair with Dorothy Huston Hodel. A good friend of and coscreenwriter with Ben Hecht on Hitchcock noir film *Notorious* (1946) and others. Hecht also was a scriptwriter on Brown's classic gangster film, *Quick Millions* (1931) starring Spencer Tracy, *What Price Hollywood* (1932), *Blood Money* (1933), *Angels with Dirty Faces* (1938), *Nocturne* (1946). Brown is heard and recorded in conversation with Dorothy Hodel on the 1950 DA surveillance tapes discussing her recent trip to Mexico.

Director/screenwriter Rowland Brown (right) with actor Spencer Tracy during the making of Quick Millions *in 1933. Coscreenwriter was Ben Hecht.*

8. **Man Ray, Juliet Man Ray:** Hodel family photographer, surrealist, and close confidant to GHH during his "Hollywood Years" (1940–1951). It is believed Man Ray met Elizabeth "Black Dahlia" Short in Hollywood (probably through GHH who may have been treating her at his First Street Clinic for a Bartholin Gland cyst infection) as early as 1943, when she posed as a nude model in Man Ray's painting, *L'Equivoque.* Many of Man Ray's artworks, both his photography and paintings, would figure in GHH's crime signatures of "Murder as a Fine Art." Man Ray was also involved in the making of the Hans Richter–directed surrealist film, *Dreams That Money Can Buy* (1947) along with his surrealist artists/ friends: Alexander Calder, Marcel Duchamp, Max Ernst, and Fernand Leger. (Blues and ballad singer Josh White and later—1950s—lover of Tamar Hodel, also had an acting role in the avant-garde film.)

Man Ray photos of "Hodel Boys" circa 1944. Left to Right: Kelvin, Michael, Steven (Taken at a different Pre-Franklin residence.) In this photograph Man Ray took the first photo (left) then as he was preparing for a second shot, an airplane flew overhead, and he caught us as we all looked up to see it. (At least, that is our mother's version.)

9. **Marion Herwood Keyes:** Top Hollywood costume designer secretary and protégé of Director Vincente Minnelli and personal secretary to GHH at his privately owned First Street Clinic, which specialized in the treatment of venereal disease. Co-employee and close friend of GHH's other personal secretary, Ruth Spaulding, who was murdered by GHH (forced overdose pills) in 1945. Costume designing film credits too numerous to list but here are a few: *Gaslight* (1944), *Mrs. Parkington* (1944), *The Clock* (1945), *The Postman Always Rings Twice* (1946), *Arch of Triumph* (1948).

Left to Right: Designer Marion Herwood, Mrs. Arthur Schwartz and photographer Paul Hesse looking over the dress. Feb 01, 1947

10. **Fred Sexton:** Artist, friend and criminal accomplice to GHH in child molestation sex acts with Tamar Hodel as well as incest with his

own teenage daughter, Michelle and subsequent child molestations with his second wife's teenage stepchildren. Fled to Mexico to avoid prosecution where he lived and died at age eighty-eight. Close lifelong friend to John Huston. Sculpted Huston's *Black Bird* for the classic film noir, *Maltese Falcon* in 1941.

Fred Sexton, lifelong artist friend of George Hodel and John Huston, sculpted the Black Bird *for Huston to use in* The Maltese Falcon.

11. **Baron Ernst Harringa:** Downtown LA gallerist and art collector with a gallery in downtown LA immediately south of the Biltmore Hotel in the historic Oviatt Building. An accomplice who with GHH is overheard on DA stakeout (tape-recorded) assaulting and possibly murdering an unidentified woman in the basement of the Franklin House in February 1950. A friend of GHH since 1925. Like GHH, left the country for many decades following the crime.

Born Ernst Franz Meyer in Germany, aka "Baron Ernst Harringa." LA gallerist and accomplice to GHH on February 18, 1950, in the assault of a woman in the basement of the Hodel residence. Possible unidentified murder. GHH recorded on tapes instructing Harringa, 'Don't leave a trace."

12. **William Copley** (artist/Beverly Hills gallerist), **Marcel Duchamp**, **Salvador Dali**, **Max Ernst** and his wife, **Dorothea Tanning:** Surrealist artists and friends to Man Ray, Juliet Man Ray, and GHH. Most of these artists were involved in the making of the film, *Dreams That Money Can Buy* (1947). Dali and Man Ray worked with screenwriter Ben Hecht on the dream sequence for Hitchcock film, *Spellbound* (1945).

13. **Henry Miller:** Novelist, friend to GHH and Man Ray. His novels, *Tropic of Cancer, Black Spring,* and *Tropic of Capricorn* were banned in the US for several decades on the grounds of obscenity and being "too sexually explicit." We recall in an earlier chapter of *BDA II* my mention of Miller's privately printed book, *The World of Sex* (NY 1940) where he writes, "...I would recommend them [men] to have intercourse with animals or to fuck in public. There is nothing in itself which is wrong or evil, not even murder. ...Some females ought to be raped to death and left lying on the spot for all to see."

14. **Edmund Teske:** Surrealist artist/photographer and friend to GHH and Man Ray. Hollywood resident formerly employed at Paramount Pictures in the photographic still department. We recall his statements to architect Steve Lamb, made in conversation in front of the Hodel home in the late 1970s when addressing the Franklin House, "It's an evil place! Artists, philosophers, accountants, and politicians we all played and paid there. Women were tortured for sport there. Murders happened there. It's an EVIL place."

In an online description and short bio of Edmund Teske, Eric Berg, a Los Angeles art collector and owner of Early California Antiques, writes:

> **Edmund Rudolph Teske** (March 7, 1911–November 22, 1996) was a twentieth-century American photographer who combined a career of taking portraits of artists, musicians, and entertainers with a prolific output of experimental photography. His use of techniques like combined prints, montages, and solarizations led to "often romantic and mysterious images."
>
> Teske began to experiment with the concept that a regular photographic image could not define a moment in life and that only multiple images portrayed together could

convey what he called "universal essences." He launched into a series of creative photographic experiments in which he both manipulated and combined multiple images to create "new pictorial realities."

Edmund Teske photograph of "Hodel Boys" taken at Franklin House circa 1947. Left to right: Steve, Mike, Kelvin Hodel. One of the cats GHH named "Satan" second cat name unknown (forgotten).

15. **Kenneth Rexroth:** Poet, author, considered one of the "Fathers of the Beat Movement." A longtime friend of both Dorothy and George Hodel. Rexroth was captured on the 1950 DA surveillance wire recordings discussing with George "great whores" they had known in San Francisco.

16. **Kiyoko Tachibana Cuddy:** "KIYO" actress in *Where Danger Lives* (1950) directed by John Farrow. *The Ten Commandments* (1956) Astrologer to the Stars, former girlfriend/lover of GHH, and future wife of the author, Steve Hodel. Hostess and regular partygoer at Franklin House. Kiyo had serial marriages as follows: John Doe, a guard at Japanese Internment Camp in 1942 (allegedly married him to gain her freedom); Brook Cuddy, photographer cameraman for CBS studios; Richard T. Herd, film-television actor in 1954; John Mickey Roth, actor and child film star in 1955; Steve Hodel (1962–1965); Rolf Aurness, 1970 World Surfing Champion, son of actor James Aurness. Kiyo died from cancer at age fifty-seven in 1978.

A young "Kiyo" in GHH's secret photo book of "Loved Ones" circa 1942

17. **Lillian Hamilton Lenorak:** Actress, thirteen film credits. *Outrage* (1950), *Phone Call from a Stranger* (1952), and nine additional films. Mistress to film director John Farrow. (Bore Farrow an illegitimate son, John Jr., who was born in 1943.) A regular visitor to Franklin House. Perjured herself in defense of GHH at incest trial. Rescued from a GHH staged "attempt suicide" by Santa Barbara policewoman, Mary Unkefer, after threatening GHH she was going to inform DA of her knowledge of Tamar's abortion and his murder of Elizabeth Short. Identified Elizabeth "Black Dahlia" Short to police as "former acquaintance of GHH." Lillian was murdered in Palm Springs in 1959 by a mentally disturbed resident (not GHH-related).

18. **Marya Marco:** Actress, a friend of GHH. Photography model for GHH at the Franklin House. Provided overnight shelter for Tamar Hodel at GHH's request shortly after the child molestation incest incident in July 1949. Tamar informed Marya, "Daddy was bad to me." (No full disclosure at that time.) In an interview with author identified herself as being one of the women in a photo in GHH's album and informed me, "I have George to thank for my movie career. His pictures of me were shown to producers who got me into films." *Song of the Thin Man* (1947), *Sleep My Love* (1948), *The Clay Pigeon* (1949), *I Was an American Spy* (1951), and seventeen additional credits.

Actress Marya Marco and author 2006. Interviewed by me and identified herself as being the woman standing by the statue in GHH's photo album. The photo was taken by GHH at the Franklin House circa 1947. Shown and did not recognize the reclining nude photo of a woman with eyes closed (believed to be Elizabeth Short).

19. **Mattie (Mady) Comfort:** Nineteen-year-old lover, ménage-a-trois sexual partner to both George and Dorothy Hodel. Actress, *Aladdin and His Lamp* (1952), *Skirts Ahoy* (1952), *The Egyptian* (1954), *Kiss Me Deadly* (1955). The part-time girlfriend of Duke Ellington, she was the original "Satin Doll" for whom Ellington, Strayhorn, and Mercer wrote the famous jazz standard. Secret Black Dahlia witness interviewed by DA investigator Lt. Frank Jemison. Acknowledged to detectives, "GHH knew Elizabeth Short." In later life post-death of GHH, Mady informed her live-in boyfriend, "We all knew he did it [Black Dahlia murder]. There was no doubt." In her written manuscripts, describes witnessing and breaking up domestic abuse and physical assaults by GHH on his wife, Dorothy at the Hodel home in 1943.

Mattie (Mady) Comfort seen with actor Robert Wagner, comedian Bob Hope, and lower photo relaxing with TIME on her hands. (Photographers unknown)

20. **Joe Barrett:** 1948-1950 resident/tenant at the Franklin House. Conscripted by DA detectives to be their confidential informant. Confirmed on televised interview in 2004 that "Lillian Lenorak knew Elizabeth Short, 'they were friends,' and that according to Lillian, "George killed Elizabeth Short." Barrett became an important witness to my later ongoing investigation from 1999-2005.

Joe Barret
Photo left taken circa 1946 and photo right taken 2005

21. **Galka Scheyer:** Art dealer/collector, painter, photographer. Famed agent for the artist's group, the "Blue Four" (Alexei Jawlensky, Lyonel Feininger, Paul Klee and Wassily Kandinsky). A friend of architects

Rudolph Schindler, Richard Neutra, and Frank Lloyd Wright. Other of her Los Angeles friends included Aline Barnsdall, bookseller Jake Zeitlin, artists Edward Weston, Stanton MacDonald-Wright, Diego Rivera, and composer/artist John Cage. Scheyer, along with artist Katherine S. Dreier, Marcel Duchamp, and Man Ray, founded the Societe Anonyme in 1920 to study modern art movements. Just two years before her death in 1945, Scheyer took the below formal Hodel family photograph.

This Hodel family photograph was taken by Galka Scheyer on November 7, 1943 (the day after my second birthday). (Top, left to right): Dr. George Hill Hodel age thirty-six, Duncan Hill Hodel age fifteen (Bottom, left to right): Author Steve Hodel age, two, Kelvin age one, Michael age four.

22. **Rudolph Schindler:** Architect. Designed and oversaw construction on Aline Barnsdall's Hollyhock House. Modernist architect; one of his most famous designs was his Kings Road House (aka Schindler House) in West Hollywood. Schindler's social circle identical to Galka Scheyer who lived in his Kings Road House in 1931, while his good friend and fellow architect, Richard Neutra, built her glass-and-concrete house in the Hollywood Hills named, "Blue Heights Drive." Schindler, at the request of Dr. George Hill Hodel, designed the below furniture for Hodel's 1940 residence at 1800 Huntington Drive in San Marino.

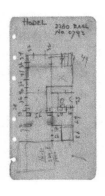

Architect Rudolph Schindler hand drawings of furniture he designed for George and Dorothy Hodel for the interior of their 1940 private residence at 1800 Huntington Drive, in San Marino. Residence (above left) is now (2017) the San Marino Chamber of Commerce (Schindler sketch designs for Hodel furniture courtesy of Schindler Archives, UC Santa Barbara.)

23. **Dudley Murphy:** Hollywood film director, screenwriter. Started his career in 1921. In 1924, Murphy codirected the experimental surrealist film, *Ballet Mécanique* with Fernand Leger, Man Ray, and Ezra Pound and music composed by George Antheil. Twenty-eight director film credits which include: *Danse macabre* (1922), *St. Louis Blues* (1929) starring Bessie Smith, *Black and Tan Fantasy* (1929) with Duke Ellington, and *The Emperor Jones* (1933) starring Paul Robeson. Close friends of Dorothy and George Hodel Dudley and his wife Virginia owned the modern Holiday House Motel in Malibu which was a hideaway-retreat and watering hole for the Hollywood elite. (Designed and built by Richard Neutra for the Murphys in 1950, today it remains on the same enchanted bluff, with spectacular views of the blue Pacific, reincarnated as Geoffrey's Restaurant and separate condominiums.)

Author Anecdote: In the early 1950s, after George fled the country and after mother and us three boys were just beginning our "Gypsy Years," Dudley and his wife Ginny "took us in" for one summer. One of the properties they owned was a small beach house just below their restaurant in a section known as "Escondido Beach." The house was unique in that it was previously occupied by F. Scott Fitzgerald and Hollywood columnist Sheilah Graham and was the very house where they had their 1930s love affair. (Their romance first told in Graham's

1958 autobiography and bestseller, *Beloved Infidel*, which the following year was made into a feature film, starring Gregory Peck and Deborah Kerr.) I have fond memories of that summer in Escondido when as boys we would swim and play with Murphy's daughter, Kit, who was our age. She had her own horse and was fond of swimming. There was also Duffy, also our age, a friend who swam with us every day. After joining the Navy and being stationed overseas, I heard that Duffy had lost a leg to a shark attack in those same Malibu waters.

Dudley Murphy was part owner of the famous Garden of Allah Hotel in the early fifties.

Author Susan Delson, in her excellent biography *Dudley Murphy, Hollywood Wild Card,* writes:

> Murphy could always be found at the center of the cultural scene: Greenwich Village when it was bohemian, Jazz-Age Paris, Hollywood in its golden era, Harlem at the height of its Renaissance. Part adventure hero, part slapstick comedian, part techno-geek, part playboy, he was a complete visionary with a directing style that was decades ahead of its time.

Still from 1924 Ballet Mécanique *directed by Dudley Murphy and Fernand Leger. Cinematography by Dudley Murphy and Man Ray, music composed by George Antheil.*

A longtime friend of George and Dorothy Hodel, Director Dudley Murphy (seated far left) at 1940 Gala Event at Hollywood's El Capitan Theatre with friends, Marlene Dietrich, Noel Coward, and Cary Grant. (Photo courtesy of Los Angeles Public Library Photo Collection)

"The Cast" as presented here primarily focuses on just those known Hollywood Insiders that were in direct association with George and Dorothy Hodel up until the time of the DA electronic stakeout in February and March of 1950.

Here's a quick review of the last days of the forty-one-day DA/LAPD surveillance of the Sowden/Franklin House, as GHH prepared to flee the country to avoid arrest.

On March 22, 1950, Lt. Frank Jemison interviewed Dorothy Hodel at her apartment on Santa Monica Pier. The transcripts of that interview (see addendum in *BDA II*) reveal Dorothy was shown photographs of both Mady Comfort and George together nude as well as a separate 1943 Santa Barbara Police booking photograph of Elizabeth Short. Dorothy stonewalled Lt. Jemison, denying she ever knew Elizabeth Short, and claimed not to know the name of the nude woman seen with George. (Before that interview, Mady Comfort, George, and Dorothy were sexual partners for years.) The following day, Dorothy went to the Franklin House and reported her conversation with Lt. Jemison and informed George that the police showed her photographs of both Mady Comfort and Elizabeth Short.

Three days later, on March 26, 1950, George was overheard talking to Baron Harringa on the wire recordings about the photo police have of him and the girl (Mady Comfort and/or Elizabeth Short?), saying, "I thought I'd destroyed them all." This was the likely catalyst for George's decision two days later to "get out of Dodge."

On March 27, George fled Los Angeles, leaving the DA Detective Lt. Frank Jemison and his men still sitting in the basement of Hollywood Police Station on a stakeout of his home, literally with their microphones up the walls.

Four days later, a newspaper reporter, who overheard the detectives discussing the case in the squad room, ran with the story which appeared in the Los Angeles *Daily News* informing Angelenos that the DA detectives are actively stalking the suspect(s) suggesting "an arrest is imminent."

Included in the article was the hint that the "Black Dahlia Avenger" may have had an accomplice(s) in the 1947 Short and French murders. The headline read, "DA aide stalks mutilation killers" and goes on to say... "The district attorney added his aide [Lt. Jemison] will continue with his inquiry until he thinks he has sufficient evidence against a party or parties and then will ask for formal murder complaints."

DA Lt. Frank Jemison

D. A. aide stalks mutilation killers

Dist. Atty. William E. Simpson said today one of his investigators is making "very good progress" in a renewed investigation of the unsolved mutilation murders of Jeanne French and Elizabeth Short, the Black Dahlia.

Simpson disclosed investigator Frank C. Jemison has been working several months on the cases, independent of the Police department. Jemison was assigned to the task at the request of the 1949 County Grand Jury.

The district attorney added his aide will continue with his inquiry until he thinks he has sufficient evidence against a party or parties, and then will ask for formal murder complaints.

The blasted body of Elizabeth Short, 22, was found Jan. 15, 1947, in a vacant lot in the southwest sector.

Exactly one month later the body of Mrs. French, 45, obscurely marked with lipstick, was discovered in a field in West Los Angeles.

Chief of Detectives Thad Brown, meanwhile, discounted reports that vital evidence in the French slaying, in the form of blood-stained clothing, had disappeared from the West Los Angeles detective bureau.

Brown said the clothing, belonging to a short-lived suspect in the case, never was recorded as evidence because its owner was absolved of any connection with the crime two weeks after it occurred.
—CHECK CLASSIFIED AD—

Daily News 3/31/50

5
REEL LIFE CRIMES IN HOLLYWOOD

"Damn, this book is Hannibal Lecter Meets
LA Confidential in *Chinatown*."

—LA Publicist after just reading
Black Dahlia Avenger in 2003

The Unfaithful (1947)

1947

Ann Sheridan   Zachary Scott   Eve Arden   LewAyres   David Goodis

THE FIRST ON-SCREEN REFERENCE to what I have termed "The LA Lone Woman Murders" was screened in that killer's most active year—1947.

The film was *The Unfaithful*, starring Ann Sheridan, Zachary Scott, Eve Arden, and Lew Ayres.

The noir romantic thriller was loosely based on a short story and later Broadway play, *The Letter* by W. Somerset Maugham. Technically speaking, it was a remake as director William Wyler released *The Letter* in 1940, starring Bette Davis, Herbert Marshall, and Gale Sondergaard.

This film version transports us from the original rainforests settings of British Malaya and Singapore to the postwar streets of Los Angeles, with many local filming locations such as Angels Flight Railway, Bunker Hill, the Bradbury Building, MacArthur Park, City Hall, Hollywood Taft Building, and The Ambassador Hotel.

Screenwriter David Goodis was a pulp fiction writer and became hugely popular when his first novel, *Dark Passage*, was adapted to the big screen and starred Humphrey Bogart and Lauren Bacall. The film is considered by many to be a film noir masterpiece. Both of these Goodis written films were released in 1947 within two months of each other.

IMDb (*International Movie Data Base*) describes the plotline for *The Unfaithful* as follows:

> A Los Angeles socialite kills a man while home alone one night and claims he was an intruder she did not know. It seems like a clear case of self-defense until the story hits the papers and people connected to the dead man come forward.

The socialite is Chris Hunter, played by Ann Sheridan. The LA case becomes high profile when she is charged with the murder of the supposed burglar who had broken into her home.

The following dialogue written by LA savvy screenwriter David Goodis shows how he was definitely up to speed on 1947 "current events" in Los Angeles.

Paula (Eve Arden), a close friend and neighbor of Chris Hunter is having morning coffee with Chris and discussing the fact that Chris had recently been attacked by an alleged burglar/robber who had broken into her home.

Chris Hunter (Ann Sheridan) on left listens as Paula (Eve Arden) discusses the high murder rate in 1947 Los Angeles

Scene: Breakfast Table, Chris Hunter residence, Los Angeles, California 1947.

PAULA:

…Of course, it's not as if he [Chris's attacker] were the only one. *Every morning you open up the paper, there's another body found on a weed-covered lot.* [emphasis mine] Believe me the day will come when parents will give their daughters a pair of brass knuckles instead of a wristwatch for graduation.

Obviously, from the dialogue he used in *The Unfaithful*, screenwriter David Goodis was familiar with the rash of Lone Woman Murders, and their frequent reference in the local newspapers.

From 1943 until the film was released in the summer of 1947, the number of women slain that the police and sheriffs suspected were connected was at seven and rising. Six more women would be added to that count before George Hodel fled the country in 1950.

Sunset Boulevard (1950)

Much to my surprise, the first celluloid named mention of LA's most horrific murder can be found as a laugh line in one of Hollywood's greatest film noirs, Sunset Boulevard (1950). The film was nominated for eleven Academy Awards and won three.

Most of us confessed cinephiles are familiar with the balcony scene and Norma Desmond's closing lines in one of Hollywood's greatest films, "All right, Mr. DeMille, I'm ready for my closeup."

But how many know that just two years after the brutal murder of Elizabeth "Black Dahlia" Short, her sobriquet would also be immortalized?

Here's a scene description and dialogue from the original screenplay, written by Charles Brackett, Billy Wilder and D. M. Marshman, Jr. The scene was written and dated "March 21, 1949," just over two years after the crime.

Ironically, shortly after this performance, Webb will become famous for his starring role in the new television show, *Dragnet* as LAPD Sergeant Joe "Just the Facts" Friday, and go on to develop a close friendship and become a drinking buddy to then LAPD Chief of Detectives, Thad Brown.

Chief Brown will also serve as Webb's "technical advisor" for the long-running hit television series. (This is the same Chief Brown that informed Webb that "the Black Dahlia case was solved. He was a doctor who lived on Franklin Avenue in Hollywood.")

In the following scene, screenwriter Joe Gillis (William Holden) has just arrived at a New Year's Eve party and is greeted by his friend and fellow writer, Artie Green (Jack Webb).

SUNSET BOULEVARD

Charles Brackett
Billy Wilder
D.M. Marshman, Jr.

March 21, 1949

ARTIE GREEN—JACK WEBB
JOE GILLIS—WILLIAM HOLDEN

DISSOLVE TO:
C-19 ARTIE GREEN'S APARTMENT

It is the most modest one-room affair, jam-packed with young people flowing over into the miniature bathroom and the microscopic kitchenette. The only drink being served is punch from a pressed-glass bowl—but everybody is having a hell of a time. Most of the men are in slacks and sweaters, and only a few of the girls are in something that vaguely suggests party dress.

Abe Burroughs sits at a small, guest-festooned piano and sings Tokio Rose. By the door, a group of young men and girls respond to the song by singing Rinso White or Dentyne Chewing Gum or something similar, in the manner of a Bach choral. Artie Green, a dark-haired, pleasant-looking guy in his late twenties, is conducting with the ladle from the punch bowl.

The door behind some of the singers is pushed open, jostling them out of their places. In comes Gillis, his hair and face wet, the collar of his Vicuna coat turned up. Artie stops conducting, but the commercial goes right on.

ARTIE

Well, what do you know! Joe Gillis!

GILLIS

Hi, Artie.

ARTIE

Where have you been keeping that gorgeous face of
yours?

GILLIS

In a deep freeze.

ARTIE

I almost reported you to the Bureau of Missing Persons.

(To the company)

Fans, you all know Joe Gillis, the well-known
screenwriter, opium smuggler and Black Dahlia suspect.

Gillis greets some of the kids by name as he and Artie push their way into
the room.

Sunset Boulevard *Apt Scene—(Left.) Joe Gillis (William Holden) greeted at the
door by (Right) Artie Green (Jack Webb) who jokingly introduces him to partygoers
as: "Well-known screenwriter, opium smuggler, and Black Dahlia suspect."*

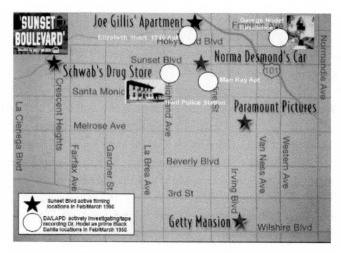

The map shows the proximity between the reel life Sunset Boulevard *film locations in 1949-50 and their counterpart real-life locations of the then active Black Dahlia investigation. The black stars on the map show shooting locations in the film: Schwab's Drug Store, Joe Gillis' Apartment, Paramount Pictures, and Norma Desmond's mansion. (J. Paul Getty Mansion at Wilshire and Irving Blvd.)*

The white circles show Hodel/Black Dahlia locations: Man Ray's apartment at the Villa Elaine 1245 N. Vine St., Hollywood Police Station (basement) which contained the wire recording machine for the DA/LAPD detective Dahlia task force. George Hodel "bugged" residence at 5121 Franklin Ave., and Elizabeth "Black Dahlia" Short's 1946 apartment at 1842 N. Cherokee Avenue.

Timing is Everything

AT THE EXACT TIME (February and March 1950) that Dr. George Hill Hodel was under active surveillance and being secretly recorded by detectives from the LAPD and DA's Office as the prime Black Dahlia suspect, director Billy Wilder was just one-mile away from Dr. Hodel's Sowden/Franklin House, on locations shooting the final scenes for what would become one of Hollywood's greatest films—*Sunset Boulevard*. The film was released in August 1950.

It is important to understand what historical, political events were unfolding behind the scenes in Los Angeles *during these very same months*.

In February and March of 1950, as the Hodel Dahlia stakeout was ongoing and in full force, the cameras were rolling on location in the making of *Sunset Boulevard*, and Deputy Chiefs William H. Parker and Thad Brown were both vying to become LA's next Chief of Police.

Thad Brown had a lock on the position as the LA Police Commission was just weeks away from taking the formal vote, Brown, with three of the five needed votes, had the majority and was destined to win.

However, Fate stepped in and one of the commissioners, Mrs. Agnes Albro, who had been diagnosed with breast cancer, died unexpectedly.

Reportedly, on August 2, 1950, in a secret meeting between the Mayor, Interim LAPD Police Chief General Worton, and four of the police commissioners, it was decided that one of the commissioners would switch his vote from Brown to Parker. Within days, Parker was appointed and would rule the LAPD with an iron fist and initiate his "proactive policing policy" for the next sixteen years.

Author John Buntin in his excellent book *LA Noir: The Struggle for the Soul of America's Most Seductive City* (Harmony Books 2009) writes:

> ...Many years later, Thad Brown would claim that he had withdrawn his name from consideration because he didn't want "Bill Parker behind me, with his knife out."

Based on my 1999-2004 Black Dahlia investigation and the discovery of the secret LA DA Hodel/Black Dahlia surveillance recordings, we now know that either murder or a serious felony assault was committed by George Hodel and Baron Harringa during the police stakeout on February 18, 1950. That recorded crime was covered up and locked away in the DA vault for fifty-three years. Based on the evidence, I would suggest an alternative reason for the selection and appointment of Parker over Brown.

Simply stated, it was FUBAR. Fucked Up Beyond All Recognition!

The Black Dahlia case was Chief of Detectives Brown's joint investigation and his officers (along with the DA detectives) while staked out and in real time overheard a woman being assaulted and crying out—and only four minutes away—*took no action to effect a rescue!*

Internally, on the QT and very hush-hush to be forever kept secret from the public—still, heads must roll. As the top dog in the Dahlia fiasco, the powers that be decided that head had to be Chief Thad Brown's.

The DA Dahlia investigation (though according to the top brass on both the DA and LAPD "was solved") would be shut down and locked away. All of the Hodel/Black Dahlia reports and recordings by order of the DA were personally hand-delivered to Chief of Detectives Thad Brown, and the investigation reassigned from the DA's Office back to the LAPD. (Those reports and evidence would shortly thereafter "disappear" from LAPD files. Another fifty years would pass before we discovered what I have called "Dahliagate," revealed only by the fact that DA Lt. Jemison had secretly locked away a second set of books and recorded transcripts.)

In the ensuing power brokerage, it was decided that Brown would be allowed to remain Chief of Detectives. Parker would take command of LAPD and together they would attempt to move forward and clean up the Department.

TRUE CONFESSIONS (1981)

> Howard Terkel: How about it, Tom? Can you get your brother the monsignor to say a mass for this cunt? It'll make the front page.
>
> Tom Spellacy: Howard, we don't even know yet whether or not she was a Catholic cunt.
>
> —Scene/dialogue from *True Confessions*

ANOTHER TWENTY-SEVEN YEARS WOULD pass before we would see the next big-screen reference to the Black Dahlia Murder.

This time it was fictionalized in John Gregory Dunne's 1977 bestselling novel, *True Confessions.*

A torture-murder. "Jane Doe" female, her nude body bisected in half and carefully posed on a vacant lot at "Thirty-Ninth and Norton." Trauma to the face and body. Identifying marks? A rose tattoo on her pubic area and a votive candle inserted in her vagina.

Elizabeth Short, "The Black Dahlia," became Lois Fazenda, "The Virgin Tramp." A wannabe actress who made porno films while she waited for her big break.

This excerpt from the book's flyleaf introduction says it best:

> An unidentified murder victim is found in a vacant lot in the shadow of the Los Angeles Coliseum. A catchy nickname is given her in jest—"The Virgin Tramp"— and suddenly a "nice quiet little homicide that would have drifted off the front pages in a couple of days" becomes a storm center that changes the lives of a score of people. Among them are: Tom and Des Spellacy, the two brothers who are the protagonists of this rich,

raucous and powerful novel of Irish-Catholic life in Southern California just after World War II.

The Right Reverend Monsignor Desmond Spellacy is chancellor of the Archdiocese of Los Angeles, a man clearly on the rise to even higher eminence in the Church. His brother, Homicide Lieutenant Tom Spellacy, is the detective in charge of the murder investigation. Once a bagman distributing payoffs to the Vice Squad. Tom was never indicted and often wonders if it was because of his brother's influence.

The book was adapted, filmed on location in Los Angeles (The Biltmore Hotel, Chinatown, Echo Park, and Olvera Street), and released as a major motion picture in 1981.

Starring Robert De Niro as Father Des Spellacy and Robert Duvall as his brother, LAPD Detective Tom Spellacy, the excellent supporting cast included veteran actors: Charles Durning, Burgess Meredith, and Rose Gregorio.

LAPD Lt. Tom Spellacy (Robert Duvall) at LA vacant lot
"Virgin Tramp" crime scene with fellow detective.

Brothers Tom (the cop) and Des (the priest) Spellacy in scene from True Confessions *(1981)*

ART IMITATING LIFE—
Chinatown *(1974)*

"George Hodel, I think, is fit company for some of Noir's most civilized villains—like Waldo Lydecker in *Laura*, Harry Lime in *The Third Man*, or even Noah Cross in *Chinatown*, the man who (thanks to the screenwriter, Robert Towne) warned us, "Most people never have to face the fact that at the right time and right place, they're capable of anything." And what had Cross done? Rape his daughter, and his city, and lived into old age."

—David Thomson *New York Times Book Review* excerpt on *Black Dahlia Avenger (2003)*

IN MY TALKS AND PowerPoint presentations over the years, during the Q&A section, this question invariably comes up: "Mr. Hodel, do you think the Noah Cross character in the movie *Chinatown* was based on your father, Dr. George Hodel?

I always answer it the same. Truth be told, I don't know.

However, here's what *we do know.*

The character Noah Cross was played by John Huston, who was the former husband of Dorothy Hodel and George's lifelong friend (at least from high school days until GHH fled the country at age forty-three).

Huston and the rest of his Hollywood insider friends knew that George as the Venereal Disease Control Officer for LA County was powerfully connected to the LA politicos, and was the "go-to" guy for discreet medical treatment for themselves or for a girlfriend who was "in trouble" and needed help.

George, like Noah Cross, was in the vernacular of that day what they called a "High Jingo": politically powerful and untouchable.

George's friends saw this play out and confirmed in his 1949 arrest for incest and abortion based on the allegations made by his fourteen-year-old daughter, Tamar.

Despite three adult witnesses being present during the sex acts, and two of them testifying during his three-week jury trial—still bingo—George was handed a "not guilty" verdict and given a "get out of jail free" card. (Fifty years later, police documents would suggest George made a $15,000 payoff to the DA's office by way of his "Hollywood defense attorney to the stars," Jerry "Get Me" Giesler.)

As relates to his daughter's (my half sister) pregnancy, George insisted he wanted her to "carry the fetus to full term and have his child." But Tamar refused, telling him she was "too young to be burdened with raising a baby."

With that, George arranged for the abortion which was performed by a friend/associate, Beverly Hills Dr. Francis Ballard. GHH then provided a perjured witness (Lillian Lenorak) in his own defense as well as at Dr. Ballard's subsequent trial.

At both trials, Lenorak testified she witnessed Tamar being examined by Dr. Ballard, "but no abortion was performed." (As we recall, she later threatened to recant her perjury and inform the DA, which resulted in GHH assaulting and drugging her, then staging her "attempted suicide" labeling her "emotionally distraught." Santa Barbara police officer Mary Unkefer, called to the Franklin House, then transported her home to Lillian's socially connected mother's residence where the mother accepted her grandson, John, but refused to take care of her daughter. Left with no alternative, Officer Unkefer was forced to take Lillian to Camarillo State Hospital for observation.

We also know that prior to the making of *Chinatown*, actress/singer, Michelle Phillips (*Mama's and Papa's*) who Tamar had known and befriended, and would later become godmother to Tamar's three sons, was well versed in all the details of the incest and trial. She also described meeting George Hodel in San Francisco in the late sixties, and described his presence as "pure evil."

Michelle would go on to relate the intimate details of the George and Tamar story to her good friend, actor, Jack Nicholson and, of course, John Huston being Dorothy's ex-husband and keeping in regular contact with her (see *BDA II*, the Huston Letters chapter), was already considered "one of the family."

It is not any stretch of the imagination to see how readily we come to the intersection of the real-life George Hodel and the fictional life of Noah Cross.

Film critic David Thomson put it best in his early *NYT* review and comparison of GHH to Noah Cross.

"And what had Cross done? Rape his daughter, and his city, and lived into old age."

Again, I will leave it to you the reader to make the call.

Here's the dialogue from the famous *Chinatown* scene where Jake demands to know the truth about the young mystery woman that Mrs. Mulwray appears to be hiding out.

Jake Gittes (Jack Nicholson) and Evelyn Mulwray (Faye Dunaway) in scene from Chinatown

PI Jake Gittes demands to know the identity of the young woman that Evelyn Mulwray is keeping in hiding.

> **Evelyn Mulwray:** *She's my daughter.*
>
> *[Gittes slaps Evelyn]*
>
> **Jake Gittes:** *I said I want the truth!*
>
> **Evelyn Mulwray:** *She's my sister…*
>
> *[slap]*

Evelyn Mulwray: She's my daughter…

[slap]

Evelyn Mulwray: My sister, my daughter.

[More slaps]

Jake Gittes: I said I want the truth!

Evelyn Mulwray: She's my sister AND my daughter! My father and I… (long pause) Understand? Or is it too tough for you?

And here's another famous *Chinatown* scene between Jake Gittes and Noah Cross.

Jake Gitties (Jack Nicholson) and Noah Cross (John Huston)

Jake Gittes: How much are you worth?

Noah Cross: I have no idea. How much do you want?

Jake Gittes: I just wanna know what you're worth. More than ten million?

Noah Cross: Oh my, yes!

Jake Gittes: Why are you doing it? How much better can you eat? What could you buy that you can't already afford?

Noah Cross: The future, Mr. Gittes! The future. Now, where's the girl? I want the only daughter I've got left. As you found out, Evelyn was lost to me a long time ago.

Jake Gittes: Who do you blame for that? Her?

Noah Cross: I don't blame myself. You see, Mr. Gittes, most people never have to face the fact that at the right time and the right place, they're capable of ANYTHING.

LA Confidential *(1974)—The Movie*

IN 1997, SOME TWENTY-THREE years after *Chinatown* was released, film director Curtis Hanson released another blockbuster film about Los Angeles, its cops, and corruption from the 1950s—*LA Confidential*.

The film starred Kevin Spacey, Russell Crowe, Guy Pearce, James Cromwell, Kim Basinger, Danny DeVito, and David Strathairn with a brilliant screenplay by Brian Helgeland.

Like *Chinatown*, the film contained no direct references to Elizabeth Short or the Black Dahlia investigation, but the ironic and highly synchronistic associations of some of the characters and locations to George Hodel and the Franklin House were mind-blowing.

As we examine what I consider to be nothing more than *happenstance,* keep in mind that it would be another two years (1999) before my father would take his life at age ninety-one (suicide by pills). And I would unwittingly be pulled into a vortex of what would become my Black Dahlia and LA Lone Woman Murders investigation.[2]

LA Confidential is set in 1953 Los Angeles.

The role of Pierce Patchett is played by David Strathairn.

Patchett is a wealthy LA behind-the-scenes shadow figure, running a vice operation and working with corrupt cops.

Pimp Patchett has a harem of high-class call girls that he has had undergo cosmetic surgery so that they resemble movie stars such as Lana Turner and others from that time period.

His distinctive Fleur-de-Lis business card reads, "Whatever You Desire."

Irony No. 1: Patchett's business cards compared to George Hodel's personal Fleur-de-lis photo album, given to me by his widow, June, days after his death. This album, with the photo of the woman who appeared to be Elizabeth "Black Dahlia" Short, would be one of the primary catalysts that began my investigations back in 1999.

---

2   When this film was released, I wasn't even aware of the victim's real name! Just her pseudonym, "Black Dahlia," and that the case was a famous LAPD unsolved from the 1940s.

Still from LA Confidential *showing Pierce Patchett's business card compared to George Hodel photo album.*

The dashing and debonair Patchett owns a large mansion in the Hollywood Hills where he has his stable of working girls "entertain" and party with his business associates and prominent LA politicos providing them with drinks, dancing, and "Whatever You Desire."

Irony No. 2: George Hodel, a dashing and debonair doctor, owned a large mansion in the Hollywood Hills and frequently threw parties with business associates and prominent LA politicos providing them with drinks, dancing, and always had women on hand to hostess and entertain.

Not only was Pierce Patchett's physical appearance and voice identical and pitch perfect to George Hodel's, but the shooting location in the film *used our former home, The Sowden/Franklin House—to shoot two separate scenes.*

"Art imitating Life" in the film with Patchett and his party girls in 1953 drinking and dancing with johns in the very room at the very home where George Hodel threw his own real-life parties from 1945–1950.

Pierce Patchett (David Strathairn)   George Hodel 1950

(Lower Left) Actor David Strathairn as "Pierce Patchett" in scene from LA Confidential. *George Hodel seated on his desk at Franklin House 1950.*

Actress Kim Basinger in the role of "Lynn Bracken" (one of Patchett's girls) dancing with a "john" at a party in the Hodel Franklin House.

Sgt. Jack Vincennes (Kevin Spacey) seated and talking with his LAPD superior, Captain Dudley Smith (James Cromwell). This dramatic scene was filmed in the kitchen of the Hodel Franklin House in 1997, some five years before its remodel in 2002.

The final irony in *LA Confidential* comes in a scene where the two LAPD detectives, Bud White (Russell Crowe) and Ed Exley (Guy Pearce) respond to Pierce Patchett's private residence and find him dead in the living room. They quickly determine it was actually a murder where the killers drugged Patchett, wrote a fake "suicide note," cut his wrists, and staged his suicide.

Compare this to George Hodel's staged "attempted suicide" of witness Lillian Lenorak at the Franklin House in 1950, where he drugged her, superficially cut her wrists, then bandaged them and called policewoman Mary Unkefer. All to discredit Lenorak as a "mental case" after she threatened to recant her trial testimony and inform law enforcement that he procured the abortion for his daughter, Tamar, and knew and killed Elizabeth "Black Dahlia" Short. (Lenorak did, in fact, inform DA investigators of what she knew after DA investigators interviewed her in Santa Barbara in early February 1950, which very likely is what initiated the electronic bugging of the Hodel residence which was installed on February 15, 1950.)

A scene from LA Confidential *where LAPD detectives White and Exley find Patchett's body in what they determine to be a "staged suicide."*

The Aviator *(2004)*

FINALLY, THERE IS DIRECTOR Martin Scorsese's *The Aviator* released in 2004, a biopic presenting us with the life and loves of legendary billionaire Howard Hughes.

The film stars Leonardo DiCaprio as Hughes, with Cate Blanchett playing his girlfriend, actress Katharine Hepburn, and Kate Beckinsale playing his backup squeeze, actress Ava Gardner.

Filmed on location in and around LA, but of special interest to us, are the interior and exterior scenes between Hughes and Gardner at the Sowden/Hodel Franklin House.

In the below stills we see Howard Hughes arguing with his girlfriend, Ava Gardner. The action revolves around the fact that Howard had his security men secretly install microphones inside Ava's residence (the Hodel/Franklin House) so he can electronically monitor her love life.

Ava, after discovering this, becomes enraged over his spying and the action spills out onto the curbside in front of the house.

Again, more Gods Laughing Irony arising from the fact that this "Made for Hollywood" fictional representation exactly mimics what occurred in real life at the Franklin House with George Hodel in Feb/March 1950.

As we know, the DA's office and LAPD secretly installed multiple microphones inside this very same residence (living room and bedroom), and tape-recorded George Hodel's sex acts, as well as his conversations and admissions as to performing abortions, making payoffs to multiple law enforcement agencies, and to killing both Elizabeth Short—The Black Dahlia—and his personal clinic secretary, Ruth Spaulding.

However, none of these facts were discovered until after gaining access to the locked secret DA Hodel-Black Dahlia Files in 2004 and due to the timing would not and could not have been known by the filmmakers.

Aviator scene filmed in the living room of former Hodel residence (Ava Gardner's home in the movie) where she is about to fly into a rage and a physical altercation with Hughes (her sometime boyfriend) after discovering he has secretly installed microphones throughout the house including her bedroom to spy on her sexual escapades.

Howard Hughes (DiCaprio) is seen here exiting the Franklin House, licking his wounds as he approaches his chauffeur/bodyguard after being assaulted by his girlfriend, Ava Gardner, who has demanded he remove all of the hidden microphones he has secretly installed in her home.

Here is the excerpt from the original *Aviator* screenplay that includes the dialogue for this Sowden/Franklin House scene.

(Living room)

AVA

Under my bed! You put a goddamn microphone under my bed!

HOWARD

Listen to me. I am concerned about you. I just wanna make sure you're okay.

AVA

And who is in that car?

HOWARD

That car is for your protection!

AVA

The only one I need protection from is you, you sick bastard! You don't own me, Howard. I'm not one of your teenage whores or some damn airplane.

HOWARD

I'll have them take all the bugs out. I need to know where you are Ava.

AVA

Why?

HOWARD

Because I worry about you, that's why.

AVA

Bullshit! What do you mean "all the bugs?"

HOWARD

There's more.

AVA

How many?

HOWARD

I don't know. Twelve, maybe and on the telephones.

AVA

Oh, Christ, Howard, on the telephone? You listen to my phone calls?

HOWARD

No, no, honey. I would never do that. I'd never do that. I just read the transcripts, that's all.

AVA

What do you wanna know, Howard? Was I screwing Artie Shaw last night?
Was I screwing Sinatra the night before? You bet. Everyone said you were a
lunatic, I didn't listen. It's no wonder Kate Hepburn dumped your demented ass!

HOWARD
Shut your goddamn mouth.

AVA
Get out, you pathetic freak. Get out!

(Exterior front of house)

CHAUFFEUR
Is everything alright sir?

HOWARD
Take out all the bugs. (whispers to him) Except for the one
on the bedroom phone.

Our former home, the Lloyd Wright–built Mayan Temple in the heart
of Hollywood, was and remains a Hollywood set. I expect it always will.

Most of these reel-to-real filmings we have examined are obviously
Twilight Zone ironic, but still happenstance. *Sunset Boulevard, LA Confidential,*
and *Aviator* all fall into that category.

However, *Chinatown*, I think, may be the one exception where, in my
opinion, we can add to its fictional storytelling the caveat—"Based on a
True Story."

Totally Bosch

Los Angeles is the construct of its mythologies good and bad, fact and
fiction. The legend of Elizabeth Short is one of the most enduring. But
now Steve Hodel has come to put the Black Dahlia painfully to rest. With
the tenacity and patience of the veteran homicide detective he once was,
Hodel goes from odd coincidence to rock-solid conclusion. Taking us on
the intriguing and unsettling journey every step of the way, Hodel's
investigation is thoroughly and completely convincing. So too is this
book. As far as I am concerned, this case is closed. Elizabeth Short's
legend is now shared with a killer who has been pulled from the shadows
of time and into the light. Everybody counts, or nobody counts, and that

includes the people shrouded in our myths. Steve Hodel knows this. And
now we do, too.

—*Michael Connelly, bestselling author: Harry Bosch mystery series*
2003 Review of Black Dahlia Avenger: A Genius for Murder

I ORIGINALLY WROTE AND posted the below article on my blogsite back in 2010 and updated it in 2015.

Since then author Michael Connelly's bestselling novels (twenty at my last count) have and are being adapted for television as the hit series, *Bosch*, now (2018) in its third season.

Author Michael Connelly's Hieronymus "Harry" Bosch—An Identity Crisis?

Los Angeles, California

November 23, 2015

I rarely read mystery novels, with one major exception-those written by bestselling author, Michael Connelly.

Prior to 2003, I had never heard of him.

My first awareness of Connelly's writings came in 2003, post-publication of *Black Dahlia Avenger* when the two of us were scheduled to speak at the 2003 Bouchercon Convention in Las Vegas.

That same year, Michael had been nominated as president of the Mystery Writers of America and would preside over the upcoming Edgar Awards in NYC. (My first book, *Black Dahlia Avenger*, was one of the six nominees in the running for an Edgar Award in the True Fact category.)

Based on those two imminent meetings with Connelly, I figured the least I could do was read one of his novels. But, which one? I threw a dart, and it landed on *The Last Coyote* (Little, Brown and Company 1995).

I picked up a copy and read it nonstop. I WAS HOOKED.

I went back and began reading his novels chronologically, and as of this writing (2010) I am just completing his fourteenth novel, *The Brass Verdict,* and find myself a bit depressed at the prospect that there is only a handful remaining. Then what do I do? (It is now 2015, and I have read all of his novels, including his just-published *The Crossing.*)

Harry Bosch—An Identity Crisis?

IN MY OPINION, MICHAEL Connelly is the best police procedural writer on the planet. He's got it down to near perfection. His character Hieronymus "Harry" Bosch is my hero. He's an "out-of-the-box" thinking detective, who plays it straight, has a high solve rate, and gets it right most of the time, but occasionally screws up. What's not to love?

But, I have to admit; Connelly has created a character whose biography so closely mimics my own on so many levels that I cannot help but IDENTIFY with Harry.

As you review the below comparisons, keep in mind while Connelly has publicly indicated that Harry Bosch "is a composite of several real-life individuals" (along with some fictional characteristics of his own)—*I am not one of those individuals.*

To my knowledge, Connelly, while giving my book one of my favorite "author blurbs," still did not know me, and it is doubtful he had ever heard of me before the publication of my book in 2003. I retired from the LAPD in 1986 after nearly twenty-four years of service. Connelly didn't publish his first novel, *The Black Echo,* until 1992.

Listed below are a few of the reasons why I have a bit of an identity crisis with my good friend Detective Hieronymus "Harry" Bosch. Harry will tell you, "There are no coincidences."

I would, for the most part, agree. So, for the moment, let's just call these—"synchronicities."

Detective 3 Harry Bosch/Detective 3 Steve Hodel Comparisons

HB: Harry Bosch (fictional)—**SH**: Steve Hodel (real life)

SH: Born at Queen of Angels Hospital, Los Angeles

HB: Born at Queen of Angels Hospital, Los Angeles

SH: His mother named him after a character (Stephen Daedalus) created by her favorite author, James Joyce in his bestselling novel, *Ulysses*.

HB: His mother named him after one of her favorite fifteenth-century artists, Hieronymus Bosch.

SH: Sent to MacLaren Hall and temporary foster homes from Hollywood in his youth due to his mother's repeated arrests for child neglect and alcoholism.

HB: Sent to MacLaren Hall and temporary foster homes from Hollywood in his youth due to his mother's untimely death. (She was a prostitute murdered in Hollywood.)

SH: Joined the military as a teenager and earned his GED (General Education Diploma).

HB: Joined the military as a teenager and earned his GED (General Education Diploma).

SH: Joined the LAPD at age twenty-one and promoted to detective after working patrol for five years.

HB: Joined the LAPD at age twenty-one and promoted to detective after working patrol for five years.

SH: Assigned to Hollywood Detective Division-Homicide.

HB: Assigned to Hollywood Detective Division-Homicide.

SH: Had one of the highest solve/clearance rates in the LAPD and was possessed of a strong disdain for any abuse of power.

HB: Had one of the highest solve/clearance rates in the LAPD and was possessed of a strong disdain for any abuse of power.

SH: Promoted to Detective III, the highest attainable rank within the Detective Bureau.

HB: Promoted to Detective III, the highest attainable rank within the Detective Bureau.

SH: Owned a home high in the Hollywood Hills and had multiple marriages.

HB: Owned a home high in the Hollywood Hills and had multiple marriages.

SH: Retired from the LAPD and became a California State Licensed PI working criminal murder cases.

HB: Retired from the LAPD and became a California State Licensed PI working criminal murder cases.

SH: After his retirement, former LAPD partners viewed him as "going to the Dark Side" because of his work for a criminal defense attorney on a high-profile LA murder case in which Hodel suspected the client was being wrongfully prosecuted and may be innocent.[3]

HB: After his retirement, former LAPD partners viewed him as "going to the Dark Side" because of his work for a criminal defense attorney of a high-profile LA murder case in which Harry suspected the client was being wrongfully prosecuted and may be innocent.

On April 6, 2016, I received this update from a reader, Brian Weatherby, who made the following comment/observation:

> Steve,
>
> Add this to your similarities between Harry Bosch and yourself: Both discovered an LAPD cover-up of murder and likely serial murder relating to his family decades after the fact. Bosch: His mother's likely killer was a drug informant that had an "untouchable" status and was relocated. George had a de facto untouchable status and got out of the country before the DA caught him.

Hopefully, these real-life comparisons to Harry's fictionally created life with all of the "been there done that" synchronicities will help to explain my feeling of close affinity and kinship toward Michael Connelly's, LAPD Detective III, Hieronymus "Harry" Bosch.

Now, let's take one final look at how Hollywood's *The Dream Factory* weaves myth and reality together with a peek into sixty seconds from the reel-real life of Elizabeth "Black Dahlia" Short.

---

3   Hodel's investigation established that the defendant was, in fact, innocent of the crime [murder] and the defendant was released by order of the court after five years of wrongful detention.

Black Dahlia Makes It to Hollywood (Blvd)

ONE OF THE MANY Dahlia Myths is that Elizabeth Short came to Hollywood to "be discovered." The "I want to be in pictures" myth—as best as I can tell, is simply *not true.*

In fifteen years of research, I have found zero evidence to substantiate that Elizabeth Short ever expressed a personal desire to become an actress. Nor, to my knowledge, has any documentation been found that she ever applied for or auditioned at any film studio to be an extra.

The only sources on this come from the fevered minds of hack writers in tabloid magazines and later fictional accounts in novels and films such as the previously referenced *True Confessions,* which portrayed her as a porno actress, Lois Fazenda, "The Virgin Tramp."

Rare WWII VJ Day Film Footage

IN EARLY 2003, BEFORE the scheduled mid-April publication of *Black Dahlia Avenger,* veteran newsman and television producer David Browning was preparing an hour show on my investigation for NBC's *Dateline.*

Producer Browning had been conducting extensive research for months fact-checking my work as well as obtaining interviews of various witnesses and gathering relevant photographs.

About one month before the scheduled airing, he called me and asked if I could meet him to review some new material.

We met and without any introduction or fanfare, he simply "rolled" some film footage and said, "Take a look."

I did and asked him to play it again and then a third time.

I couldn't believe my eyes. David had found a ninety-second piece of 16mm film footage from Los Angeles. The location was the 6600 block of Hollywood Boulevard.

It was taken on, August 15, 1945—VJ Day!

The film showed six or seven young women riding in an open convertible down Hollywood Boulevard. A sailor runs up to the car and kisses several of them, including a dark-haired woman.

David had edited the footage to zoom in on and highlight the black-haired beauty.

After the third viewing, he smiled and said, "So, what do you think Steve?

"No doubt in my mind. It is definitely Elizabeth Short."

He agreed.

I was stunned. "Where did this come from?"

David went on to explain he had found it while reviewing hours of stock footage from that period.

Thanks to the keen eyes of veteran television producer (now a producer for CBS's *Sixty Minutes*) Elizabeth Short debuted first in 2003 on the *Dateline NBC* episode "Black Dahlia" with Josh Mankiewicz. She then was seen in a subsequent program (also produced by Browning) in 2005, CBS's *48-Hours*, "Black Dahlia Confidential," hosted by news reporter, Erin Moriarty.

(Lt to Rt) Producer David Browning, Reporter Erin Moriarty, Researcher/ partner Roberta McCreary and author at Sowden/Franklin House for CBS's 48-Hours, *"Black Dahlia Confidential," shoot 2004.*

Incredibly, a part of the Black Dahlia lore and legend has become a reality. This, almost lost to history movie footage, is the Black Dahlia's only "role."

Elizabeth Short made it *into pictures* in Hollywood—on Hollywood. Her audition, bizarrely caught in a Zapruder-like few seconds as she passed by in the back of an open convertible, was immortalized on film, on VJ Day, in August 1945. However, she would not be *discovered* and debuted to the public for another sixty years.

Known photo
Elizabeth
Short

VJ Day August 15, 1945, Elizabeth Short with friends celebrating the end of the war. This is the only known film footage of "The Black Dahlia" in existence. To view this 1945 footage online go to http://stevehodel.com/videos

6
TAMAR NAIS HODEL 1935-2015

1950

Tamar "Through the Years." The 1950 photo shows her at age fifteen and was taken in Mexico just months after she had testified as a victim at her father's incest child molestation trial in Los Angeles. Her mother, Dorothy Anthony Barbe, is seen standing to her rear.

Tamar, a sultry twenty-something

IN 2015, I WROTE the following blog on my website shortly after my sister's death.

Tamar Nais Hodel Dies at 80 in Honolulu, Hawaii

October 18, 2015

Los Angeles, California

Two weeks ago, today, my half sister, Tamar Nais Hodel, passed away in her sleep. She was eighty years old.

She bore, five children. Two daughters, Fauna and Fauna II (Deborah Elizabeth), and three sons, Peace, Love, and Joy. My heartfelt condolences go out to each one of them.

I have written much about my half sister's life, and through my writings, she has come to be known as, "the daughter of Dr. George Hill Hodel, the Black Dahlia serial killer, and the victim of his incest and sexual molestation."

Sadly, from early childhood, Tamar suffered extreme physical, sexual, and psychological abuse at the hands of her (our) father. Sexualized at an early age, her life continued out of control (sex, drugs, etc.) for decades. The cycle continued. The abused, became the abuser, creating more pain and suffering for her own five children. Each child's suffering unique to him or her.

Much could be said about Tamar. She had hoped to tell her own story, in her own words, but that was not to be.

I am not going to attempt to expand on her life, about which I know little. I do know that she had a natural ability to accept all people of all races and will let her close friend, folk and blues singer Josh White, speak for her.

One of my favorite songs exemplifies my sister's spirit. The song made popular by Josh in the forties is "Free and Equal Blues." Listen carefully to the lyrics, and you will better understand a part of Tamar that sought for Goodness and Fairness.

THE INTERVIEW

IN JULY 2004, I made arrangements for Tamar to fly to Los Angeles for a short visit. She needed to have some dental work done and wanted a specific Orange County dentist to do the work. This was the first time I had seen my half sister in person in over twenty years.

In fact, I recall the exact date time and location of our last visit—it was memorable.

Tamar and I were in the bar at the Ilikai Hotel, Waikiki Beach, Honolulu, Hawaii, preparing to go to dinner. The date was March 5, 1982.

I was there on an extradition preparing to bring back a suspect who was in custody at Hawaii 5-0 (the real one). A short three-day trip. I was on my fourth scotch when I got a page from the hotel to "please call the front desk."

It was my supervisor, Detective III Russ Kuster calling from Hollywood Homicide.

"Steve, need you back ASAP. Can you catch the next flight? John Belushi is dead at the *Chateau Marmont*. Looks like an overdose, but who knows? Press is all over us. You're the senior man here. I want you to handle it."

I respectfully but firmly told Russ that there was "no way" I could get there. I had started processing the paperwork on my in-custody suspect and had to be at the Honolulu courthouse the following day.

Russ didn't like it but took no for my answer.

Tamar and I had dinner. That was twenty-two years ago.

Several days after Tamar's arrival in Los Angeles, we met, and I made arrangements to have a private videographed interview conducted by a top television journalist friend and his cameraman son.

I wanted to record and preserve as many of Tamar's memories as she could recall related to her growing-up years and the time spent with our father and us three brothers at the Franklin House.

The videotaped interview lasted ninety minutes.

Not wanting anything to get lost in translation, I will here omit the question portions of the interview and just present Tamar's verbatim responses as she recalls and reflects on her early memories of "The Franklin House Years."

While the interview is long, I have decided to present it in its entirety, unedited.

With Tamar's passing, it is literally the last word on the subject. Further, as a daughter/victim/witness, Tamar provides us with details and insights into George's personality and actions that are new and revelatory.

I will include my comments and observations in brackets when and if I feel they are necessary for clarification purposes.

Tamar Nais Hodel in Los Angeles July 2004 Age: 69

Video Interview of Tamar Nais Hodel

July 2004

Studio City, California

(Verbatim transcript, Interviewer's questions omitted.)

My earliest memories about my father were—I was about nine, and I begged my mother…my mother and father were separated and I wanted to see my father. He lived in a house at that time in South Pasadena. It was a wonderful house because you went round and round and round up the driveway to this magical lush house. And there were only two houses on the hill. So, I arrived, and there was this person. He had a purple bedroom that you could never enter. That was forbidden, and there was purple hangings and purple sheets, and I got in trouble once for peeking in. He was very stern. I was very surprised. How stern he was, and he ran the house. He was very stern with Steven's mother, Dorero. [This would be the yet unidentified home we lived in circa 1943 as described by witness Mady Comfort where she had her sexcapades with George and Dorothy.]

Well, I'd seen him up until I was about two or three. But, then I hadn't, and I'd wanted my father. I needed my father. We really had no contact except for recordings he'd make and send to me. I'd lived in a matriarchal home. A household of women and I'd had no idea. I never was raised to obey men. And he you obeyed, or it was very severe punishment.

Well, he just loved purple. I hear in the office in the Philippines he had oodles of purple. Well, he was royal you see. I remember him years later, on the intercom at the Franklin House, saying, 'This is God Speaking." And, we'd run. [Laughs]

Yes, saw him more around 1946. Again, I wanted to go live with my father. My mother, who I'm sure was glad to get rid of me, sent me off to my father. He had the Franklin home and my goodness, what an impression. What a feeling walking up to that house for the first time. It was a magnificent house.

Though he was very strict, he was more mellow then, than before. I was about eleven then. We sunbathed nude in the house because the house was completely private, like a Spanish home. I thought it was marvelous. It was a very interesting group of people. Besides my father, there was my grandfather and his ex-wife from France. An—... I don't remember her name. I'm sure Steve knows. And, there were some artists living in the back, in the studio, and a strange maid named, Ellen. Various people were always coming and going. John Huston often came. They [George and John] were kind of archrivals. Even though they were friends, they would kind of try to outdo each other, as to who was the most important. And John really had it made, 'cause he could pick up a guitar and try and sing. [Grandfather's ex-wife from France was Andree Clotilde Hodel (nee Servel), a music teacher graduated from the Sorbonne, in Paris, France. She married grandfather in LA on September 23, 1940. Andree was at the Franklin House in 1945. However, they were obviously divorced shortly after that, as Grandfather in 1946 would remarry a lab technician named Alice, employed at his son's First Street Clinic, who would remain his wife until his death in 1954.]

Andree Clotilda Hodel. (Passport photo)

Andree and George Hodel Sr. 1937 Trip to Naples, Italy (Pompei)
Andree Hodel, circa 1945

O yes, very Bohemian. Actors and dancers and actresses. I don't know any other...I grew up a Bohemian from San Francisco, so it's all I know. I found the world strange after I left that. His home, and the court trial and everything, because I had no idea what middle America was like. Surprise. [laugh]

It was a magnificent house. I used to sunbathe up in that balcony in the front. For fun. Just to look like a statue lying on the front of the house. [Tamar, then age thirteen, would pose nude on the elevated stone entrance high above the steps. She would freeze in place pretending to be a statue. Passersby on the sidewalk would stare up in amazement, and she would move, laugh at them and run back inside the house.]

There were always woman lined up to see my father. I mean they would take their turns going in the bedroom. We were lucky if we got to see him. That was mostly his life. Women and giving orders about everything. Yes, beautiful women lined up, and they were in competition with each other. [Taking an educated guess (though I could be wrong), I suspect "women lined up at his bedroom" may have been "working girls" (possibly even LA's foremost madam Brenda Allen's stable of 114 prostitutes) being treated for an STD and getting a shot of the newly released miracle drug, penicillin.]

I don't remember us going to the clinic and working or anything. I just remember that there were always women there [Franklin House] who were taking up his time. We were resentful because we wanted to be able to see him. Once in a while, we got to go out on outings, to the theater, or a play or something. We always went late, so he would be explaining what we were missing, prior to our entering the theater.

He acted like a king and had a lot of power. In his voice and in his attitude. I can't say I spent any fun times with him. I don't ever remember him like that.

Well yes, my mother had sent me a doll. Oh yes, right after the Dahlia thing happened he said: "We couldn't sunbathe nude because we were being watched." I didn't know why. He didn't explain. But, we followed his orders. Then a short time after that my mother sent me a baby doll that I had wanted. It had lamb's wool hair, and I asked him [George] to name her because he always picked such wonderful names. He smiled, and he said, "Call her Elizabeth Ann." And, I did, but I thought that wasn't a very unusual name, but I did it. It wasn't until somewhere in the eighties when someone handed me a book. 'Cause I'd always said that I thought my father killed the Black Dahlia. But, I didn't know for sure. This friend brought me a *Good Housekeeping* or something like that, and I opened it up an article on Elizabeth Ann Short. And that was just another little piece that felt that he had. [As mentioned previously in *BDA*, addressing the "Elizabeth Ann" story. In questioning Tamar on this, she definitely recalls father telling her to name the doll "Elizabeth" and thought he also said "Ann" but acknowledged to me she could be in error on the middle name. The FBI and the LA newspapers referenced Short's middle name as "Ann" and the misnomer seems to have stuck. I suspect it was something more than "coincidental" that Tamar chose to name her second daughter, born in 1954, "Deborah Elizabeth."]

The nude sunbathing was around the same time. Because he was being watched at that time. I didn't know anything about why but looking back on it all.

No, the Dahlia murder wasn't talked about in the house, but it seemed to give him immense pleasure to tell me to call her (the doll) Elizabeth. That's all I know. But, he said weird things too. Very strange things. He would leave notes for the milkman to deliver "pints of cum." He would tell me things like that. [Laughs] I mean what do you say?

[RE: the "police watching us" comment.] You have to understand that anything he (George) said was like an edict. You just followed what he said. Because he was an "authority." I didn't think about it I just did what he said.

Occasionally, people would break into the house. And, he had an electric eye over one portion of the house where the library was and where the library opened to go down to this little place down below, which was a, I don't know what? Private room? So, he had his electric eye beamed there. And he had his stolen treasures from the communists and his artwork in the front room. That's the way he was. That's the way things were. [I can only assume by this statement that Tamar never actually saw inside the secret small storage area behind the sliding bookcases. She was under the impression that it led downstairs to the basement. It did not. It was merely a room about 5'x12' built in 1926 during Prohibition to hide the booze.]

When Steven told me he was writing a book, I said to myself, 'Hah, now he will investigate and see whether—I thought he was writing a book about the LAPD. So, if he's doing that, he's going to find out about the Black Dahlia, and we'll know. 'Cause, I wanted to know.

You see, all the years that my father was alive, I wanted to talk to him. After the court trial, we saw each other on a couple of occasions but didn't really talk. And I wanted to. As I got older, and a little more conscious of everything that happened, I wanted to speak with him. I also wanted him to say that he was sorry for the life he gave me. Because, when he said that I was a liar, that altered my life completely, and I had no family support. He took everything away by protecting himself in that way. And, he did it fiercely. So, I wanted to speak with him before he died. But, I was afraid to go. Many times, people would say, "Look, I'll pay your fare, and you can go to talk to him." This was in San Francisco and in the Philippines. Once, when they gave me the fare to go to the Philippines, I called him and said I was coming. He said, "Oh, I'm just leaving tomorrow, I'm just flying out, but I'll come and see you, I promise." But, he didn't.

Yes, I was afraid, and in the end, my son Peace said, "You have to resolve this. You have to go talk to him, and I'll pay your way." But, I was afraid. I was afraid if I walked in that house and I talked to him honestly, the way I wanted to speak. And, I wasn't angry. Honestly, I was hurt, but not angry, that I would never ... There was the possibility that I would never leave. I felt that he might kill me. That's what I thought. Just to shut me up.

Because he said that this [the incest] never happened. I knew that there was more than one murder and I knew in my heart that he had killed women. And, I wanted to say to him, "It's much easier on this side, to say, and I'm the one person you can talk to, 'cause I'm not going to go run and tell anybody. I just want to talk to you about this. Because if you don't handle this before you die, it's a lot harder to do it on the other side." So, that was where I wanted to come from but, I was afraid. And I didn't know who I could take with me. To make sure I got out of there. I just had this sense of dread, and actually, I think I was right.

Yes, I thought there was a possibility that my father might kill me that I was gambling, and that was too high a risk to take. I was afraid of him. I want you to know I loved my father. I feared my father. And, I wanted to make peace with my father. But, I didn't want to die to have that conversation, and I was sure that that was possible. So, I didn't accept the offer to go. And, when I found out later that he had called my older brother Duncan to his bedside a week or two before he died he said to him, "I just want to tell you that everything that Tamar said [incest allegations] was a lie and wasn't true." So just think, if he was saying that just before he died, I was correct, it wasn't safe for me to go.

John Huston was a tall, very powerful man also. Almost overshadowing my own father. As I said, they were in competition with each other. But, my most vivid memory of John and I'm sorry to say this for Angelica's sake, but it's the truth. When I was eleven, we were sunbathing nude before we were told not to, and John was drunk. And, he tried to rape me. I was rescued by my stepmother, Steven's mom, Dorero. She pulled him off and said, "John John, no." And, everything was OK, but I will not forget that.

No, it was not a party. And I never did experience a party as has been described so often. I'm talking about normal everyday life at the house. John was a frequent visitor. I had actually left the center [courtyard], and I was nude, going into my bathroom. He came after me, and he pinned me down to the floor, and Dorero heard me and heard him, and she came and pulled him off and said, "Leave her alone."

Well, that was in keeping with what I knew about men and the house, I mean, I hadn't had lots of conversations with him. We children were kind of seen but not heard, you know. I mean it was in keeping with…women were there to serve men…I don't quite know how to explain it. I was shocked that that happened, but she got him away so quickly that I didn't think about it again, except in recollection with what I know about John.

John used to come to the house. Even in the house in South Pasadena, he came, and I know that Dorero always said that there was a rivalry between my father and he. He was a very colorful person. You definitely noticed him when he was around.

There was a lot of sex going on in my father's bedroom, but I never saw a party ever. Now, I've heard these incredible stories, and things were printed and said in the newspaper that I never said. Because I never witnessed parties. The only time that the whole thing happened with my father that came out in the court trial was one time.

I had come home from school, and I was allowed in my father's bedroom. So, I went in, and he had a few other people there, and he was hypnotizing one of the people, Barbara. He was hypnotizing her, and Fred Sexton was there, whom I'd known over the years. Known him and his wife, Gwynn. [Actually, Sexton's wife's name was Gwain.] Another woman was there. [Interview stopped while an airplane flies over the residence.]

[Interviewer states that "Huston had a reputation for not particularly being a nice man by all accounts." Tamar agrees.]

No, not a nice man, not at all. Did you ever see that ridiculous film that was made, *White Hunter Black Heart*? That was so ridiculous.

Yes, there was always a line of women waiting to see him. Taking up his time so we couldn't talk to him. We would be there for dinner. At the dinner table, but he was like the king. It was a mini version of *The King and I*. He ruled, and we followed. He didn't pay a lot of attention to us.

When I was eleven he gave me, he had a library of erotica, and he started to give me the books. I was a great reader a fairy tale reader anyway, and so we just progressed to …which at puberty was very interesting to me, the erotica. And the erotica, I must say was not vulgar, it wasn't, it was quite beautiful compared to what I've seen of what pornography is today. It was fascinating. So, that is how I guess he prepared me. And he used to tell me, "When you're sixteen, I'll make love to you, and you will be a woman." So, I thought, oh, well that's wonderful. I had no… I didn't have a middle-class background, and I didn't know what the standards were.

Lenny Bruce and I were good friends, and Lenny tried to explain to me how other people thought. And how you had to get inside their heads to understand what was going on. Well, I didn't have that experience until after Juvenile Hall. Then I began seeing how other people thought and how shocked they were to find out about how I lived and how I grew up. I never fit into…I didn't go to games. I didn't do any of those things, so I didn't have people giving me feedback about what was going on.

And when the event [incest] happened with my father, which was only one time and I went to my girlfriend at school, Sonia Biberman, her father was Herbert Biberman and told her I was pregnant. I'd got pregnant just like that. And, she said, "You'll have to have an abortion." And, I didn't know what that was, but, I knew it was something better than having a baby. He [George] wanted me to have the baby. He thought that would be great and he would send me off somewhere to have the baby. I didn't like that idea at all, so…[Tamar initially disclosed the incest and sex acts with George and the three adults to my mother, Dorothy, who told her she "feared for Tamar's life." Tamar ran away and after three days of searching the police found her hiding out at her girlfriend Sonia Biberman's home. Sonia's parents were apparently away in Europe at the time.]

We looked up to the Great George Hodel. We were privileged. I didn't have any girlfriends. I had just started Hollywood High School, and I knew Sonia who lived in the area. Well, actually, it was her aunt and uncle that were Gale Sondergaard and Larry, you know the harmonica player. [Interviewer provides the name Parks, then corrects it saying, "No, Adler."]

Yes, you're right, Larry Adler. And they had had a beautiful estate, so I had met her and become friends. And when this happened, and I became pregnant, I told her about it.

Even when I was eleven and he [George] gave me the erotica, and he attempted to teach me how to give him oral sex I failed miserably on this adventure. I was embarrassed because I failed HIM. So, I told my mother about it when I went back to visit, and I said what had happened, and she said, "I will have to talk with your father." Then, I never heard anything. She never responded, or came back to me and said anything. So, that just kind of slid by. And years later when I was about eighteen, I said, "Why didn't you help me? Why didn't you speak up for me? Why? Why? And she said, well she had gone to him and said what had happened, what I said, and he told her that I was a pathological liar and that I had said the same thing about her and her mother." That so turned her off and frightened her that she assumed he was telling the truth. [Perfect example of GHH's deviousness and quick-witted ability to discredit the witness. We are reminded of his quick actions with Lillian Lenorak after she threatened to go to the DA and admit she perjured herself and lied in court for George. What does he do? Drugs her, stages her "attempted suicide," bandages her (the rescuer), and sets her up as a "mental case" not to be believed.]

Yes, I grew up in a very closed world. I had no idea what the rest of the world was like. An unusual world, it was Bohemian. I have a friend who used to refer to George as "The First Avant-garde." I know I've had a very unusual upbringing, to say the least. There were many good things. There were many wonderful things. I mean even going to a play with him and you missed the first act. The way he described what you'd missed you felt privileged even though you missed the first act you got to…

Yes, Man Ray. He was our family photographer. He took a lot of pictures of me when I was about twelve. He and his wife. I didn't like him very much, but I loved having my picture taken. He just felt creepy. He never did anything untoward, but he just didn't feel good to be around. He just felt like a dirty old man. He took nudes of me. They weren't lewd; they were nudes. I don't know what happened to them? I used to have some of them. Years ago, my mother didn't like them. I'd love to be able to find some of those prints. That would be great if somebody somewhere saved any of them.

He [Man Ray] reminded me of my grandfather, who was a dirty old man, who had made passes at me when I was about eleven. Those people weren't charming. George was charming. You have no idea how charming he was. And, it's going to be difficult to find someone to play him because he was so powerful. He was so powerful; I remember how shocked I was –I remember in San Francisco in the sixties. We were crossing Broadway, and the street was packed with cars, and he just raises his arm up in the air and walks without looking to the right or to the left. So, that's kind of the way he was. He behaved as though he was the king. [I found this comment interesting as I had a similar incident with Dad in downtown LA sometime in the seventies. After a visit with him, I dropped him across the street from his hotel and without even looking he began crossing the street. A car slammed on its brakes and hit the horn. Dad just raised and shook his fist and keep crossing with other cars having to brake for him. My reaction was identical to as Tamar had described it—a king whose subjects must yield to at all times.]

Women were there to serve him in every way. But, you see, now that I know for sure that he has murdered a number of women, I have to look at it all so differently. Knowing. I go back to an incident that I go back to when I was pregnant with my son Joy. He came to visit me. After the court trial, George would appear. Not tell you he was going to be there, he'd just come. And, he always came when I was about to give birth to a baby too, which seemed very strange to me but…He'd arrive, and he took me to dinner at the Beverly Hilton I think it was. Anyway, we were walking along, and they had redecorated the Hilton, and they had these large Rhododendron-like flower pattern on the carpet and he asked me what I thought of it.

I told him I thought it was unattractive. I thought it was ugly. He said, "No, no. What pattern do you see?" I said I thought it looked like Rhododendron flowers to me. He said, "No no. Look. It looks like lips. Nether lips."

So this is slowly sinking in. I'm pregnant, right, walking along with him. When I finally saw he meant it was the shape of a vagina, I said, "Yes." Then he took his foot, and he stomped on it, and he said, "Did that hurt?" And, he smiled. Then the elevator doors opened, and we went into the elevator, and I thought, Oh my God. He always threw curveballs like that. I'm the kind of person that don't react and say quick what's on my mind. I'm stunned for a while when people act like that. Now, I'm thinking back and putting all the pieces together and realizing what a terribly sadistic cruel person he was, though brilliant. But, he must have been so troubled.

Because he came to visit in San Francisco, again appearing out of nowhere when the Mamas & the Papas were doing their first concert. And, I had asked The Legion of Mary, I'd become a Catholic at that point, to light candles for the concert. Because John [Phillips] had said, "Oh my God, we're doing our first live concert, and we need candles, Tamar." So, the Bay Area was doing candles.

He [George] arrived with two beautiful young women. I was living in a housing project in North Beach. I invited him to come with me to see Michelle [Phillips] at the Fairmont, and we went to the hotel and knocked on the door, and Michelle opened the door. I said, "I'd like you to meet my father, Dr. George Hodel." And, she nearly fainted. Her eyes rolled. And she pulled it together, and she put out her hand, and she said, "I've known you since I was twelve." Because I had always talked about him and raised Michelle from age twelve.

We went in, and fans were throwing so many drugs and everything you could think of. A knock would come on the door, and you would open the door and... An ounce of hash arrived, and he said, "Oh we've got too much," and John threw it in the wastebasket. I reached in and retrieved it. I mean it was crazy like that. And, they were ordering a large meal before the concert and then my father took charge. He [George] reminds me of Anton Walbrook in *The Red Shoes*. Yes, an impresario. Definitely an impresario, and he said, "No no no. You don't eat a large meal before a concert." He changed the order. Called and had everything changed to hors d'oeuvres.

He passed the hash pipe around to everybody, but I noticed that he didn't smoke. So the following day, after the concert I said to the two women, how strange it was that he hadn't smoked. And she said, "Oh, he doesn't smoke anymore. He doesn't do that anymore because the last time he smoked in Tokyo he had me lock him in the bathroom and told me not to let him out all night and he said, "Don't let me out because sometimes I do terrible things." My hair stood up. And she said, "He cried all night. While in there he cried." So when I heard that that is what led to why I wanted to talk to him. Because I thought that I knew so much about him that I could help. That's what I thought. No, she didn't expand on it. If only I could remember her name. I'm sure she's alive. She was a young woman in the sixties. If only she'd come forward, and maybe she will. If she wasn't enchanted by him.

[Asked about drug use in the Franklin House] No, not that I knew of. I never saw that. Well, yes he smoked hashish because he was a doctor so he could do anything. But, an interesting piece of information was that years later in Hawaii, in the fifties, someone called me. Two people called me. One called to tell me that he wanted to reach him [George] because he [George] had developed and worked for the arresting cure for leprosy when he was in Hawaii.

And the other that he [George] had developed a hashish oil in the thirties, and it was legal then, and there was a paper written about it. He'd written a paper. Then I remembered that my mother told me, that George had developed this oil that made you high for three months. She complained because she was cleaning up after everybody that partied at their house.

[Tamar asked to explain what happened regarding the incest allegation in the summer of 1949]

Well, I came home from school. I was allowed in the bedroom. There was this session going on. He was hypnotizing this girl named Barbara whom I hadn't met before. Fred Sexton was there, and someone else was there. Someone I knew. Connie? I'm not sure. We watched with fascination all the hypnotism. I was given a drink. I don't know what, but I was given a drink, and I drank it. Pretty soon, and I don't know why? I don't know what happened, but I was taking off my clothes, or my clothes were being taken off, and Fred Sexton was attempting to have sex with me, and that made George very angry, and he kicked him out of the room.

Now, while this was going on, I felt as though I was looking down on myself from up high in the ceiling. I mean I was in shock about everything that was going on. I can't explain to you what happened other than my consciousness left my body for a few moments and then Connie, I think that was her name? I call her Connie, maybe Corine, but I think she was called Connie, was in the room. [Her name was Corrine Tarin, age twenty-seven. The other woman was Barbara Sherman, age twenty-two.] She was upset with what was going on, and there was just my father and I. And, my father had sex with me. And, remember he had said when I was sixteen this was going to happen and it was a privilege, and I would become a woman.

But, it wasn't like that at all. I thought this was a very romantic thing that was going to happen, but no. And he felt angry, guilty, weird. My impression of his consciousness was entirely different. Both while and after it was happening. I mean I was probably in a lot of danger at that point, but I didn't know it. It just didn't feel right in any way, shape, or form, and it certainly wasn't what he had said was going to happen. Then I left the room, and it was maybe five in the morning by this time. That never happened again. But, I became pregnant by my father, yes, and he thought that was amusing. As I said, I didn't think it was amusing at all.

I was scared. Because he said, I had to go away somewhere and have this child. And, I didn't want to go away anywhere. Oh, yes, he had Barbara have oral sex with me. I remember looking down at myself from the top of the room which was a strange sensation. I don't know if I was drugged. I can't say. It would be logical looking at it now that that's what happened.

After that, he [George] began acting very strange. After school, I had to be home at a certain time, or I'd be in trouble. If I came home with a friend from the school like a boyfriend, because I was beginning to become interested in boys, he didn't like that at all. He just started acting crazy. I remember that on one occasion somebody must have turned off the refrigerator or the freezer knob, not me, but somebody did, and he was so furious that this had happened that he took me from my room and I wasn't dressed and very vulnerable. And he started throwing everything out of the refrigerator at me, at the walls, everything, and it was the biggest mess because somebody had defrosted something valuable he had in there. Then he told me to "clean it up." I got help from Dorero and the maid and so forth.

I didn't tell anybody about the incident in the bedroom with my father until I knew I was pregnant and then I told Sonia. Only Sonia. Because my mother had never said anything. She felt like she wouldn't help me in any way. So, I told Sonia. I told him, and he said, "Well, you will have to have this child." Sonia said, "You'll have to have an abortion." So, that was a second choice, even though I didn't know what it was. I hadn't a clue. I started asking my father for an abortion. And he said he didn't believe in that. I kept asking him, and he finally said, "All right," and he arranged for this abortion. And, his friend took me to have the abortion. The person that drove me there was a very strange man that used to eat raw fish from his fish tank. Very strange man. One of the group of people that were associated with my father.

So, I went to have the abortion, and I found out what an abortion was. Without any anesthetic. That was terrible. And I kept screaming for them to stop, but you cannot stop in the middle of an abortion. Afterward, I was sick. I was crying and the person who had driven me there was to drive me home. I was nauseous and needed to throw up out the window so he took me to his place and he put down a rubber sheet on the bed because I was bleeding and he raped me. Then took me back to my father's. I told my father what had happened, and he was furious not so much at the rape, but that I might have become infected after having had an abortion. His behavior just got more and more bizarre.

By this time, even though I didn't know how the outside world was, I was being harmed and hurt so much that I didn't know what to do or where to turn. I told Dorero what had happened. She said, "This has gone too far. You must leave. Run away. You must get out of here immediately."

She told me this story, and it frightened me. I always believed her. She said that my father had murdered this woman who used to work for him and he had broken up with her. He heard she was writing a book about him. Two manuscripts for publishing. One with the names changed and one with all the actual names. I'm going to give you the story in bits and pieces because that's one thing she told me, this story.

When she told me the story about the woman that had written these books, the next thing she told me was that she got a call from George in the middle of the night saying that she, Dorero, was to go to the apartment, so she went. She was given the books, two manuscripts to destroy, which I always hoped that she didn't, that they're hidden somewhere. She was dying. The woman was in the process of dying, and he [George] was allowing her to die. [This is his First Street Clinic secretary, Ruth Spaulding, a suspicious death, alleged "suicide" investigated by LAPD in 1945 as a possible forced overdose. GHH admits to committing this crime on the 1950 DA electronic surveillance recordings.]

Then later, in the police report in 1949, I talked to them about that. Why I ran away. Among other things. And they [police] said, "A woman had died, and he was there and may have called them when she was dead. When her body was taken away, and they were suspicious about it. They were investigating it, and the neighbors had said that she was so excited about it the night before because she was going to see Dr. Hodel again." I don't know the name of that person. I heard it then. If I could only recall it. I don't know how to dig up that information, but I know that he did. Is responsible for her death. I have a feeling; Steve doesn't think so, I think those manuscripts could be somewhere. She was supposed to burn them, but if she had any smarts at all, she didn't.

George told Dorero just to "come to the apartment; I need you to come." So she went. She was there. The woman was dying. I think the official thing they said: "she died of an overdose." But, she was still alive when Dorero was there. His only concern was that she take the books and get them out of there and destroy them. And, she said she destroyed them, but I don't know. How could Dorero, who is a mystery writer, how could she have done that?

[RE: What police told Tamar while she was in custody at Juvenile Detention and in the trial.]

They [police] told me they were investigating him [George] for this woman and also for the Black Dahlia. I didn't know much about the Black Dahlia because I hadn't read the papers when it all happened. But, yes, they did tell me that. They were out to get him. They thought they had enough evidence to get him. They wanted to get him bad. It was a strange situation for me to be in.

Because I wasn't out to get him, but they were. And, once I told the truth when they picked me up and said, "We know all about you and your father," I thought they meant they knew all about me and my father and what had happened. So, I told them what had happened, that I'd gotten pregnant, had a miscarriage, or rather had an abortion, and all that happened and why I'd ran away. Of course, they didn't know all that and were very glad to hear all that, it just got worse and worse. Every day they came and took me out to lunch and asked for more information. I was glad to get out of Juvenile Hall every day.

The information they wanted to know was about the incest and whatever else I could tell them about my father. Everything. They were out to get him, period. I don't know who these people were or who they represented. Yes, Ritzi was one of them. [William Ritzi was the Deputy DA who prosecuted George at the trial.]

When I was going to court. They had the jury there, but he [George] wasn't present. The defendant wasn't present. Isn't that strange, but he wasn't. I told my story about what had happened. I didn't tell it from the point of view that I was ashamed, or that I was guilty. I just told it from the way I knew it, which seemed to play into the hands of the defense attorneys because it looked as if I wasn't horrified. I only saw my father once during that court trial which was at the end of the long hallway away, and the police detectives were taking me from a room out into the hallway, and they were taking me back in, and he gave me a look like, it really was the look that could kill. He was with Duncan, my older brother, and I, just like I am telling you, I just told what I knew had happened and I listened to the attorneys and the prosecution, and they wanted to get him. [I suspect Tamar is confused on some of the court hearing dates versus the actual trial. Hard for me to imagine the defendant, George Hodel, not being present during her testimony. It is a basic right for the accused to confront their accuser, especially during court testimony.]

But I was kind of in the middle of all this. They said they were "rescuing me" from the beautiful house and putting me in Juvenile Hall, I mean that was a strange rescue. The way they handled that. Then they said that "I hadn't had any love" so they wanted to adopt me when the trial was over which wasn't true at all, they had no intention of adopting me. This was the detectives, I guess, the people that took me out to lunch every day.

I was in Juvenile Hall when the verdict came in. I was in shock pretty much throughout the whole thing then they transferred me to San Francisco. I don't know what I thought. Because I wasn't on a trip to get him. I just told the truth because they asked me. And I had nothing to judge it all by. I was fourteen during the trial.

I did see him again. While I was still in Juvenile Hall, my mother arranged to take me out for the day and took me, we went to a point just on the other side of the Golden Gate bridge and like on the highway, off the road, like on the shoulder. I don't know what I said, and I don't know what he said, but he [George] was there. This was a while after the trial after I was transferred to San Francisco. [This is strange. A secret meeting obviously arranged by George. For what purpose?]

When the police told me they were investigating him for the Black Dahlia, it clicked a little something. I'm very intuitive, I just know things, I can't explain things to you on how I know them, well that was like another piece of the Dahlia story coming together as it turns out. Bit by bit these pieces have been added, and I just felt he had. And, I was really glad that Steven was writing his book because he'd find out. [Again, Tamar, nor any other family member, did not know I had been investigating the Black Dahlia until 2003, just weeks before the book's publication. All they knew was I was writing a book about my years on the LAPD.]

[RE: Press mentioning Tamar claimed GHH was the Black Dahlia Killer during the trial.]

Yes, there was something in the newspaper back then, but I don't remember saying that. Yes, most likely it was what the police had told me.

Otherwise, I would have flown to see my father and talk to him, but I was afraid of him. When he arrived, though, he was the great Dr. Hodel and I was an outcast from that point on. From my family on my mother's side and everybody. I mean I was an outcast. So, when the great Dr. Hodel would arrive every few years to say hello with his pomp and circumstance, which there was plenty of, it was the honor of his arrival. I always thought that someday he'd say that he was sorry that he loved me and he would help me.

I think he was motivated by something to do with his mother. I don't know what, but my mother told me that he hated his mother. Hated her. But, when she died, he wept. That was the only time she had ever seen him weep. It must have been way back. But, he never said anything. It was not like he ever spouted anything about women that would make you alert. He was like no other person I've ever met.

If only Steven, and Kelly [my brother Kelvin] and I and those that knew him could express, could bring back to life who this person was and how he was, you would understand more. I'm hoping that there is footage somewhere. There are voice recordings of his voice.

I never stopped loving my father, but it was me seeking his love. He was a dangerous, dangerous man and I'm still in the process of reconciling all that. It's hard because I loved him so much. And then, I wanted his love. I wanted him to say, "I'm so sorry for what happened to you, Tamar. You're so precious to me." But, as I said, I couldn't take the chance to go see him in person, in case I was right that he'd murdered women and I might be one of them.

I didn't hate him when I heard he died or anything. People don't understand, "Why don't you hate your father?" I don't hate anybody actually. I hate situations, but hate, it's ugly. I didn't have that feeling. I just wanted it to be right again. I wanted him to understand that not only do fathers not sleep with their children, but adults don't sleep with children. They should allow them the natural way that they are going to develop and not do that to them. And the harm that comes from all this is what happens to how you feel about yourself. You don't feel protected. The protection is gone.

My daughters have always been upset that I loved him still. How could I love him still? But, I really feel, sometimes you love somebody because you want their love. That's different maybe. We were bonded. We were attached. My daughter, my second daughter [Deborah Elizabeth aka Fauna II] had an experience that I didn't know anything about when she was about thirteen.

The time that he [George] came and he talked about the Rhododendron flowers. You know, the nether lips on the carpet was the same visit. He took her out to dinner. And she came back, and she didn't say anything to me about anything. It was years later, after she had raised children, talking to me on the phone and going back and we were fixing everything that needs fixing in a relationship, as we are going over everything, she told me that he [George] had taken her that night to dinner and she had had a drink of something with him and she started to faint. He took her back to his hotel, and there was a period of time that she was out and when she came to she was nude, and he was taking pictures of her.

And she had no idea what had happened or anything. He brought her back, and she didn't tell me because she thought he was the great Dr. Hodel, and even though she didn't like what had happened, she "thought I knew." That's what she told me. That would have helped so much if I had known.

She told my mother later. She went to help take care of my mother. When she was there, she said, "I want you to know what happened. This happened to me too. So, if you don't believe Tamar, this is what happened." After that point, my mother refused to speak to her anymore. She disowned us completely. She didn't have children or grandchildren anymore. That was the end of that. She just shut off, and that was the way it was the rest of her life.

Once, in Honolulu, I'd gotten into trouble for something I didn't do. But, nonetheless, I had to get an attorney and all that. I'd called my mother and asked her to please call George and see if he will send money for the attorney. I need an attorney in this case. She said, "Well, after what you've done to your father?" She's still saying I'm bad Tamar who said these things about George. I don't understand it.

[Asked about Dorero and what she thinks she knew.]

I think Dorero knew a lot. Poor Dorero took with her more than anything any of the people my father was involved with. I think she knew of murders. And a lot of other things we don't know about and I would like it very much if people, when they read the book, or hear a program, or whatever, any information we can get helps weave the tapestry of our understanding and throws more light on the story of what really happened.

No, Dorero never talked to me about the Dahlia case. Remember, I was the one that had caused trouble. I hardly dared bring the subject up with my family.

Yes, the police were sure of something, and they wanted to get him. Because I didn't have that great fire to go get him, that wasn't where I was coming from nonetheless, I was in the middle of it, and that was the team I was on. I was afraid about what my father would say about all this. I wanted to talk to him, but there was no way possible.

But Dorero only told me about that one thing. [GHH's secretary murder]

Interestingly enough, my mother got a call, telling her that I had run away. Dorero did that I'm sure. And my mother came and then George had to put out a missing person's report because he just couldn't say, "Oh well." But, Dorero saved my life. Because she knew all that had happened and knowing what had happened to others, I'm certain that's why she told me to "get out of there and run away." And, why she called my mother to come NOW. Dorero was one of the most loving people I've ever known. She felt more like my mother than my mother. She was just a lovely, loving woman. But for whatever reasons, she was bound to him.

[Asked why nothing came out from her about her knowledge of GHH being Dahlia suspect.]

Well, here was my dilemma. I needed to know if he truly murdered those women. I hadn't seen him murder them. And, according to my code of ethics, you don't say that someone has done something unless you know for sure that they've done it. It's just not right. So, I wanted to know. I felt it deep in my soul that he had. My children heard the whole story growing up. We always said there was more than one woman. There were other murders. But who are you going to talk to about this? Not my family. They were in denial. Certainly, can't tell the general public. I mean it was bad enough when I just told my life story. You know, they say, well, I grew up and went to high school, and I played basketball.

My story is just... People's jaws drop. And, this is just the first part of my story, because it goes on. On and on and on, not with George but... My whole life has been very unusual.

[Asked if Tamar could speak to George Hodel now what would she say.]

Well, I would say, knowing ...How can I explain this? I know that there is no such thing as death. And I know that he is still an entity, a being, I would say why I was trying to reach you, to tell you how important it was that you not go to your death with this on your conscience. That you needed to repent for that. To tell your sorry for those wronged. And, to know that you were loved, regardless of all this.

Even, a son that is a murderer, they still love their son. But, I would also say how horrified at how he treated me. It was way more than the physical part. It was his lying about me. His presenting his daughter to the world as a "pathological liar." Who her brothers weren't supposed to speak of, let alone speak to. That was a terrible thing. I just have an anger and a hurt about that. I will resolve it, at some point I have to let it go, but I'm appalled. The more I find out, the more appalled I am.

That's replacing the feeling of, oh I love you, and I want to have peace with you. He's my blood. I still have love, but what would I say to him? Just, he should have listened to me. He promised me that... Every time that I was going to see him, he promised me that he was "going to give me ten days, that I'm going to come to Hawaii and visit with you and we will talk and get everything straightened out, and we will have ten days." But, he didn't keep his promise. And I think that was to his detriment. Certainly to mine.

If I could have talked to him safely, I think he would have listened to me. To some degree, because we were a lot alike in some ways. Aside from murders. There was such a genetic bond. I think he would have seen how sincere I was. Where I was coming from. And at least considered it. Even though he made jokes about not believing in things. Not believing in God. Or if he did believe in God maybe he'd be a Taoist. That kind of thing. But, I think he would have listened. But that opportunity is missed. By me too, because I was afraid to go. And I have letters at home that I had written long letters, that I never sent. I could only get so far. In the letters, I said what kind of life I had after the trial. My self-esteem, what happened, how I was treated, what it was like. Because you see, I'm intelligent and had I had some positive reinforcement and support, I would be in a different position now than I am in today. He could have made my life very different.

Yes, he was a selfish man. Very very selfish. I remember occasions when he would fly in, and we would go to the airport together. Sometimes we would have to meet him at the airport and just have a little bit of time with him. I remember one time when Steve and Michael and Kelly were trying to find him. I was with him, I'd found him. And he laughed. He thought it was so amusing that they were running here and running there. It was amusing to see people run after him. To gain his approval. He was really a very shallow man. Shallow because he was so unkind. And he didn't appreciate the love he had from all his children.

Even when my older brother Duncan was hurt. When he was in the Navy, someone beat him up, and he had a bad head injury that still plagues him to this day. He has to go into a harness to help his neck. My father wouldn't give him any money to help him, and he could have. He could have helped us all so much. I don't understand.

The Cycle of Abuse

Lolita—*A sexually precocious young girl. A character in the novel* Lolita *(1955) by Vladimir Nabokov. Lolita is a female given name of Spanish origin. It is the diminutive form of Lola, a hypocorism (a pet name) of Dolores, which means "suffering" in Spanish.*

—*Wikipedia*

Tamar was Lolita ten years before Lolita was introduced to the public in the Nabokov novel.

(Ironically, Tamar would befriend and, along with her close friend, Michelle Phillips, would become a sort of "technical consultant" to Sue Lyon. Tamar, eleven years older, and Michelle, just two years older than Sue, both attempted to explain to their then (1960) fourteen-year-old friend, the subtleties of her upcoming role, as a twelve-year-old seductress in the novel.)

Stanley Kubrick's Lolita was released by MGM in 1962 and starred James Mason as Professor Humbert Humbert, Shelly Winters as Charlotte Haze, and Sue Lyon as her fourteen-year-old daughter, Lolita. (All three actors are seen in above clip, lower right.) (In the Nabokov novel, Lolita was actually twelve, but the studios advanced her age to try and avoid accusations of "pedophilia.") Sue Lyon, in her role as Lolita, was nominated and won the Golden Globe Award for "Most Promising Newcomer-Female."

Tamar was sexualized by her father in 1946 at age eleven by his insistence that she perform oral sex on him. This was reinforced in the following years by his repeated indoctrinations of her to his private collection of erotica as "artful pornography" along with his promise "to make love to her and make her a woman when she became sixteen." George assured her that sex between father and daughter was a family norm; after all, "all the great families of the world, including the Pharaohs, did it."

I am not a believer in the "Bad Seed" theory. I do not believe anyone is really "born bad." Rather, I subscribe to the Nurture and Nature doctrine.

While the science of genetics as our potential gifts and curses is undeniable, still our surroundings, our environment during those critical "formative years" to my mind, is equally influential—hence, my belief in the coequality of influence of Nurture and Nature.

Further, I believe in the power of Responsibility (one's ability to respond).

How we, as individuals, respond to internal and external influences determines our success or failure in life. Some choose to become predators and populate the world as criminals; others choose the equally destructive path of becoming prey, continually remaking themselves into "the victims."

The stronger individuals, the *responsible* ones, choose to attempt to live the middle path through life. A path of self-determination regardless of "the hand they were dealt." They forge their own path keeping in check, as best they can, their dark inclinations and try to live and work by controlling their urges and impulses and attempting to follow their internal moral compass, their Conscience, which becomes their guidance and their "higher angels."

As I see it, Tamar, after being sexualized and victimized by her father, chose to continue to live in that world. Indoctrinated at eleven by her father, she drank the Kool-Aid and believed that "giving herself sexually could and would bring love."

Nineteen teenage boys from Hollywood High School were arrested and admitted to engaging in some form of sexual activity with Tamar "up on Mulholland Drive." Most or all of the juvenile boys it is believed were "counseled" with no formal charges to follow.

During the 1949 pretrial investigation, a number of adult males implicated as being associated with Tamar were also brought in by LAPD detectives and "questioned and released."

According to Fred Sexton's daughter Michelle (a then friend and playmate of Tamar's), her father later told her that Man Ray was very concerned about being implicated in the Hodel scandal. He purportedly even went so far as to provide authorities with a note from his doctor, indicating he was "impotent, and could not have had sexual relations with Tamar." (Though she never claimed he did.)

I am not going to attempt to here provide a detailed biography of Tamar's life following her sexualization but will merely highlight some of her behavior in the years following the incest trial.

In 1950, immediately after the trial, Tamar, age fifteen, traveled with her mother to Mexico and met and married an artist "to escape and get away from her mother's influence." The marriage was short-lived.

Back in San Francisco, Tamar visited an Italian American who she claimed forced sex upon her that resulted in her becoming pregnant and she gave birth to Fauna Hodel on August 1, 1951.

Tamar, believing that the baby would be better off being raised by a "Negro family," lied about the unnamed father being a Caucasian, and told the Catholic sisters at the hospital that "the father was Negro" and Fauna was adopted and raised by a black family.

Tamar then married musician/singer Stan Wilson, and a second daughter, Deborah Elizabeth Wilson, was born in San Francisco on October 24, 1954.

The births of her three sons, Peace, Love, and Joy Hodel, followed, and by the end of the sixties, Tamar had given birth to five children by five separate fathers.

My younger brother, Kelvin ("Kelly"), at sixteen, was dating a girl by the name of Rusty Gilliam. Rusty was the older sister of Michelle Gilliam, then thirteen, who a decade later would become Michelle Phillips of The Mamas & The Papas fame.

Brother Kelly introduced our half sister Tamar to the Gilliam family, which consisted of Gil Gilliam, a handsome, free-spirited LA County probation officer, divorced and raising his two daughters as a single father. Gil, very much a ladies' man, would go on to marry five more times.

Over the next three years in Los Angeles, Tamar and Michelle became very close and Tamar would on occasion sleep with her father Gil, just to keep things "copasetic."

By 1961, Tamar decided she wanted to move north to San Francisco, and Michelle, now seventeen, would accompany her with little or no objection from her father Gil, who in June of that year would marry a sixteen-year-old.

Tamar's life of sex, drugs, and rock and roll and her befriending of the young teenager, Michelle Gilliam, who within a short few years would metamorphose into Michelle Phillips of The Mamas & The Papas is well documented in Michelle's autobiography, *California Dreaming*.

In an early chapter on Tamar in *Black Dahlia Avenger* back in 2003, I wrote:

> Maybe it was my own design and not simply the passage of time that kept the true story of Tamar and the family scandal a dark mystery to me for many years. Even in my adult mind, Tamar was the image of the adolescent temptress Lolita. She would go on to blaze a trail from the beat generation of the middle 1950s to the street generation of the late '60s, bouncing off poets, folk singers, druggies, and hippies.

> Tamar was described by singer Michelle Phillips in her book *California Dreaming: The True Story of the Mamas and the Papas* as her "very best friend, who got me interested in folk music, or at least into folk music people." Michelle's description of Tamar is a snapshot of the young girl who, a decade earlier, unwittingly had come within a hair of playing a critical role in the Black Dahlia investigation.

Phillips writes:

> So, off we went to Tamar's. As soon as I set eyes on her, I thought she was the most fabulous, glamorous girl I had ever met. She had a wonderful lavender-colored room, with lavender pillows and curtains, lavender lead-glass ashtrays, all of that. I thought it was just great. She had just acquired a new pink and lavender Rambler, buying it on time.

> She hung out with a very hip Bohemian crowd—Josh White, Dick Gregory, Odetta, Bud and Travis. Tamar was incredible. She gave me my first fake ID, my first amphetamines ("uppers" to help me stay awake in class after late nights). This was a girl after my own heart, and we became very close…and now she was my idol.

In August 1961, Michelle, who thanks to Tamar's underground connections had obtained a fake ID passing herself off as twenty-one, came home to their Fillmore Street apartment to find Tamar unconscious.

Depressed, she had taken an overdose of sleeping pills. Michelle called for an ambulance and Tamar was transported to San Francisco General Hospital.

An article in the *Oakland Tribune* headlines the incident, "Alimony Late; SF Blonde Tries Suicide."

Oakland Tribune, August 25, 1961

Alimony Late; S.F. Blonde Tries Suicide

Tamar Hodel, pretty ex-wife of folk singer Stan Wilson, apparently tried to take her own life early today by gulping a quantity of sleeping pills, according to San Francisco police.

The 26-year-old blonde was found unconscious in her apartment at 3153 Fillmore St. by her roommate, Micelle Gilliam, 21, at 1:30 a.m. She was given emergency treatment at San Francisco General Hospital, where she is reported in satisfactory condition.

Miss Gilliam said the former Mrs. Wilson had been brooding recently because Wilson, touring Australia, is three months behind on alimony payments. Wilson, 38, is a former Oaklander.

Eighteen months later, on February 5, 1963 (the day following my acceptance and entrance into the LAPD Police Academy, and apparently desirous of following in our father's footsteps) my half sister was arrested in San Francisco as an accomplice in performing abortions.

The article in *The Fresno Bee* read, "Abortion Ring Is Broken Near UC Campus" described "the arrest of a statuesque blonde (Tamar) and the issuance of a warrant for a Van Nuys doctor." Tamar was arrested for two counts of assisting in abortions and for possession of narcotics.

A month later Tamar pled guilty to one count as an accomplice to abortions and was sentenced to no jail time and a straight three years probation.

Tamar's prosecutor, in this case, was none other than Edwin Meese III, who would go on to be appointed by President Ronald Reagan as the seventy-fifth Attorney General of the United States. (1885–1988)

5, 1963   THE FRESNO BEE

Tamar N. Hodel— Bail
set as

Abortion Ring Is Broken Near UC Campus

BERKELEY — AP— The police announced the breakup of an abortion ring near the University of California campus with the arrest of a statuesque blond and issuance of a warrant for a Van Nuys doctor.

Police Inspector Bruce R. Baker said Tamar N. Hodel, 27, former wife of folk singer Stan Wilson was arrested on charges of conspiracy and possession of narcotics. She was released on $3,150 bail.

Doctor Sought

Baker said he has a warrant for Dr. John R. Sedgwick, Jr., of Van Nuys, who is being sought in Southern California.

According to Baker, a San Jose music teacher brought two San Jose State College coeds to Miss Hodel's home six blocks from the Berkeley campus, and abortions were performed on both last Wednesday night.

One of the girls now is in the Santa Clara County Hospital in San Jose. The music teacher was questioned and released.

Probation In Illegal Surgery

Shapely Tamar Hodel 27 who pleaded guilty to one count of abortion, was placed on three years probation today by Superior Court Judge William J McGuiness

Miss Hodel, attractive ex-wife of folk singer Stan Wilson, was charged jointly with Dr. John R. Sedgwick, 43, Van Nuys physician, of performing illegal operations on two San Jose College coeds in her Berkeley apartment at 3600 Fulton St early this year

But one count of abortion was dropped when Miss Hodel pleaded guilty May 24

Judge McGuiness said he was reserving imposition of a jail sentence on Miss Hodel out of deference to her physical condition.

She injured her back in a fall down a flight of stairs and made previous court appearances in a wheel chair. Her attorney, Herman Mintz, said today her condition was still far from perfect

In announcing his intention to reserve imposition of a jail term, Judge McGuiness commented

"Her actions throughout were characterized as a deliberate calculated and utter contempt for the law."

Her attorney argued that Miss Hodel could be rehabilitated through probation

Dr. Sedgwick is still a fugitive

Tamar's troubled and abusive childhood led directly to her own self-inflicted troubles and abuses.

All five of her children were impacted by Tamar's dramatic and out-of-control life.

A shocking example of how totally "out of control" and abusive Tamar's life was with her children has been documented in a June 2015 feature article in *Dujour Magazine*.

The article, "The Sins Of The Father: Uncovering the Secrets of the Black Dahlia Murder"was written by journalist and best-selling author, Sheila Weller. Here is an excerpt from Weller's excellent article.

…

> As for Tamar, she remained artistic, precocious—and wounded. At 16, she married a black artist in Mexico, then left him after he beat her so badly she attempted suicide. In San Francisco, she married a second time. He was Stan Wilson, a black folksinger and activist. She became a people-connecting socialite in the interracial avant-garde, spending evenings at the Hungry i with Harry Belafonte, Maya Angelou, Lenny Bruce and Bruce's stripper wife, Honey. She had a daughter with Wilson and named her Deborah. Though Tamar was, this now-adult daughter says, "very brave" in confronting the hate of being married to a black man in the early 1950s, her parenting almost helplessly followed the sick route etched by her sadistic father and her own enabling mother: She introduced Deborah to sex at age 10—the girl's evenings with men paid the rent after Tamar's divorce. And Tamar did not protect her from the family's psychopath patriarch. When Deborah was 12, Hodel took the girl to a fancy lunch, slipped a drug in her drink "and I woke up hours later spread-eagled and undressed" in her half-clad grandfather's presence.

Intentionally or not, each of Tamar's children suffered significant emotional abuse at the hands of their mother.

As best as I can tell, all five of her children have risen to the challenges, have overcome their environmental neglect, and did not succumb to the many existential pitfalls that were placed before them.

Good on them.

Aside from her children, Tamar also made several other deliberate and very bad choices.

The first was obviously a direct and early result of her sexualization by her father. It involved her decision to have sexual intercourse with one of her younger half brothers during that summer of 1949. That brother was then less than ten years of age.

That incident occurred just prior to her running away and subsequent arrest and disclosure to the police about her father and friends having sexual relations with her during the "hypnosis session."

The second seduction was with a separate half brother and occurred a decade later.

Tamar, now a woman in her early twenties, was living in Los Angeles.

Her brother was in his mid-teens. That incestuous relationship occurred over many months and resulted in Tamar informing him that "she was pregnant and needed money for an abortion." (Unknown if she was really pregnant, as this was a line she used with many men on many occasions through the decades.)

These separate acts were never formally reported and remained "family secrets" while she lived.

I only mention them now to attempt to illustrate a truth of how extremely destructive and far-reaching "the sins of a father" can be.

George not only made Tamar a victim, one of the abused, but he also aided and abetted in helping create those character imperfections, those flaws and weaknesses within her own psyche, that would allow her to make bad choices that led to her actively becoming an abuser.

A seemingly never-ending cycle.

We know that George Hodel was abused. Certainly, emotionally, and very likely sexually, probably by his own over-controlling, dominating mother. Or, if not her, then another close family member?

Sadly, my half sister, Tamar Nais Hodel, led a tragic life.

But, much of it came from her deliberate choice to perpetuate her victimness. Her criminal arrests were never her fault. Always, "A Victim of

Circumstance." Always, "Their drugs, not mine." "I was just in the wrong place at the wrong time."

Had Tamar taken control and become responsible for her life, things could and would have been much different. She could have been living not at affect, but rather with effect.

Rest in Peace Tamar.

I will close this Tamar chapter with two remarkable emails I received from my half sister just one year after the initial publication of my book, *Black Dahlia Avenger: A Genius for Murder in 2003*.

Tamar was living in Honolulu, on welfare and struggling just to exist. She was renting a small unit in a federally assisted housing project.

Constantly behind on her rent and utility payments, her dream was to write her autobiography and tell her own life story, which was far more fascinating and inclusive than just "the incest trial."

Sadly, that never happened.

Here, again in her own words, unabridged, is the overview of her life she sent to me, along with a second follow-up email with the names of the people and acquaintances that played a role, large or small, in her amazing life.

Steve

From:	"Tamar" <Tamar@hawaii.rr.com>
To:	"Steve Hodel" <steve.hodel@verizon.net>
Sent:	Monday, January 12, 2004 10:22 PM
Subject:	FEEDBACK PLEASE

An overview...of my project.

I am writing an Autobiography in three parts titled "The Tamar Chronicles"

Book One will cover my early and quite interesting childhood growing up in the North Beach Bohemian sector of Beautiful San Francisco in 1935 ....leading into a life changing experience after going to live in Los Angeles with my Father Dr. George Hodel... and my Brothers Michael, Steven and Kelly (and my Beautiful Step-Mother Dorero) at 5121 Franklin Avenue...Lloyd Wright's Mayan Temple Edifice in Old Hollywood.

A most intense and quite unusual two years followed at the Franklin House prior to my running away from my father ...in 1949 ..and being catapulted into newspaper headlines in an infamous incest trial... appearing in LA Confidential and Keyhole magazines, etc. available throughout the U.S.

(This part of the story has been partially covered in My brother Steven's recently published book "Black Dahlia Avenger" by Steven Hodel..exposing my father as a serial killer...misogynist and the person responsible for the murder of "The Black Dahlia")

Life as I knew it... totally shattered.

My Father was defended shamelessly by Attorney Jerry Giesler and Robert Neeb.... "All a Fantasy of a young girl " ! A smear campaign was created and I was labeled inaccurately as a liar and a "bad seed ".

At the close of the court trial and my father's acquittal ...I was transferred from The Los Angeles Juvenile Hall to San Francisco Juvenile Hall as a Ward of the Court ...suddenly I had become the criminal...without committing a crime!

I was incarcerated for almost one year. The system had no idea where to place me...In the end ...I was released to my Mother in San Francisco...the first day home I walked across the street to see my childhood friend David age 15, and as I approached...I was startled to hear his Mother call out to him not to speak to me ...telling me "to get away from her son...You Whore...You Whore "!!! He did not even speak...I returned home...shocked and confused...later that day David slipped away from his Mother's watchful eye to tell me that the case had been in all the newspapers and Sex Magazines...that I was a Scandal !! Considered to be A Very BAAAAAD Girl...He asked me to meet him at his friends home nearby that evening so that he might show me the news clippings and magazines...I arrived at his friends house... (a bachelor, about 25 years of age)...who kept me supplied with good tasting drinks (I learned later that I was being given Sloe Gin in mixed drinks)...I drank and waited...no David...finally I passed out and awakened to being raped by his friend ...as soon as I could walk...I went home...and soon discovered that I was pregnant!!!

Still a ward of the court....a Baaaaad Girl

and pregnant....I asked my Mother for help...She refused to help saying"she would not help ... not after what I had done to my Father !!"

That I should take care of it on my own !

Wow!

A long series of painful attempts "to handle my pregnancy on my own " followed...all unsuccessful. That is a whole chapter to itself...

My Mother turned me into the court as a runaway...I had not ...I was simply trying "to take care of it myself as instructed "At the final point of this effort...too many people were becoming involved that could be hurt for helping me...including Gus Hall the distinguished leader of The Communist Party

Rather than endanger any others...I turned myself into The Juvenile Court.

A very kind and loving Black man tried to help me...offered to marry me...which he thought would ..give me my freedom as an adult...the court said no...it was actually illegal at that time in California !

By the time that I was about two months pregnant..I was placed in an Unwed Mother's Home....and although my pregnancy was truly an unwanted one...my baby became the only family that I had in the world...and I wanted so very much to keep her...I was informed that would not be possible...unless my Mother agreed to be responsible...As they

1/13/04

assumed that the father of my child was black (due to my friend who asked permission to marry me)...and...All my heroes were black...(I was not favorably impressed with the white race... I had been very shocked by the way I saw blacks being treated at Juvenile Hall...(I was embarrassed to be white) and I was also surprised by the fact that most of the beautiful black girls...had no idea that they were beautiful) Sooooooooooo as they thought that the baby's father was black, I continued to allow them to think so. Understanding that I would not be allowed to keep her...I wanted her to be in a loving environment. At that time (1950) I naively thought just being in a black family would accomplish this...

When she was born, I did not get to hold her ...I was only allowed to see her through a glass window in the arms of a nun...and as I looked at her trying to project my absolute helplessness at the whole turn of events...she flashed an accusing look of betrayal.

I was not to look into her eyes again until 20 years later, when we were reunited in Honolulu. She (Fauna) has made a film about her long search for her mother... and growing up white in a black family, called "Pretty Hattie's Baby" with Alfre Woodard, Charles Dutton, Jill Clayburgh, Tess Harper, Bobby Hosea and Allison Elliot.

After Fauna's birth, I was whisked away to Mexico City "to forget". I was told that I must never attempt to find my daughter, that she had been adopted by two wealthy Interracial Artists....and that I must never interfere.

At the time I believed my Mother....however as it turned out my Mother actually had her given to a maid at The Silver Dollar Hotel in Reno Nevada !!

In Mexico City in 1951 ...I met a dazzling array of Artists including Diego Rivera and Frida Kahlo...had bit parts in two films with Jorge Mistral "La Bestia Magnifica "and "La Mujer Que Tu Quieres "...met and married

(divorcing two years later) a handsome Negro Art Student when I was 16...During that time I traveled to New York City and met and fell in love with the man I would love alllllllll the days of my life... (to this very day even though sadly he left the body in 1969) the beautiful and noble Josh White ...Folk Singer and Story Teller and Civil Rights spokesman par Excellence...

1/13/04

I returned to Mexico City...divorced my first husband and moved back to San Francisco

at age 18.

In San Francisco I met and married Stan Wilson, (Folk Singer and part owner of the famed "Hungry i") The Place To Gather if you were young, intelligent and hip.

I had my second daughter with Stan named Deborah (she later changed her named to Fauna also,...thinking at the time that we had no way to find her sister. When she found us in Honolulu... in 1973 they became Fauna I and Fauna II.)

There was in the 1950's a delightful and interesting group in the then Bohemian North Beach, San Francisco....Maya Angelou ..The Smothers Brothers, Lenny Bruce, Mort Sahl, Phyllis Diller, Odetta Felious, Bud and Travis ...and many more who were part of the Music and Art Scene in California...a very deep and interesting time.

There were many adventures and challenges traveling "On The Road" with Stan..it was considered quite scandalous and shocking in the 1950's for a Black man and a White woman to marry..

Buying the Lime Lighter and Cosmo Alley from Herb Cohen and Theodore Bikel and inheriting Les McCann and Gene McDaniels.

And Paul Mazursky.

Book Two..will continue with Michelle Phillips ..Uniting with my father again...and many more adventures all the way through the 60's with Dick Gregory and Scott Mackenzie and Lenny Bruce ...The Flower children days ...Michelle and John Phillips ...Timothy Leary ...moving to Honolulu and giving birth to my three sons...Peace on Earth, Joy To The World and Love.

Book Three...will cover the 70's, 80's and 90's in Honolulu ...and ...Now.

1/13/04

Tamar's second email contained the long list of names.

From: "Tamar"
To: Steve Hodel
Sent: January 12, 2004

Subject: PARTIAL LIST OF CHARACTERS SO FAR (AS I THINK OF THEM)

(Tamar in her email inadvertently repeated several names)

Robinson Jeffers
Eleanor Roosevelt
Paul Robeson
Marion Anderson
The Ballet Theatre
The Ballet Russe
Leonide Massine
Alexander Danilov
Alexander Oumansky
Dr. George Hill Hodel
John Huston
Dorero
Man Ray
Fred Sexton
Kiyo
Tim Holt
Jerry Giesler
LA Confidential
SF District Attorney
 Hot Lips Page
Mexico City
San Francisco
Los Angeles
Dr. Charles White
Joe Adams
Billy Ekstine
June Ekstine
Trini Lopez
Faith Petric Craig

Fauna
Mexico City
Jose Guttierez
William Byers
John Wilson
Vernon
Michelle and Russell Gilliam (Phillips)
Gil Gilliam
Frida Kahlo
Diego Rivera
Elizabeth Catlett
Apollo Theatre
Josh White
Dizzy Gillespie
Duke Ellington
The Theresa Hotel
John D. Thomas
Harlem

Cosmo Alley
Paul Mazursky
Leon Bibb
Michelle Gilliam Phillips (again)
and Kelly
John Hawker
Gogi Grant
Ketty Lester
Kitty White
The Renaissance (LA)

Billy Daniels
Hungry I
Stan Wilson
Deborah Elizabeth Wilson
Enrico Banducci
Mort Sahl
Maya Angelou
Tommy and Dick Smothers
Phyliss Diller
Harry Belafonte
Earth Kitt
Professor Irwin Corey
Frank Werber
Harry Smith
The Gateway Singers
The Limelighters
The Purple Onion
Billy Holiday
Honolulu
Tempest Storm
Lenny Bruce and Honey
The Clouds
Doris Duke
Liberace
Peggy Lee
Tom Moffatt

Dick Gregory
Langston Hughes
Scott McKenzie
The Journeymen
John Phillips
The Church Catolico
(St. Peters and Pauls)
Father John Hester
The Mamas and the Papas
George Harrison
Dr. Paul Fleiss
Warren Beatty
Wendy
Tex Watson
The Rathskellar
Harvey Ragsdale
The Kingston Trio
Theodore Bikel
Skip Weshner
Susan Oliver
Steve McQueen
Sally Kellerman
The Lamplighter
Les McCann
Gene McDaniels

So Many Secrets

TAMAR'S LIST OF NAMES included her short-lived marriage as a teenager to William Byers, in Mexico, which she had informed me, was "to get away from her mother." A cursory check of Byers' name revealed a *Jet Magazine* article from March 1953, which documents a despondent Tamar had attempted suicide by pills.

True to the times, the married couple are described as "her Negro husband" and Tamar as "a twenty-three-year-old White student."

Student's White Wife Tries Suicide In Mexico

Desperate after her first quarrel with her Negro husband of less than a year, Tamar Hodel Byers, 23-year-old white student at Mexico City College, took a heavy dose of sleeping pills in an attempt to commit suicide. William Charles Byers found his wife unconscious in their Mexico City home, rushed her to a hospital where emergency treatment saved her life. Byers, a native of Washington, D. C., now studying in Mexico under the GI Bill, said he and his wife had been "perfectly happy," could give no reason for her suicide attempt.

7

Dr. George Hill Hodel:
A New Life and a New Wife in the Territory—
Hawaii-1950-1953

G EORGE HODEL, IMMEDIATELY AFTER his October 6, 1949, arrest for incest and child molestation retained nationally renowned criminal defense attorneys Jerry "Get Me" Giesler and his partner, Robert Neeb to represent him. GHH secured their services by signing over his Sowden House as a $10,000 retainer ($102,000 in today's dollars).

Post-trial in 1950, George then prepared his own sales brochure, "For Sale, SHANGRI-LA in Los Angeles" and put the house on the market asking "$44,500 Liquidation Price" (roughly a half million in 2017 dollars).

(Lt) GHH Deed of Trust on Franklin House signed over as collateral to his attorneys Jerry Giesler and Robert Neeb. (Rt) GHH prepared 1950 Sales Brochure "SHANGRI-LA in Los Angeles" asking "$44,500 Liquidation Sale."

"Get out of Dodge"

THE DA STAKEOUT AND Bugging Tapes occurred in Feb/March 1950, and we know that GHH disappeared in late March just as Lt. Jemison was about to arrest him for the murders of Elizabeth "Black Dahlia" Short and Jeanne French (the "Red Lipstick Murder").

Also, now armed with the newly recorded confession of having killed his secretary, Ruth Spaulding, it is likely Lt. Jemison would have charged that crime as a third count of murder.

By the fall of 1950, George Hodel had relocated to the Territory of Hawaii and was initially hired as "Resident Psychiatrist for the Territorial Hospital."

Civil Service OK's Doctor Contracts

Territorial civil service commissioners yesterday approved two contracts hiring doctors for territorial institutions.

COMMISSIONERS approved a contract employing Dr. Edwin K. Chung-Hoon, chief of the Territory's Hansen's disease medical services, division of hospitals and settlements.

The contract was negotiated between Dr. Chung-Hoon and Dr. Charles L. Wilbar Jr., president of the board of health, Dec. 1.

DR. CHUNG-HOON will be responsible for planning, developing and managing a Territory-wide medical program. He will receive $850 a month.

Also approved was a six month contract by Thomas B. Vance, director of institutions, hiring Dr. George Hill Hodel, resident psychiatrist at the territorial hospital, at a monthly salary of $600.

Jan 17, 1951, Honolulu Advertiser

The *Honolulu Star-Bulletin* on August 23, 1952, announces the marriage of Dr. George Hill Hodel to Hortensia Laguda. Married in "Sonora, Mexico" and currently living "at home on Black Point Rd." (GHH also married my mother, Dorothy Huston Hodel, in Sonora, Mexico, ironically on December 7, 1940, one year to the day before the bombing of Pearl Harbor in Honolulu, Hawaii, which marked the US entry into WWII.)

The article goes on to describe GHH as "staff psychiatrist at Kaneohe Territorial Hospital in charge of the rehabilitation program and chief of the psychiatric clinic at Oahu Prison and lecturing faculty at University of Hawaii." (What could be more perfect? GHH as territorial prison psychiatrist with at least a dozen Los Angeles murders on his CV is now "counseling psychopath to the psychopaths.")

In a later (1957) article, the same newspaper announces that Mrs. Hortensia Hodel is now revisiting Honolulu. It goes on to inform readers that she is the cousin of former (1953) Philippine Vice President, Fernando Lopez, and that her husband "Dr. George Hill Hodel, a former staff psychiatrist at Kaneohe Hospital until 1954, now practices in Manila."

Hodel-Laguda Marriage Revealed to Friends

Disclosed to their friends in Hawaii is the marriage of Miss Hortensia Laguda of Manila to Dr. George Hill Hodel of Honolulu.

The couple was married in Sonora, Mexico, recently upon the completion of a world tour by Miss Laguda.

The bride is the daughter of Mrs. Paz Lopez Viuda de Laguda of Manila and the late Salvador Laguda. She is a graduate of Santa Scholastica College in Manila and also attended Norfleet School and Juilliard School of Music in New York.

The bridegroom, a graduate of the University of California Medical School, is a psychiatrist on the staff of the Territorial Hospital in Kaneohe, in charge of the rehabilitation program.

He is also chief of the psychiatric clinic at Oahu Prison and is on the lecturing faculty of the University of Hawaii.

The couple is now at home on Black Point Rd.

Honolulu Star August 23, 1952

WHEN the President Wilson docked yesterday on its voyage from the Orient, it brought Mrs. George Hill Hodel, who will combine business with visiting island friends.

She is the former Hortensia Consuela Laguda of Manila and Ilo-Ilo, the Philippines, and is a cousin of Fernando Lopez, former vice-president of the Philippines who visited here in 1953 en route to Washington, D.C.

Mrs. Hodel was educated in convent schools in Manila and at the Peet School in New York City.

She is the wife of Dr. Hodel, psychiatrist, who was on the staff of Territorial Hospital, Kaneohe, until 1954 and who now practices in Manila.

Mrs. Hodel will visit Mr. and Mrs. John Dominis Holt in Aiea for two weeks.

Honolulu Star August 14, 1957

Dr. George Hill Hodel in Hawaii circa 1953 with an unidentified woman, possibly staff worker?

BLACK POINT ESTATES AND SHANGRI-LA: *"The Good Life."*

NOT BEING FAMILIAR WITH Honolulu digs, I decided to check out the 1952 article's reference indicating that George and Hortensia were living "at home on Black Point Rd."

Here's what I discovered.

Ironically, after George Hodel sells his "Shangri-La Los Angeles" home, he then moves to Black Point Road, next to the "Shangri-La" home of heiress, Doris Duke in Honolulu, Hawaii.

Black Point Road appears to be and likely always was the Beverly Hills of Honolulu.

A 2017 realtor describes the community as, "…approximately seventy-five homes elevated on an oceanside black lava rock knoll wedged between Diamond Head and Kahala."

Originally developed in the 1920s, current market values show home sales range from $2 to $10 million.

Arrows show locations of "Black Point Road" and the Doris Duke Shangri-La residence (now a museum) at Black Point Road Estates. Duke home was built in 1936-1938

University of Hawaii 1951

GEORGE HODEL, THE STAFF psychiatrist, teaches a graduate course in *Dynamics of Human Behavior.* The catalog description for Professor Hodel's teaching course reads:

> "Personality growth and development from infancy through old age. Interpretation of the individual's

behavior in the light of physical, psychological, and social factors which have contributed to his maladjustment."

(Once again, you can't make this stuff up.)

University of Hawaii

SCHOOL OF
SOCIAL WORK
1951 - 1952

GRADUATE PROGRAM FOR PROFESSIONAL STUDY
November 1951

GEORGE H. HODEL, M.D., University of California; Staff Psychiatrist and Director of
Rehabilitation Program, Territorial Hospital, Kaneohe; Lecturer in Social Work

310 DYNAMICS OF HUMAN BEHAVIOR (2) I   Mr. Hodell
  Personality growth and development from infancy through old age. Interpretation of the individual's behavior in the light of physical, psychological,
and social factors which have contributed to his maladjustment.

Hawaii 1951

Hawaii 1952

Hawaii 1953

Two Thumbs Up from "The Gov" and Off to the Far East

THE BELOW LETTER WAS written in September 1953 by then Hawaiian Territorial Governor, Samuel Wilder King.

It is a letter of introduction and recommendation for Hawaiian-based psychiatrist Dr. George Hill Hodel.

The "To Whom It May Concern" refers to all Asian and Far East countries, colleges, hospitals, research centers, etc.

I will let Governor King speak for himself and his esteemed researcher. (The letter was given to me by June Hodel, along with other personal effects, just a few days after my father's death in May 1999.)

Samuel Wilder King, 11th Territorial Governor of Hawaii
In office February 18, 1953–July 26, 1957. Appointed by President Dwight D. Eisenhower

TO WHOM IT MAY CONCERN:

      The bearer of this letter is DR. GEORGE HILL HODEL, Psychiatric Consultant to the Psychological and Psychopathic Clinic of the University of Hawaii. Dr. Hodel is a psychiatrist who served for two years as Staff Psychiatrist at the Territorial Hospital of Hawaii and also as Psychiatric Consultant to the Hawaii Prison System.

      Dr. Hodel is conducting a research on racial and cultural factors in mental illnesses, crime and other forms of personality disturbances. This research was first sponsored by the Territorial Hospital and is now under sponsorship by the University of Hawaii. The purpose of his present trip to the Orient is to compare the findings with regard to mental illness, crime, etc., among the various peoples of Hawaii with similar findings as they may exist in the homelands of the various races who are being studied.

      Any courtesies or assistance which can be rendered to Dr. Hodel in the conduct of this important study will be cordially appreciated.

Samuel Wilder King

SAMUEL WILDER KING
GOVERNOR OF HAWAII

29 September 1953

Unbeknownst to the governor, he has just requested all doors and cooperation be provided to his mental health/crime expert.

An academic, a man with not only significant "book learning" but who also brings with him decades of "hands-on experience."

At this stage in his "dual career," George Hodel, working nights and pulling double duty as a serial killer had committed a minimum of sixteen sadistic murders and is well on his way to double that number before completing his "research" at age ninety-one. (This victim count only takes into consideration his crimes from 1943–1950 and omits "The Early Years" and those that followed in the 1960s.)

After three years in Hawaii, Dr. George Hill Hodel, with his wife, Hortensia, moves on to Manila, Philippines, where he will establish his private practice as a consulting psychiatrist.

Within a few years, he enters the newly developed field of market research as "Director General" of INRA-ASIA (International Research Associates) throughout the Far East, including Hong Kong, Japan, and Australia, as well as conducting additional projects throughout Europe.

I have not yet conducted any extensive research of my father's activities while in Hawaii from 1951-1953.

The obvious question is: *Did George Hodel continue to commit murders in Hawaii?*

Given his "track record" it is hard for me to imagine he could go three years without killing. I strongly suspect there are some cold cases collecting barnacles at Hawaii 5-0.

Very likely that there were victims in Hawaii, but unfortunately any investigation will have to be put on a back burner for the immediate future.

I currently have my hands full with attempting to ferret out his crimes from "The Early Years" (the 1920s and 30s) in California.

Any of you, my readers who feel like searching for any unsolved lone woman murders in the Hawaiian Islands from 1951–1954, have at it and don't hesitate to contact me on any possible findings at steve@stevehodel.com.

***

IN THE SPRING OF 1986, my father received a communication sent to INRA—Manila.

It was from Dr. Wayne P. Chesbro, MD, President, UCSF Class of '36, inviting him to attend the fiftieth-anniversary class reunion ceremonies on May 17, 1986, to be held in San Francisco.

Dr. Chesbro also asked for a capsulated report of George's professional life to be shared with his classmates. Father responded with a three-page letter.

Below is a scan of his letter providing us with a complete employment history on GHH coming directly from the mouth and hand of the "Director General" himself.

George did not attend his fiftieth class reunion, but in 1990, he and his wife, June Hirano Hodel, did permanently relocate back to San Francisco and leased a thirty-ninth-floor penthouse suite in the downtown Financial District, where he would live out the final decade of his life.

Here is that letter to his classmates sent from Manila in February 1986.

INTERNATIONAL RESEARCH ASSOCIATES (ASIA)

EXCELSIOR BUILDING
161 ROXAS BOULEVARD
PARAÑAQUE, METRO MANILA, PHILIPPINES
MAIL ADDRESS: P. O. BOX 912, MANILA

TELEPHONES: 832-0834,
832-0840, AND 832-0871
TELEX: ITT 46288 OR EASTERN 63428 (INRA)
CABLE ADDRESS: INRAFAREAST, MANILA

February 17, 1986

Wayne P. Chesbro, M.D.
President, UCSF Class of '36
620 Cragmont
Berkeley, California 94708
U. S. A.

Dear Wayne:

Greetings across the miles and across the years! You were always a leader, in the old days. I am glad to see that you continue to be unafraid of responsibilities.

It was good to hear from you, and to know that the Class of '36 is having its 50th reunion on May 17. If at all possible, I'll attend. If this is not possible, please extend my warmest greetings to our fellow-classmates.

My work and related travels bring me Stateside regularly -- once or twice a year.

I was at UCSF last year for a medical problem, but that happily proved to be a minor and correctable one. Am in apparent good health, working hard, and enjoying life immensely.

It is hard to compress one's professional life into a capsule report, but let me try. You can pass this word on to our classmates if I cannot make it to the reunion. For the first 12 years after graduation I was in public health, with the New Mexico State Department of Public Health and later with the Los Angeles County Health Department. Being in the U. S. Public Health Service reserve, was assigned to a United Nations mission to China, at the end of World War II -- in the field of public health administration. While in China, fell in love with the Orient, and resolved to return.

In 1950 took a residency in psychiatry at the Hawaii State Hospital (then Territorial Hospital) and served as Director of Rehabilitation Therapies there. Taught at University of Hawaii. Conducted psychosocial research on behalf of the Hawaii Department of Institutions and the University of Hawaii.

In 1953 I was invited to become the Luis Guerrero Memorial Lecturer at the University of Santo Tomas in Manila, Philippines. (This university is

Wayne P. Chesbro, M.D.   - 2 -   February 17, 1986

older than Harvard). Have stayed in Asia ever since -- the Philippines, Japan, and Hong Kong mainly. Established a psychiatric and psychological center in Manila in 1955. In 1960 we were approached by the U. S. State Department to conduct studies on the Smith-Fulbright Fellowship Exchange Program. This led to more and more studies of an attitudinal and motivational nature. These are what have mainly occupied me ever since, for the past 30 years.

Have been for many years the director of International Research Associates (INRA-Asia). INRA is part of a 32-country research and consultancy network. Here in Asia, we have three main divisions and areas of specialization. One is the Physicians Research Institute, based in Hong Kong, which conducts medical and pharmaceutical studies in 12 Asia-Pacific countries. Our surveys include such subjects as the attitudes and motivations which influence doctors' therapeutic decisions and their prescribing patterns, etc. These studies are sponsored by some 30 pharmaceutical manufacturers.

The second main area is in the field of travel -- a subject which has always been of great interest to me. Our International Travel Research Institute (INTRA) has conducted attitudinal and motivational studies for 40 airlines, 70 hotels and hotel chains, 20 governments and inter-governmental organizations, etc. We now have multi-country surveys under way for the World Tourism Organization (WTO), the United Nations Development Program (UNDP), and the Association of Southeast Asian Nations (ASEAN). INTRA conducts research studies in 55 countries throughout the world.

All of this may seem a long way off from medical practice, and of course it is. But the same intellectual and diagnostic challenges exist. Some of our studies are very fascinating. We conducted the benchmark surveys in the United States, Japan, and other countries on fear of flying, sponsored by the Boeing Company. Another challenging study, also on behalf of Boeing, was to analyze the passenger reactions and preferences for airplanes of the future -- before these airplanes had been built. (To do this, we tested travelers' reactions to small-scale, medium-scale, and full-scale cross-section models of future aircraft types, in various countries).

A substantial portion of our work, over the years, has been on behalf of the U. S. State Department and other government agencies. Many studies have been carried out on the image of America and the American people, as perceived by the general public and by leadership groups in different countries. At present we are conducting multinational surveys for the United Nations. No two of these research tasks are ever quite the same. There is no danger of monotony. The same is true -- is it not? -- in medical diagnosis and practice.

Wayne P. Chesbro, M.D.   - 3 -   February 17, 1986

This, then, is my capsule report to my classmates. It has been and continues to be an exciting professional life.

Across the Pacific, cordial remembrance and good wishes to our Pamassus colleagues.

Fraternally,

George Hill Hodel

P.S. The enclosed photos are among those which I took at UCSF in 1935 and 1936. If any of you would like to have a print, just let me know. It may help to refresh our remembrance of how fortunate we were to learn from those giants who made the rounds, in those great days.

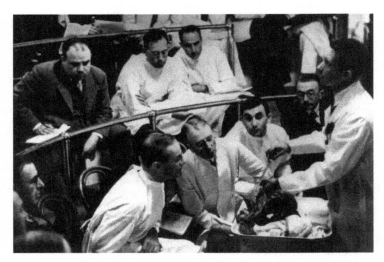

Photo was taken by GHH in 1935 at the Operating Theater at San Francisco General Hospital. This and several others were enlarged and became part of a mural exhibition in the medical school building in the 1930s, where they remained on display for many decades. (Though the operating surgeon seen performing the lecture strongly resembles GHH it is not he, as Dr. George Hill Hodel is taking this photograph.)

8

"Modus Operandi (MO) in the Twenty-First Century—Thoughtprints"

Thoughtprint: The motive within a thought. The ridges, loops, and whorls of the mind, which like the "points" found in a fingerprint, contain the potential to link an individual to a specific time, place, crime, or victim.

—Steve Hodel (Term originally coined by author in his first book,

Black Dahlia Avenger 2003)

1966 In front of LAPD Parker Center "The Glass House."

Officer Steve Hodel and Chief Thad Brown

THE ABOVE PHOTOGRAPH WAS taken in 1966, in front of what was then known as the LAPD's, PAB (Police Administration Building). Shortly after this photo was taken, it was renamed Parker Center in honor of Chief William H. Parker. Immediately after Parker's death in 1966, then Chief of Detectives Thad Brown was named as Los Angeles's interim chief of police. (This was standard for a high-ranking officer to be selected and assume temporary command, while other staff officers prepared to compete for the exam, orals, and permanent selection.)

In 1966, with only three years on the job, I was a rookie officer working Hollywood Patrol and was sent, along with a dozen other officers from Hollywood Division, to attend Thad Brown's swearing-in ceremony in the police auditorium.

Immediately after the ceremony, a department photographer approached me in the lobby as I was walking out the front door and asked, "Officer, would you like to have your picture taken with the new chief?" Surprised and honored I readily agreed, and Chief Brown smiled as we walked out in front of the building where this photograph was taken. About three weeks later, I received this copy through the Inter-Department mails. I threw it in a box and forgot about it.

The photo had no real meaning or significance to me, other than the obvious honor of being with the chief. However, we now know it had tremendous meaning and importance to Thad Brown. He knew then, what I would not discover for another thirty-five years. Thad Brown KNEW I was the son of the Black Dahlia killer, and he just could not resist the "photo-op."

It would not be until after the completion of my investigation and the publication of my first book in 2003 that we would learn from an LAPD reserve officer about the conversation between Thad Brown and actor Jack Webb, his close friend who played LAPD's Sgt. Joe Friday. *In that confidential conversation, Thad Brown disclosed to Jack Webb, "We know who killed the Black Dahlia. The case was solved. It was a doctor in Hollywood, who lived on Franklin Avenue."*

Chief Brown's statement made to his friend and drinking buddy Jack Webb was his independent and separate confirmation of what we discovered locked away in the secret DA Dahlia/Hodel Files, which identified Dr. George Hill Hodel, living in Hollywood at 5121 Franklin Avenue, as the killer.

Those files, opened in 2003 as a result of my investigation, named Dr. George Hodel as the Black Dahlia killer and contained his tape-recorded confession (146 pages of transcripts) to the murder of Elizabeth "Black Dahlia" Short, as well as the murder of his personal secretary, Ruth Spaulding. (LAPD admitted they had investigated him in 1945 for her suspected murder as a possible "forced overdose," but were unable to obtain sufficient evidence for prosecution and the investigation remained listed as a "suicide" by pills.)

The secret tapes also contained Dr. Hodel's admissions to "payoffs to Law Enforcement" and to performing illegal abortions at his clinic, as well as *the real-time recording of a felony assault and or murder of an unidentified woman in the basement of the Franklin House residence.*

In addition to LAPD Chief Thad Brown, three other high-ranking law enforcement officers connected to the original 1947 investigation would independently confirm in private conversations with friends and relatives that the case was "solved."

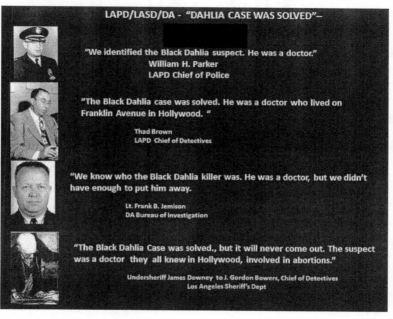

LAPD/LASD/DA - "DAHLIA CASE WAS SOLVED"-

"We identified the Black Dahlia suspect. He was a doctor."
William H. Parker
LAPD Chief of Police

"The Black Dahlia case was solved. He was a doctor who lived on Franklin Avenue in Hollywood. "
Thad Brown
LAPD Chief of Detectives

"We know who the Black Dahlia killer was. He was a doctor, but we didn't have enough to put him away.
Lt. Frank B. Jemison
DA Bureau of Investigation

"The Black Dahlia Case was solved., but it will never come out. The suspect was a doctor they all knew in Hollywood, involved in abortions."
Undersheriff James Downey to J. Gordon Bowers, Chief of Detectives
Los Angeles Sheriff's Dept

In 2005, Dr. Richard Walton contacted and advised me he was writing a textbook on cold case investigations and asked if I might be willing to contribute a summary of my concept of "thoughtprints" which I had introduced to my readers several years earlier in my book, *Black Dahlia Avenger*.

I agreed, and the following year his excellent textbook, *Cold Case Homicdes: Practical Investigative Techniques* was published.

Here is a scanned reproduction of my summary, *"Modus Operandi (MO) in the 21st Century–Thoughtprints"* as published in Dr. Walton's textbook.

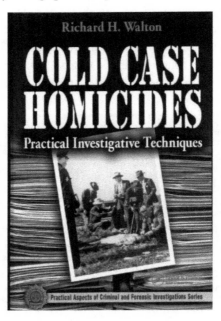

MODUS OPERANDI (M.O.) IN THE 21ST CENTURY — "THOUGHTPRINTS"

In his international bestseller, *Black Dahlia Avenger: A Genius for Murder*, retired Los Angeles Police Department homicide detective Steve Hodel introduces us to the term, *"thoughtprints."* Beginning in 1999, Hodel began to research the possibility that his father, the late Dr. George Hodel, was responsible for one of the most infamous unsolved homicides in Los Angeles history, the 1947 "Black Dahlia" murder. In doing so, he uncovered compelling evidence that suggested his father was responsible for this and other unsolved murders. During his investigation, he conceived the idea of "thoughtprints" and provides this definition:

Our thought patterns determine what we do each day, each hour, each minute. While our actions may appear simple, routine, and automatic, they really are not. Behind and within each of our thoughts is an aim, an intent, a motive.

The motive within each thought is unique. In all of our actions, each of us leaves behind traces of our self. Like our fingerprints, these traces are identifiable. I call them thoughtprints. They are the ridges,

110   Cold Case Homicides: Practical Investigative Techniques

loops, and whorls of our mind. Like the individual "points" that a criminalist examines in a fingerprint, they mean little by themselves and remain meaningless, unconnected shapes in a jigsaw puzzle until they are pieced together to reveal a clear picture.

If we are careful and clever in committing our crime, we may remember to wear gloves and not leave any fingerprints behind. But rarely are we clever enough to mask our motives, and we will almost certainly leave behind our thoughtprints. A collective of our motives, a paradigm constructed from our individual thoughts, these illusive prints construct the signature that will connect or link us to a specific time, place, crime, or victim."

In his book, Hodel cites numerous examples of Dr. George Hill Hodel's thoughtprints. I asked Hodel if he might provide us with a few examples of thoughtprints, and if he would explain how they might be useful to cold case investigators. Here is his response:

First let me clarify a misconception. Thoughtprints have absolutely nothing to do with anything psychic or metaphysical. They can apply to any crime. However, in the specialized field of homicide investigation, they should be thought of as a tool to complement M.O. and signatures.

As with the "Zodiac" unsolved murders in the San Francisco area in the 1960s and early 1970s, the slayer in the Black Dahlia case taunted police with notes and documents mailed to the news media. Figure 4.7 shows notes mailed to a local newspaper after the homicide. I believe the sender reveals training as a journalist and crime reporter through the pasted headline "copy" he sent to the press and the police as the "Black Dahlia Avenger." During the investigation, I learned that my father had training as a journalist and crime reporter for newspapers.

In another instance, as illustrated in Figure 4.8, the careful posing of the victim's arms and body mimicked the surrealist photograph, The Minotaur, created by Dr. Hodel's personal friend Man Ray. This artist's photograph illustrated a nude woman bisected at the waist (see Figure 4.9). The nude victim was found bisected at the waist and similarly posed.

Within months of the murder, George Hodel's 11-year-old daughter asked him to help her name her play doll. Interviewed decades later, the woman recalled that Hodel told her to name the doll, "Elizabeth Ann." As revealed during my investigation, The Black Dahlia's dossier from the FBI revealed the victim's name as Elizabeth Ann Short.

In another instance, I discovered a witness statement that described attendance at a "Hollywood" party at George Hodel's Hollywood house. The witness told officers that the doctor used lipstick to write words on the bare breasts of a partygoer. After concluding that the evidence strongly suggested Dr. Hodel stomped a woman to death months later, my research indicated that Dr. Hodel wrote a taunting message to the police on her nude body—using lipstick.

The concept of thoughtprints can best be utilized by cold-case investigators, by providing them a fresh start, and emphasizing the need to "think outside the box." I suggest that investigators should look for connections in a suspect's background, profession, or personal life. These could link him or her, to the crime, the victim, or the location. One of the best sources for finding potential thoughtprints comes through the reinterview of close friends. In very cold cases, careful research and review of all newspaper articles from the period can be invaluable. In the Dahlia-related serial killings from the 1940s, I extracted the documented statements of over seventy-five witnesses, and after placing them in chronological order, discovered they yielded critical information on both the victim and the suspect. Another huge potential source for latent thoughtprints is the original crime-scene photographs. Investigators can re-scan them at high-resolution, then magnify and zoom in, and conduct a present day "walk-through," right from a laptop. Reexamine the scene, inch by inch, quadrant by quadrant.

Good luck and good hunting.

Steve Hodel
Los Angeles, California
January, 2005

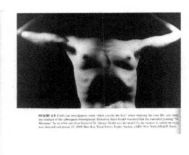

FIGURE 4.9 Cold case investigation which "2008 outside the box" when studying the case file, and Amy the standout of the subsequent investigation. Detective Steve Hodel insisted that the outraged joining "The Minotaur" by an artist and close friend of Dr. George Hodel was the model for the torture in which the victim was bruised and posed. (© 2008 Man Ray Trust/Artists Rights Society (ARS) New York/ADAGP, Paris).

FIGURE 4.7 Detective Hodel's investigation revealed that the printer suspect, his father, Dr. George Hodel had training as a journalist and crime reporter as well as that of a surgeon. (Courtesy of Steve Hodel)

FIGURE 4.8 During photo images and the case investigators, cold case investigators may consider "posing" would cause as well as it these, never reuse. (Courtesy of Steve Hodel)

In the past decade as my investigation expanded from Los Angeles's Black Dahlia and the Los Angeles Lone Woman Murders to Chicago, Manila, and most recently to the San Francisco Bay Area dozens, of new thoughtprints have been found.

As presented in the updated chapters of this book, within just the past year, two dramatic George Hodel MO latent thoughtprints (the Dahlia / Red Lipstick, "Mountain View Ave" body-posing, and the Man Ray homage to George Hodel by way of his "1969 poster Minotaur Unsalable") have been raised.

Having studied and followed my father's crime signatures from the 1940s through the 1970s, I have become "sensitized" to his unique thoughtprints.

Dr. George Hill Hodel was a creature of habit and history. Those two characteristics, combined with his megalomania and need to let the world know he was a "master criminal," have led to his undoing.

As I move forward in my attempts to ferret out more of my father's crimes from long, long ago, way back into the 1920s and 1930s, I am armed with a distinct advantage—I now know and can identify most of his thoughtprints.

I know how he thinks and how those thoughts led to his criminal actions.

Stay tuned much more to come in what I expect will be my final investigation which is ongoing now as *Dr. George Hill Hodel: The Early Years.*

9

"...By Gun, By Knife, By Rope"

Zodiac, San Francisco Chronicle *Halloween Card 1970*

The Victims: 1943-1969

In *Most Evil II* (Rare Bird Books 2015) page 195, I wrote:

The Avenger/Zodiac Victims

Zodiac in 1971 first took credit for "17" murders, then, three years later, in 1974, claimed he had killed "37," informing police and press that they were "missing a hell of a lot more of them down there [in Southern California]."

In my investigation to date, I am crediting my father, George Hill Hodel, with twenty-five murders, spanning the period of some twenty-five years (1943 to 1969).

These crimes I have previously classified as "Category I" murders—definites.

In Black Dahlia Avenger, I originally included some additional cold case murders (Category II's [probables] and Category III's [possibles]) which would add another twelve or so, bringing his total kill count to approximately "37."

I am not including those additional crimes in this summary and am only listing the names of the Category I victims that I am confident were slain by George Hodel, as Avenger / Zodiac.

Here are those twenty-five victims, along with the dates of their murders and the law enforcement agency currently responsible for the cold case investigation. I have included a photograph of each victim, when available.

1 ora murray 7.26.43
2 georgette bauerdorf 10.11.44
3 ruth spaulding 5.9.45
4 josephine ross 6.6.45
5 frances brown 12.10.45
6 suzanne degnan 1.6.46
7 elizabeth short 1.15.47

8 jeanne french 2.10.47
9 Laura Trelstad 5.11.47
10 marian newton 7.16.47
11 lillian dominguez 10.2.47
12 gladys kern 2.14.48
13 louise springer 6.13.49
14 mimi boomhower 8.18.49

15 jean spangler 10.7.49
16 jane doe franklin house 2.18.50
17 cheri jo bates 10.30.66
18 lucila lalu 5.28.67
19 Betty Jensen 12.20.68
20 David Faraday 12.20.68
21 darlene ferrin 7.4.69

22 michael mageau 7.4.69 (survived)
23 cecelia shepard 9.27.69
24 bryan hartnell 9.27.69 (survived)
25 paul stine 10.11.69

*In nearly every listed murder the cause of death, be it "By Rope" (strangulation), "By Gun" (gunshot wound), or "By Knife" (stab wound), also included some form of blunt force trauma to the face and or body—suggesting a frenzied and vicious overkill.

What follows is a chronological overview, identifying each one of my father's "Category I" crime victims by name, location, and the investigative agency responsible, along with a brief synopsis of each crime. These twenty-five crimes span nearly three decades from 1943 to 1969.

Following in the footsteps of his revered predecessor, "Jack the Ripper" Dr. George Hill Hodel also created and provided his own pseudonyms, "Black Dahlia Avenger" and "Zodiac."

Like "Saucy Jack," George Hodel was intent on ensuring that the police and press correctly identify and credit him by name to each of his crimes as part of his own marketing/public relations program.

Beginning in 1943, I will designate what I believe was his killer "persona" either publicly declared by him or not, in each of George Hodel's separate crimes as follows: **LWM** (Lone Woman Murder), **CLK** (Chicago Lipstick Killer), and **ZK** (Zodiac Killer).

1. ORA MURRAY—LWM "By Rope."

July 26, 1943, Los Angeles (Los Angeles Sheriff's Department)
"The White Gardenia Murder"

Victim, age forty-two, met suspect who introduced himself as "Paul from San Francisco" at a dance hall in downtown Los Angeles. Ora was invited out by Paul to "show her Hollywood." Driven to an isolated golf park, strangled, and savagely beaten with a tire iron causing severe blunt for trauma to her head and face. The cause of death: "constriction of the larynx by strangulation and concussion of the brain and subdural hemorrhage." Her killer ceremoniously draped a sarong over the victim's body and placed a white gardenia next to the body. What went unnoticed was that the suspect's crime had been patterned after a recent Suspense Theatre Hollywood radio play, *The White Rose Murders*, starring actress, Maureen O'Hara. The show had aired in Los Angeles on July 6, 1943, just twenty days before his "reenactment." The slaying of victim Ora Murray was identical to the radio script, originally written by popular novelist/screenwriter, Cornell Woolrich.

Above is the gruesome scene at the Fox Hills Golf Club parking lot, where the semi-nude body of Mrs. Ora E. Murray was found last July 27.

Los Angeles Sheriff's detectives at 1943 Ora Murray crime scene

2. GEORGETTE BAUERDORF—LWM "By Rope."

OCTOBER 11, 1944, Los Angeles (Los Angeles Sheriff's Department)
"THE BATHTUB MURDER"

The victim, age twenty, was followed home from the well-known Hollywood Canteen where she volunteered as a junior hostess, helping entertain servicemen during WWII. After gaining entry, Georgette was assaulted inside her residence apartment, beaten, asphyxiated by having a gag (medical ace bandage) forced down her throat. The cause of death was "obstruction of upper air passages by inserted cloth." Her killer then post-mortem carried her body to the bathroom, placed it inside the tub, and turned on the water. A witness in the building later in the morning heard the sound of running water and, in checking the apartment, found her body in the bathtub.

Robbery not a motive as valuable jewelry and money were left behind, however, the suspect did take her car, which was found abandoned near downtown Los Angeles. On the one-year anniversary of the Baurdorf slaying, her killer left a taunting typewritten note, later published in the newspapers taking credit for her murder. He bragged he would "appear at the Hollywood Canteen in uniform on or about October 11."

Further, he informed the public he had killed her due to "Divine Retribution—catch me if you can." Newspapers identified this as "The Bathtub Murder" and LA Sheriffs would, a year later in 1945, actively investigate it as possibly being connected to several "Chicago Lipstick/Bathtub murders."

1944 Bauerdorf investigation. The note typed by killer was smeared with red medical antiseptic Mercurochrome to imitate blood. (Jack the Ripper used red ink to simulate blood in his mailings to press.)

3. RUTH SPAULDING - LWM
(FORCED OVERDOSE PILLS)

MAY 9, 1945, LOS Angeles, (Los Angeles Police Department)

The victim, age twenty-seven, was single and lived alone in a downtown apartment in Los Angeles, California. Victim employed as a personal secretary to Dr. George Hill Hodel at his First Street Clinic. Ms. Spaulding was having an ongoing sexual affair with Dr. Hodel, and they had "recently broken up." Ruth had written several manuscripts and threatened to expose several of Dr. Hodel's known criminal activities. (These included false diagnosis to patients, illegal billings, performing abortions, etc.) Dr. Hodel on the pretense of "making up and getting back together" came to victim's apartment where he drugged (possibly by injection?) and forced her to ingest a lethal amount of sleeping pills. After staging the "suicide," he then called his wife, Dorothy Hodel, to the scene, while the victim remained unconscious but still alive and breathing, and gave her the incriminating manuscripts and ordered her to "take them and burn them." His wife complied. Dr. Hodel remained in the apartment with the victim until she became comatose and at death's door, then transported her by taxi to Georgia Street Receiving Hospital where she was pronounced dead one hour later. LAPD investigated the death as suspicious and "possible foul play," but their investigation was terminated nine months later, when Dr. Hodel left the country after joining UNRRA and going to China in February 1946. Four years later, on the secret DA Hodel/Black Dahlia electronic recordings Dr. Hodel would be recorded admitting to overdosing and "killing his secretary" and expressing concern that "maybe they [police] have figured it out." He was recorded stating, "Supposin' I did kill the Black Dhaliah. [sic] They couldn't prove it now. They can't talk to my secretary [Spaulding] anymore because she's dead. They [Georgia Street Receiving Hospital] pronounced her at twelve thirty-nine."

FILE NO.   304

LOS ANGELES COUNTY
CORONER'S REGISTER

2234

Name of Deceased	Ruth Spaulding	Married—Single—Widowed—Divorced	
Male or Female—Race Cauc	Age 27 Years 3 Month 22 Days—Nativity California	
Date of Call May 10, 1945	Time of Call 12:45 AM M. By Whom B. B. OLSEN DEPUTY CORONER	
Name of Person Reporting Case Miss Todd	Address Georgia Street Hospital	
Residence of Deceased 1206 W 2nd Street, Los Angeles	
Place Where Death Occurred Georgia Street Receiving Hospital	
Date of Death or When Found Dead May 10, 1945	Social Security No. 555 18 4492	
Body Brought in by MacDougall DEPUTY CORONER	Embalmed by No. 1895	
Body Received at Morgue May 10, 1945	Time 10:30 AM M. Deputy Coroner Seară	
Report by L.A.P.D. Dr #72 408	
Inquest at Coroner's Office	Date May 11, 1945	
Undertaker Pierce Brothers	
Order for Delivery Signed by V E Spaulding	Relation to Deceased Father	
Address 367 N Orange Dr. Los Angeles	City	
Informant Same	Address	
Embalming Fee Exemption by	
Date of Accident, Suicide or Homicide May 9, 1945	Time 11:45 P M.	
Place of Accident, Suicide or Homicide 1206 W 2nd Street, Los Angeles	
Nature of Accident, Suicide or Homicide Barbital poisoning.	
Probable Cause of Accident, Suicide or Homicide	
Autopsy Surgeon Frank R Webb, M.D.	Jury—No Jury—Investigation	
Cause of Death Barbital poisoning. Due to ingestion of lethal dose of barbiturates. Suicidal.	

LA County Coroner's Register listing "Probable Cause of Death, 'Barbital poisoning,' due to ingestion of lethal dose of barbiturates. Suicidal." Incredibly, this coroner's document confirms Dr. Hodel's electronic surveillance statement made nearly five years later, showing the coroner was notified of the death at 12:45 a.m., which would have been just six-minutes after she was pronounced dead at Georgia Street Receiving Hospital at 12:39 a.m.

4. JOSEPHINE ROSS—CLK "By Knife, By Rope"

JUNE 3, 1945, CHICAGO, Illinois (Chicago Police Department)
"THE BATHTUB MURDER," AKA "The Lipstick Killer Murder."

The victim, age forty-three, was accosted in her apartment on Chicago's Northside, mid-morning shortly after having breakfast with her two daughters, who then left the shared apartment. The police investigation revealed her intruder entered the apartment and a violent struggle ensued. The victim was attacked with a knife and received defense wounds to her hand and thumb. She was then struck on the head with five powerful blows which likely rendered her unconscious.

The assailant stabbed her five times in the neck and severed her jugular vein, which was the cause of death.

When discovered, she was found holding several black strands of hair which she had pulled from her attacker's head during the struggle. The suspect then committed the following highly unusual acts postmortem: 1) He placed the victim's body in the bathtub and washed it clean using a douche bag found in the bathroom. 2) He towel-dried the body and carried it to the victim's bed. 3) Using strips of medical adhesive tape, he covered over the lacerations he had inflicted on her face. 4) He tied a woman's silk stocking tightly around her throat. 5) Finally, he draped a red skirt over her head. A witness observed the suspect exit the apartment building using an exterior fire escape and provided the following description: "A tall male, thirty years, black wavy hair, wearing a light-colored sweater." (GHH was thirty-seven, but could easily pass for younger.) The crime was later connected as one of the three "Lipstick Murders," but this one was initially known as "The Bathtub Murder." (As mentioned previously, LA sheriffs would investigate this as possibly connected to the Bauerdorf "Bathtub Murder" that occurred in Los Angeles just nine months prior.)

Josephine Ross Apartment

Josephine Ross with daughter Jacqueline

5. FRANCES BROWN—CLK "By Knife, By Gun"

DECEMBER 10, 1945, CHICAGO, Illinois (Chicago Police Department)
"THE BATHTUB MURDERS," "THE Lipstick Killer Murder"

The victim, age thirty-three, had recently been working in Washington DC and was newly discharged from the US Navy as a WAVE. (Women Appointed for Voluntary Emergency Service). This crime was identical in almost every respect to the murder of Josephine Ross, which occurred just six months prior and only one-quarter mile away. The knife-wielding suspect entered her apartment, approached her in her bedroom, and a struggle ensued and victim received multiple knife cut "defense wounds" to her hands. The suspect then stabbed the victim in the neck with a large bread knife which he had removed from the kitchen. In addition, she was shot twice, once in the right arm and a second time in the forehead, which caused instantaneous death. As in the Ross attack, the killer dragged her body to the bathroom and used a douche bag to wash the blood away. He then removed her pajamas and wrapped them around the bloody knife and left it embedded in her neck, leaving her posed in the tub. As a final taunting act, he went to the south living room of the apartment, removed a framed picture, placed it on the floor, and, using a lipstick tube, wrote in bright red letters ranging from three to six inches in size:

For heavens sake catch me
Before I kill more
I cannot control myself

Killer's taunting message left on Brown's apartment wall, hence the Chicago
Press' dubbing the crime "The Lipstick Murder"

Chicago Tribune *dubs Brown's murderer, "The Lipstick Killer."*

Miss Frances Brown, a former WAVE, who was shot and stabbed to death in her apartment on Dec. 10, 1945, by slayer who left macabre message in lipstick on the wall.

Ex-Navy Wave, Frances Brown

Chicago PD investigation identified the murder weapon as a .38-caliber handgun. The suspect gained entry to the apartment by climbing an exterior fire escape and entering an open window. After turning the radio on loud, he exited through the front door. The night manager observed the suspect in the hallway at approximately 4:00 a.m. and described him as: "Male Caucasian, thirty-five to forty years, dark complexioned wearing a dark overcoat and dark fedora hat." A tenant who resided directly under the victim's apartment later reported hearing possible gunshots around 3:00 a.m. Several days after the murder, this witness received a threatening phone call from the possible suspect who stated, "I'm the lipstick killer. You'll get it next if you don't keep your mouth shut."

6. SUZANNE DEGNAN – CLK "By Knife, By Rope"

JANUARY 7, 1946, CHICAGO, Illinois (Chicago Police Deptartment)
"THE LIPSTICK KILLER MURDERS"

The victim, age six, wearing pajamas, was asleep in a large family residence on Chicago's north side. She was abducted from her bedroom. Police theorized a wooden ladder was used to possibly gain entry through a second-floor window. A ransom note was left in the bedroom. The child was strangled to death and taken to the basement of a nearby apartment building where her body was surgically dismembered, the body parts washed clean, wrapped in paper and/or rags which the killer(s) placed in six separate nearby sewers. (After nearly a day of police searching for the kidnapped child, a man (likely her killer) called the family residence and suggested the police "search the storm drains in the neighborhood.")

Police located what they described as "The Murder Room" (a basement) at 5901 Winthrop Avenue, just two city blocks from the victim's home.

Residents of this location admitted hearing noises, footsteps and running water at 3:00 a.m., but took no action.

The below ransom note was written and left inside the victim's bedroom. The note written by the killer, feigning illiteracy, demanded $20,000 in small bills.

NOTE—Here is one side of note found in victim's room. It reads: "Get $20,-000 reddy & waite for word do not notify F B I or police Bills in 5's & 10's."
—Associated Press wirephoto

Degnan Ransom Note left in victim's bedroom

It is my belief that in committing this crime, Dr. George Hodel was paying homage to two of the world's most infamous crimes; those of Jack the Ripper and the 1932 kidnap-murder of the Lindbergh Baby. Why?

Because the MO similarities between Degnan and Lindbergh are too unique to simply call them "coincidences." It had to be deliberate. George Hodel was recommitting the Lindbergh kidnap, but unlike the suspect Richard Hauptmann (later arrested, tried, convicted, and executed), GHH would outwit the police and get away with his copycat crime, proving to the world that he was much smarter than his predecessor and truly in a class of his own as a master criminal.

Here are a few identical and unique MOs used in both the Lindbergh and Degnan crimes:

- Wealthy home in an upscale neighborhood selected
- Ladder used to gain entrance to child's second-floor bedroom
- Handwritten ransom note left in bedroom
- Feigns illiteracy note containing many spelling mistakes

This MO coupled with a side-by-side comparison of the wording in both notes, in my opinion, informs us that the Degnan is a copycat crime to Lindbergh.

1932 Lindbergh Ransom note left in bedroom read:

> Dear Sir!
>
> Have 50.000$ redy 25 000# in 20$bills
>
> 15000$ in 10$ bills and 10000$ in 5$ bills
>
> After 2–4 days we will inform you were to deliver the mony.
>
> We warn you for making anyding public or for notify the Police
>
> The child is in gut care.
>
> ...

1946 Degnan Ransom note left in bedroom read:

> Get $20,000 reddy & waite for word do not notify FBI or Police
>
> Bills in 5's & 10's
>
> Burn this for her safty

A second note *written in lipstick* was found on a telephone post outside and near the "Murder Room" on Winthrop Avenue.

Lipstick printed sign on post near building where body of Suzanne Degnan was dismembered, discovered yesterday.

"Stop Me Before I Kill More"

Suzanne Degnan, age six | Degnan northside home | Degnan parents

January 8, 1946, Chicago Tribune *"Jack the Ripper" like headlines.
The city will remain terrorized and in fear for many months following
the Suzanne Degnan crime.*

A third note, allegedly written by the "Lipstick Killer," was mailed to
the Chicago police. In this note, the killer threatens to commit suicide. (In
later Avenger and Zodiac mailings, the killer also publicly announced his
intent to commit suicide). Also, like the earlier Bauerdorf typed letter to
police, the writer claims he can be found at a specific location. Police went
to the address but found no suspect.

> Why don't you catch me. If you don't **ketch** me soon,
> I will **cummit** suicide. There is a reward out for me.
> How much do I get if I give myself up. When do I get
> that 20,000 dollars they wanted from that Degnan girl
> at 5901 Kenmore Avenue. You may find me at the Club
> Tavern at 738 E. 63rd St. known as Charlie the Greeks.
> Or at Conway's Tavern at 6247 Cottage Grove Av.
>
> Please hurry now.

Chicago PD, in the months following these "Lipstick Killer" murders
was under tremendous pressure to solve the crimes. Citizen vigilante mobs
were ready to move on anyone who even had the slightest suggestion of
being a possible "suspect."

Multiple arrests (at least six) on different males were made oftentimes with
heavy-handedness with the police using excessive force. One elderly individual,
Hector Verburgh, age sixty-five, who was employed as a janitor at the same

Winthrop Avenue apartment where the Degnan girl was dismembered, was arrested, tortured, and hospitalized. After his release a few days later without being charged, his attorney sued and won a large settlement from the City for police brutality. Mr. Verburgh, when interviewed by the press, had this to say:

> Oh, they hanged me up, they blindfolded me. I can't put up my arms; they are sore. They had handcuffs on me for hours and hours. They threw me in a cell and blindfolded me. They handcuffed my hands behind my back and pulled me up on bars until only my toes touched the floor. I no sleep, I no eat, I go to the hospital. Oh, I am so sick. Any more and I would have confessed anything.[4]

William Heirens: "The Lipstick Killer"

On June 26, 1946, a seventeen-year-old, opportunist daytime burglar by the name of William Heirens entered an unlocked apartment, took a single dollar bill from a wallet on a dresser, and exited. On his person, he also had a gun taken in an earlier burglary. The teenage burglar was spotted by a witness and took off running.

An off-duty policeman chased him, fired several shots at him and Heirens took out the pistol and threw it at the pursuing officer.

A second officer gave chase and broke a flower pot over Heirens' head. Heirens was arrested and booked for burglary.

Chicago PD detectives, figuring Heirens must have something to hide to flee from the police, though it was six months after the Degan murder, decided to make Heirens the next "Lipstick Killer suspect."

Though still a juvenile, Heirens was deprived of sleep and food, grilled around the clock, beaten, prevented from speaking with an attorney or his parents, subjected to a spinal tap without anesthetic, and injected with sodium pentothal ("truth serum"). He had ether poured on his testicles and was given a lie detector test without his consent. (Though concealed for more than a decade, the results of that exam according to experts showed Heirens was telling the truth when he stated he did not kill Suzanne Degnan, Josephine Ross, or Frances Brown, the three "Lipstick Killer" victims.)

---

4   In 1948, the City of Chicago agreed to settle Hector Verbugh's claim for wrongful arrest and police brutality for a sum of $20,000 (a considerable amount in 1948 dollars).

Teenager Bill Heirens being booked for Degnan murder after June 1946 arrest

August 1946 Heirens is seen "Center Ring" in a legal circus attended by twenty "officials" (attorneys, Chicago police, arresting officers, detectives and sheriffs, all wanting to be present) when on the advice of his defense attorney Heirens is about to plead guilty to the "Lipstick Murders" to save himself from being executed. When asked by State's Attorney Tuohy (seated at the desk directly across from Heirens) if he is offering to plead guilty because "You are in fact guilty of these murders?" Heirens says, "No" and the meeting is quickly and unexpectedly adjourned to allow Heirens "to think it through." A month later in September, he will "cop a plea" to save his life, then recant it immediately after being transferred to the State Prison.

The evidence exonerating Heirens of the three "Lipstick Killer Murders" is overwhelming.

Too much to attempt to detail here, but for those interested, I recommend you read author and paralegal Dolores Kennedy's excellent book, *William Heirens: His Day In Court* (Bonus Books, Chicago 1991).

Dolores worked hand in hand with attorney Steve Drizen and his team at the Center on Wrongful Convictions at Chicago's Bluhm Legal Center, Northwestern University School of Law.

Judge Luther Swygert of the US Court of Appeals had this to say about the Heirens Case in 1968:

> The case presents the picture of a public prosecutor and defense counsel, if not indeed the trial judge, buckling under the pressure of a hysterical and sensation-seeking press bent upon obtaining retribution for a horrendous act. The State's Attorney and defense counsel usurped the judicial function, complying with a community scheme inspired by the press to convict the defendant without his day in court.

In a notable book, *Your Newspaper: Blueprint for a Better Press* (MacMillan Co. 1947) written by Nine Nieman Fellows[5] the authors point directly to the many journalistic abuses employed by the *Chicago Tribune*, in that reportage of the Heirens investigation.

Here are a few Heirens-related excerpts from that book. Pages 48–50:

> The Heirens murder story in Chicago illustrated how newspapers sometimes lose their sense of proportion. William Heirens, a seventeen-year-old University of Chicago sophomore, was arrested by Chicago police in June 1946 and held for questioning in connection with the kidnap-murder of six-year-old Suzanne Degnan and the murder of two women. Heirens denied knowing anything about the crimes.

---

5   The Nieman Foundation for Journalism is the primary journalism institution at Harvard. Founded in 1938, its stated goal is "to promote and elevate the standards of journalism in the United States and educate persons deemed specially qualified for journalism."

When he was held for the grand jury for assault and burglary (not for murder), the four Chicago dailies began to go to town, calmly and professionally, almost as if the Degnan case were secondary to their circulation war. The assigned reporters began hunting for private clues, trying to fasten the murders on Heirens, and recorded their progress on page 1. For more than a month, while Heirens insisted that he was innocent, Chicago journalism relived Ben Hecht's and Charles MacArthur's *Front Page*.

The *Hearst Herald-American* started off by importing a mystery story writer, Craig Rice, from her Santa Monica home to write about it, and brought the artist, Burris Jenkis, Jr., from New York to illustrate her articles. After interviewing the suspect in jail, Mrs. Rice decided he was innocent, and she wrote: "He's the kind of boy you could trust your teenage daughter with. I keep wanting to call him Bill." With its three rivals screaming "Murder!" the *Herald-American* dropped Craig Rice like a hot potato.

The papers printed every morsel of information they could learn about the boy, hounded his parents, and told in detail how the three victims had been murdered, how the little girl was strangled, dismembered with a knife and her body disposed of in Chicago sewers. Heirens college room was ransacked, his notes and books were gone over by reporters.

...

Justice and circulation

By the middle of July, the newspapers began reporting that Heirens had confessed. The State Attorney's office and Heirens' counsel denied it. But the papers went ahead with the stories just the same. The result was utter confusion to the reader, but—the story sold papers. Marshall Field's *Chicago Sun* jumped thirty thousand in circulation in one day.

The *Chicago Tribune* rocked its competitors by scoring a beat on an alleged confession, with a front-page streamer head, *HOW HEIRENS SLEW 3*. The *Sun* hit the streets at the same time with a contradictory streamer: HEIRENS: NO CONFESSION. But the *Tribune* story forced the *Sun* to reverse itself in later editions with the eight-column headline, HEIRENS CONFESSION. When Heirens finally confessed to the three murders in August, the *Sun* outdid the *Tribune* by running the confession in full—twenty-two columns.

The *Tribune*, trying to live up to its slogan of being "the world's greatest newspaper," claimed four "great beats" during the case. In a three-column story, the *Tribune* wrote:

"For the first time in newspaper history, the detailed story of how three murders were committed, naming the man who did them, was told before the murderer had confessed or was indicted...So great was public confidence in the *Tribune* that other Chicago papers reprinted the story solely because the *Tribune* said it was so. Never has a newspaper's contemporaries, and competitors paid a higher tribute to its reputation for veracity... For a while, Heirens maintained his innocence, but the world believed his guilt. The *Tribune* had said he was guilty."

The Harvard team of Nine Nieman Fellows, experienced reporters/ scholars all, ended their chapter's condemnation of the Heirens coverage by quoting journalists who covered the Heirens story from abroad.

...

The *Tribune* could boast about "beats" perhaps without regard to its responsibility as a newspaper in giving a man a fair chance. But the British press was shocked at this type of journalism. *The London Sunday Pictorial* attacked the handling of the Heirens case under a five-column headline, "CONDEMNED BEFORE HIS TRIAL—AMERICA CALLS THIS JUSTICE."

Writing of the case a week before the confession, the London paper said: "A seventeen-year-old student held by police for questioning has been tried and found guilty of three murders—in the columns of Chicago newspapers. Yet he has not even been charged. It will be hard to pick a jury which has not already read that he is a guilty man.... The whole trial by the press has been carried through while Heirens—as yet innocent in the eyes of all civilized people—is merely held for questioning."

Nieman Fellows, Class of 1946 authors of your Newspaper: Blueprints for a Better Press *(MacMillan Co. 1947)*

First row: Ben Yablonky, Robert Manning, Mary Ellen Leary, Cary Robertson, James Batal, Louis Lyons (Curator), Charlotte FitzHenry, Professor Arthur M. Schlesinger Sr. Second row: Arthur Hepner, Leon Svirsky, Richard Stockwell, Frank Hewlett.

Inarguably, Heiren's was convicted in a sham Trial by Press. Front-page-style reporters presented sensational and manufactured "evidence" to a lynch mob readership who demanded blood and revenge for the three "Ripper-like" horror murders.

All four Chicago newspapers followed the *Trib*'s lead and placed the completely fabricated "twenty-two-column confession" detailing how Heirens supposedly committed his "Lipstick Murders" on Page One. No fact-checking on this one. Too big a story, they all just closed their eyes and nodded their heads, Yes, the confession came from an "official and reliable source."

The faux confession was good enough for the public. No need for a real trial.

***

GIVEN A CHOICE TO live or die, the teenager chose to live, and a month after the newspapers' imaginary confession, which was above the fold nationwide along with a full "Jekyll and Hyde" photo spread of Heirens in *LIFE Magazine*, Bill was forced to "cop a plea."

Never mind that:

1. Heirens passed a lie detector test that showed he was telling the truth that he was innocent and not involved in any of the three murders.
2. The bisection of the Degnan girl was performed by a skilled surgeon and was a delicate and complicated medical procedure known as a "hemicorpectomy."
3. Heirens during his "confession" when asked how he did it informed his interrogators that he "used a hunting knife and did it in the dark in the basement, then threw the knife away." Based on the skill required, which the Degnan Coroner indicated was "beyond his own capabilities," this would have been a physical impossibility. (This was the exact same surgical bisection operation performed on Elizabeth Short less than a year later in Los Angeles.)
4. Witnesses to the crimes say the suspect was twice Heirens' age and a "tall thin man."
5. The fingerprints claimed to be found at two of the crimes scenes that the police claimed were Heirens' only appeared six months after the crimes and only after his arrest in June 1946. And they were "rolled fingerprints" never found at crime scenes and were only a type obtained during police booking procedures.
6. Heirens in his formal "confession" was unable to give any details of his crimes and for the most part could only say "yes" or "no" to police interrogators and was unaware of how many shots were fired at his victims. (Forced to guess, he claimed "one," but Frances Brown was shot twice.)

No preliminary hearing. No grand jury indictment. No trial. No witness testimony. No evidence offered forth. He was brought before the Court, pled guilty on the condition that he would receive "Life with Parole and not be executed," and was speedily sent to prison. "Case Closed."

FOCUS THE LIPSTICK KILLER

'Lipstick Killer' dies at 83

3 murders in 1940s shocked Chicago and family of slain girl is relieved that their fight is over

The Chicago Tribune March 7, 2012 headlined death of William Heirens who died in custody while serving his 65th year in prison.

William Heirens died in prison on March 5, 2012 while serving his sixty-fifth year for crimes HE DID NOT COMMIT.

Imagine being locked in a six-by-six-foot cell and waking up every day knowing you *are* innocent and counting as the clock ticks off the days, the months, and the years of your life.

Bill Heirens did just that. He counted each day until the clock and his heart stopped on the 23,979th day of his imprisonment.

My heart felt thanks and utmost respect to all of you who brought a little hope and light into Bill's life.

Especially to Dolores Kennedy his best and closest friend. Dolores never gave up and fought the good fight on behalf of Bill until the very end.

7. ELIZABETH SHORT—LWM "By Rope, By Knife"

JANUARY 15, 1947, LOS Angeles, California (Los Angeles Police Dept)
"THE BLACK DAHLIA MURDER"

The victim, at age nineteen, left her home in Medford, Massachusetts and came to California. It is believed she originally met Dr. George Hill Hodel in 1943, as a patient at his First Street VD Clinic in downtown Los Angeles. She was treated by him for a "Bartholin Gland infection," a sexually transmitted disease.

Short is introduced to Hodel's surrealist artist friend and photographer, Man Ray and poses for an oil painting, *L'Equivoque* in 1943. Dr. Hodel becomes "a suitor" and dates, wines, and dines Short on her occasional visits to Hollywood while she is working at the military base at Camp Cook in the Post Exchange as a sales clerk. Short is arrested in 1943 in Santa Barbara for "minor possession" for being present underage in a bar and is sent home to her mother in Medford, Massachusetts.

Based on information contained in the secret DA Hodel/Black Dahlia Files we learn that Short traveled to Chicago, Illinois in June 1946 and began making inquiries into the three "Lipstick Murders." Police reports indicate she became intimate with four separate newspaper reporters and informed them that "she was personally acquainted with a police officer that was working on the Degnan/Heirens case." Short visits Los Angeles in the summer/fall of 1944 and again in the summer of 1945 and is photographed on VJ Day riding in an open convertible with five other women.

In the fall of 1946, Short returns to Los Angeles and resides at various apartment houses in the Hollywood area. In November 1946, she became fearful for her life and fled to San Diego where she hid out at a private residence for approximately six weeks.

In late December or early January 1947, Short was seen and identified as being in the company of Dr. George Hodel. Both were standing in line waiting to attend a Jack Carson radio show at the CBS Columbia Square Radio Playhouse in Hollywood. On that occasion, George Hodel approached the head usher, Jack Egger, who would later become a prominent witness in the investigation. George produced a police badge identifying himself as "a Chicago police officer" and the usher allowed both Short and Hodel to jump the line (a common courtesy shown to law enforcement) and escorted them to Studio A to see the show.

On January 9, 1947, Elizabeth Short permanently returns from San Diego and is dropped off at the *Biltmore Hotel* by an acquaintance.

During the following week, on separate days and nights she is seen by more than a dozen witnesses at locations in Hollywood and in the downtown section of LA.

The victim was last seen on the afternoon of January 14, 1947 near the intersection of Fifth and Main Street, in downtown LA, where she spoke with Officer Meryl McBride, an LAPD uniformed policewoman working her beat.

Officer McBride described Short as being both "excited and fearful" as she ran up and informed the officer that "a former suitor was inside a bar down the street and he just threatened to kill me."

Officer McBride accompanied Short back to the bar and recovered the victim's purse, but the man was gone. Officer McBride returned to her footbeat.

An hour later, McBride observed Short a second time exiting a different bar. This time she was in the company of "two men and a woman." McBride approached her and asked, "Are you all right?" Short replied she was and that she was going to the Greyhound Bus Station down the street to meet her father who was coming into town.

McBride again returned to her duties and this was the last known live sighting of the victim.

The following morning, January 15, 1947, Elizabeth Short's body was found carefully posed on a vacant lot in the Liemert Park section of Los Angeles, some six miles south of Hollywood.

She had been sadistically tortured for hours. Ligature marks were found on her hands, ankles and around her neck, indicating she had been tied then sexually assaulted and anally raped. She had also been force-fed feces. Numerous cuttings were performed on the body and her right breast was removed. (Possibly retained as a "trophy.") A "hemicorpectomy" surgical operation, identical to that of victim Suzanne Degan, had been performed. Her body was posed in the *Minotaur* position (hands bent at the elbows and placed over her head) on a street named "Degnan." (George Hodel thought he was on Degnan, but unbeknownst to him the street changed names mid-block.) Physical evidence (large paper cement sacks) used to transport the body parts from the original crime scene to the vacant lot would later be connected by this investigator establishing Short had been slain at Dr. George Hodel's Hollywood residence, 5121 Franklin Avenue.

Secret DA Hodel/Black Dahlia Files discovered in 2003 would establish that Dr. George Hill Hodel was her killer, and that electronic surveillance recordings were made containing his confession to this crime as well as other murders and criminal activity.

8. JEANNE AXFORD FRENCH—LWM "By Knife"

FEBRUARY 10, 1947, Los Angeles, California (Los Angeles Police Department) "THE RED LIPSTICK MURDER" aka "Jeanne French: The Flying Nurse Murder"

The victim, age forty, was married, and was last seen dining at a restaurant in West Los Angeles, with a man closely fitting the description of George Hodel. At dinner, the waitress who served them later indicated they were "speaking

French." A male employee observed the couple exit the restaurant and enter the suspect's vehicle, which he described as a 1937 black sedan identical in description to the 1937 black Packard owned and driven by Dr. Hodel.

The killer drove the victim to an isolated vacant lot in the 3200 block of Grandview Ave where he stripped her naked, beat her with what LAPD Police Captain Donahoe described as "a heavy weapon, probably a tire iron or a wrench, as she crouched naked on the highway." The victim's nude body was dragged from the street to a dirt lot where she was literally stomped to death. The coroner's physician, Dr. Newbarr, found the cause of death to be "ribs shattered by heavy blows, one of the broken ribs having pierced the heart creating hemorrhage and death."

As part of his "posing," the suspect ceremoniously draped the victim's blue coat trimmed with red fox-fur cuffs and her red dress over her nude body. A man's white handkerchief was also found lying nearby. Police recovered black hair follicles from under the victim's fingernails, indicating a violent struggle had occurred prior to her demise.

In a final taunt to the police, as well as to identify himself as "The Black Dahlia Avenger," the same man who tortured and slew Elizabeth Short and posed her body on a vacant lot just three weeks earlier, removed a red lipstick stub from the victim's purse, and wrote a message in large red letters across her nude body. It read:

"Fuck You BD"

Top: Jeanne French nude body at the crime scene. Bottom: Close-up of "Red Lipstick" message written on victim's body taken at the LA Coroner's office.

9. LAURA ELIZABETH TRELSTAD—LWM "By Rope"

MAY 11, 1947, LONG Beach, California (Long Beach Police Dept)

> *"George [Hodel] drowned himself at times in an ocean of deep dreams.*
> *Only part of him seemed present. He would muse standing before one in*
> *a black, flowered dressing gown lined with scarlet silk, [emphasis*
> *mine] oblivious to one's presence."*
>
> —*Newspaper article, "The Clouded Past of a Poet"*
> *describing a young George Hodel by Ted Le Berthon,*
> Los Angeles Evening Herald, *December 9, 1925*

The victim was a thirty-seven-year-old married mother of three children who had left a party after arguing with her husband.

Mrs. Trelstad went to a Long Beach bar where she continued drinking and engaged fellow patrons in an argument whereupon the bartender refused to serve her any further drinks. A sailor who had been drinking with her put her on a homeward-bound bus.

Police located the bus driver who recalled the victim being aboard his bus on May 10, 1947. He recalled her due to an incident in which she began arguing with him for passing her stop at Thirty-Sixth Street and American Avenue. She exited the bus at approximately 11:30 p.m. The bus driver recalled seeing a "tall, well-dressed man" follow her off the bus.

On May 11, 1947, at 5:00 a.m., the victim's body was found by an oil field pumper arriving at work at the Signal Hill Oil fields, in Long Beach.

The victim had been severely beaten about the face and body, raped, and then strangled *"with a piece of flowered cotton cloth, believed torn from a man's pajamas or shorts." [emphasis mine]*

LA County Coroner, Dr. Newbarr, found the cause of death to be "asphyxia due to strangulation, and a skull fracture and hemorrhage and contusion of the brain."

Police detectives at 1947 body dump locaton of Laura Trelstad
near Signal Hills Oil Fields

Police informed the press that "the victim had been murdered elsewhere and the body then dumped in the vacant lot close to the oil rigs." Vehicle tire tracks and footprints were found near the body. Police obtained plaster castings of the footprints.

The fact that the coroner's office affirmed that victim was raped suggests that slides of sperm cells were obtained during the autopsy. If this is confirmed and they still exist, a strong possibility exists that DNA could be obtained and compared to the full DNA profile of George Hodel currently in my possession.

10. MARIAN DAVIDSON NEWTON—LWM "By Rope"

July 16, 1947, San Diego, California (San Diego Police Dept)

The victim was an attractive thirty-six-year-old divorcée vacationing in San Diego from her home in Vancouver, British Columbia.

This crime was identical in nearly all respects to the first Lone Woman Murder of Mrs. Ora Murray that occurred in 1943.

Ms. Newton, accompanied by a female acquaintance, Edna Mitchell, whom she had met at her hotel, decided to go to Sherman's, a popular nightclub/dance hall and local San Diego attraction that "sported nine different bars and the largest indoor dance floors in the world."

Witness Mitchell would later describe the possible suspect to police as a man who kept dancing with Marian and who was later seen accompanying her from the club. Mitchell described him as "tall, over six foot, thin, possibly in his thirties, with dark hair, wearing a tan sport coat, slacks and a bright-colored tie." The witness earlier in the evening informed the victim that she didn't like the look of the guy and warned her "not to get into a car with any man she met at the club."

The victim's body was discovered by a couple on a hike in the Torrey Pines Mesa area just north of San Diego.

FOUND SLAIN—Mrs. Marian Davidson Newton (above), 36-year-old Vancouver, B. C. divorcee, was found slain near San Diego, Calif. Marks on her throat indicated that she had been strangled. (AP wirephoto)

1947 AP Press Photo article of Marian Davidson Newton

On scene, homicide detectives determined that Marian Newton had been strangled with a thin wire or cord.

She suffered blunt force trauma to the body, heavy bruising and had been raped.

Two men's handkerchiefs were found near the body. One was stained and one was not.

The victim's purse and identification had been thrown from the suspect's vehicle and were found in downtown San Diego at the intersection of University and Albatross Streets.

San Diego detectives believed there may have been a connection to this crime and the wave of Lone Woman Murders in Los Angeles and met with LAPD who, despite the strikingly similar MO, expressed doubt to this "outside agency" that the crimes were connected.

11. LILLIAN DOMINGUEZ—LWM "By Knife"

OCTOBER 2, 1947 , Santa Monica, California (Santa Monica Police Dept)

This LWM crime was not discovered by me until 2009 and was first summarized in Chapter 11 of *BDA II*, "The Black Dahlia's Three Greatest Myths—Myth No. 1—A Standalone Murder."

The victim, age fifteen, was a student at John Adams Junior High, in Santa Monica, California. She was walking home from a school dance with her sister and a friend.

At the intersection of Seventeenth Street and Michigan, a man approached them and as he walked past he stabbed the victim in the heart with a long thin stiletto-type knife and kept walking.

Lillian yelled out to her friends, "That man just touched me." She took a few more steps and blurted out, "I can't see," then collapsed to the ground and died.

The suspect was only seen from the back as he walked by, so no accurate physical description was ever obtained.

On October 9, 1947, one week to the day of Lillian's murder, her killer left a taunting note under the door of a furniture store that read, "I killed that Santa Monica girl. I will kill others."

See earlier chapter as referenced for further details.

Author reproduction of taunting note left by Dominguez killer. The original note was not published in the newspapers, nor was the "Los Angeles furniture store" address, where it was left made public. Was it like other Avenger Notes, left in downtown LA near Dr. Hodel's medical practice?

12. GLADYS EUGENIA KERN—LWM "By Knife"

FEBRUARY 14, 1948, LOS Angeles, (Los Angeles Police Department)
"THE REAL ESTATER MURDER"

This victim was a fifty-year-old married woman employed as a real estate agent. Her office was located in the Los Feliz district of Los Angeles (one mile from the home of Dr. George Hill Hodel).

Victim's killer, posing as a home buyer, accompanied her to a vacant private estate in the Hollywood Hills where he and possibly a second man attacked her with an "eight-inch jungle knife" which was left at the scene (found in the kitchen sink, wrapped in a man's handkerchief).

Cause of death was found to be "multiple stab wounds to body."

On the afternoon of the murder, a Japanese gardener working near the "For Sale" residence observed "two men walk out of the house and down the steps."

Later descriptions from witnesses who had seen the suspect with Mrs. Kern prior to going to the residence described him as "tall, well dressed, wearing a business suit."

An LAPD police artist obtained the below composite drawing which was published on the front page of the local newspapers.

Kern Police composite of killer compared to Dr. George Hill Hodel's appearance in the late 1940s and early 50s. No mustache was recalled by witnesses so I have airbrushed it out in Hodel photos for comparative purposes.

The day following the murder, Kern's killer left a long rambling note in a mailbox at Fifth and Olive Streets, revealing the murder.

The writer, feigning illiteracy, gave a detailed description of the crime prior to the body being found by police.

The note was found just two blocks from Dr. Hodel's medical office and was posted in the same mailbox in which the Black Dahlia Avenger had left a Dahlia-related note to police a year earlier.

1948 Kern Murder Note left in mailbox at Fifth and Olive St. downtown LA.

13. LOUISE MARGARET SPRINGER–LWM "By Rope"

JUNE 13, 1949, LOS ANGELES (Los Angeles Police Department)
"THE GREEN TWIG MURDER"

This twenty-eight-year-old victim was married and the mother of a two-year-old boy. Her husband, Laurence Springer was a hairstylist of wide reputation employed at a salon on Wilshire Boulevard.

Louise, also a hair stylist, worked in a department store at Santa Barbara and Crenshaw, just two blocks from where the body of Elizabeth "Black Dahlia" Short was found.

On June 13, 1947 at 9:05 p.m., the victim finished work and was picked up by her husband in the couple's brand-new 1949 green Studebaker convertible.

Louise discovered she had left her eyeglasses inside and her husband volunteered to go get them as he also needed to pick up some cigarettes in the tobacco store adjacent to the beauty salon. He was absent for only ten minutes.

On his return, his wife and their vehicle had disappeared.

After frantically searching the parking lot, he phoned LAPD, who responded, searched the immediate area, and took a "missing report" assuring him that his wife would "likely return in a day or two."

Three days later, the abandoned convertible was found near downtown Los Angeles. The victim's body was found in the back seat, covered with a beautician's tarp.

The cause of death was found to be by "ligature strangulation" with a white precut clothesline cord tied tightly around her neck, which police speculated her killer had brought with him.

Robbery was not a motive as her purse, jewelry, and money were found in the car.

The second shocking discovery appeared in an article in the *Los Angeles Examiner* of June 17, which read:

...

BODY VIOLATED

And with a fourteen-inch length of finger-thick tree branch, ripped from some small tree, the killer had violated her body in such a manner as to stamp this crime at once and indelibly in the same category as the killing of Elizabeth Short, "the Black Dahlia."

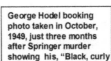

George Hodel booking photo taken in October, 1949, just three months after Springer murder showing his, "Black, curly hair."

Photo showing "Springer Murder Car" Article reads, "The discovery has touched off the wildest man hunt since the slaying of the Black Dahlia."

Neighborhood witnesses looking out their window observed a "tall, thin man with black curly hair" exit the Kern vehicle on the night of the kidnapping and walk away. The parked "abandoned" vehicle was not reported to police for several days.

I have upgraded this crime from its original "Category II" (Probable) in *BDA* (Arcade 2003) due to additional information and findings as presented in *BDA II* Chapter 11, "The Black Dahlia's Three Greatest Myths: Myth No. 1—A Standalone Murder."

14. MIMI BOOMHOWER–LWM (Unknown cause of death body not found)

AUGUST 18, 1949, LOS ANGELES, (Los Angeles Police Department)
"THE MERRY WIDOW MURDER"

The victim Mimi Boomhower was a Bel-Air socialite and "prominent heiress," age forty-eight.

Mrs. Boomhower was last heard from on August 18, 1949, when she spoke with her business manager and informed him "she was meeting a gentleman at 7:00 p.m. at her home" whom the manager believed was a prospective buyer for the mansion.

Police surmised the victim was abducted from her home with a possible motive of robbery, though numerous items of value had been left inside her private residence.

Mimi Boomhower was never heard from or seen again nor was her body ever found.

The possible suspect(s) left her purse just a few miles from her hillside mansion at a phone booth in Beverly Hills.

The following message to the police was written in large printed letters on the Boomhower purse:

POLICE DEPT.—

WE FOUND THIS AT BEACH THURSDAY NIGHT

(Left) Police and press noted the similarities of the Boomhower crime to the murder of real estate agent Gladys Kern in February 1948 and headlined the connection, "Wealthy Widow Feared Victim of Knife Slayer. Police Recall Still Unsolved Kern Killing." (Right) Photo of purse left at a phone booth on which probable suspect(s) handprinted message to police.

Handwriting analysis of the letters on the purse was conducted by court-certified Questioned Document Expert, Hannah McFarland.

Her comparison to known samples of the hand-printing of Dr. George Hill Hodel resulted in a finding that it was "highly probable that he wrote the message to police." (QDE McFarland also analyzed and found that the lipstick hand-printing on the body of Mrs. Jeanne French was "highly probably written by Dr. George Hodel.")

15. JEAN ELIZABETH SPANGLER–LWM (Unknown cause of death, body not found)

OCTOBER 7, 1949, HOLLYWOOD, California (Los Angeles Police Department)

The victim was a twenty-seven-year-old Hollywood actress who had been a former dancer at Black Dahlia witness Mark Hansen's Florentine Gardens nightclub. She was recently divorced and living with her five-year-old-daughter Christine in an apartment in Hollywood.

Tracing her movements on the evening of October 7 until she was last seen in the early morning hours of October 8, 1949, police determined the following:

The victim was seen with a handsome dapper-dressed male sitting in his dark-colored sedan parked in the Hollywood Ranch Market lot. (The descriptions fit both George Hodel and his vehicle, a 1937 black Packard. The location was just seventy-five feet from his good friend Man Ray's residence apartment at the Villa Elaine, 1245 N. Vine St. It should be further noted that George Hodel was released from jail on the incest/child molestation charges on the previous morning, October 6, after posting cash bail.)

On the early morning hours of October 8, the victim was seen seated with two men at a front row table at the Cheese Box Restaurant, 8033 Sunset Boulevard.

They were having an argument and as the restaurant's radio personality "Al the Sheik" Lazaar approached the actress for a live interview, the man, fitting Dr. Hodel's description, brusquely signaled to him "no interview" and Lazaar veered away. (As to the public argument, I find myself asking, "Could it be related to the fact that GHH had been arrested the day previous and charged with having sexual relations with Tamar, his fourteen-year-old daughter?)

The last sighting of the victim was by a gas station attendant at a service station just a few blocks from the restaurant, shortly after the argument.

The driver pulled his car to the gas pumps and had the attendant fill the tank, saying, "We're going to Fresno."

Jean Spangler shrank down in the front seat and as the car pulled away she yelled to the witness, "Have the police follow this car." The attendant immediately called LAPD who responded but were unable to locate the vehicle or Jean Spangler.

Jean's sister-in-law, Sophie Spangler, who was babysitting Jean's daughter, Christine, phoned the police and made a formal "Missing Report" on Saturday, October 8 at 9:00 a.m.

Spangler's purse was found twenty-four hours later on Sunday at 11:00 a.m., discarded off the roadway in Fern Dell Park, a short distance from the Hodel residence.

Like the previous victim, Mimi Boomhower, Jean Spangler's body was never found and the exact cause of death remains unknown.

Spangler's divorce attorney, S.S. Hahn (who was also the attorney who represented my mother, Dorothy Hodel in her 1945 divorce from George Hodel) shortly after the disappearance of his client publicly announced that "foul play is suspected."

Long Beach Independent October 12, 1949

LAPD officers pointing to where victim Jean Spangler's ripped purse was found in Ferndell Park. More than two hundred officers searched this west side area of Griffith Park on foot and horseback.

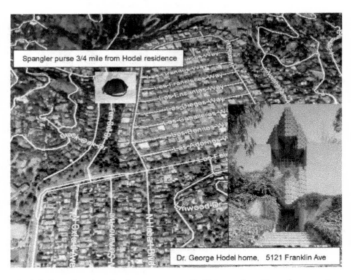

Aerial photo showing the three-quarter-mile distance from Spangler purse to Dr. George Hodel's then private residence at 5121 Franklin Ave.

Jean Spangler's updated findings and linkage to Dr. George Hill Hodel were presented in *BDA II* (2014 ed.), Chapter 24, "Odor Mortis: The Smell of Death—Jean Spangler Background and Last Known Movements."

16. JANE DOE—LWM (Possible drugging and blunt force trauma, body not found)

FEBRUARY 18, 1950, HOLLYWOOD, California, (Los Angeles Police Department jurisdiction. No known investigation ever conducted by LAPD. DA detectives initiated a cursory investigation based on electronic surveillance tapes, but the suspected crime was never made public.)

The victim was an unidentified female "Jane Doe" who had gone to the residence of Dr. George Hill Hodel on the afternoon of February 18, 1947.

Unbeknownst to Hodel and others at the residence, the LADA was electronically staked out at the home and recording conversations and activities.

The victim was overhead being offered alcoholic drinks, and was possibly drugged.

Dr. Hodel is overheard saying, "Let's have another drink. Does your husband know you're here?"

In the afternoon hours, the victim was recorded crying and attempting to call the telephone operator but dropped the phone and was disconnected. It is believed she was attempting to call for help.

Hours later, Dr. Hodel and an accomplice, later identified by me as "Baron Ernst Harringa," a longtime Hodel acquaintance and DTLA art gallerist, are recorded going downstairs to the basement.

An object is heard striking what is believed to be the Jane Doe victim. She screams. More blows are overheard, and more screams, then Dr. Hodel is recorded saying to "The Baron," "Don't leave a trace."

Based on these recorded statements and actions, DA Detective McGrath conducted a follow-up investigation and interviewed a plumber who had been summoned to the Hodel residence to "clear a drain in the basement." McGrath inquired if he had "seen any signs of digging in the basement." Witness stated, "He wasn't looking for anything like that and just did his job and left." McGrath made a formal report documenting his investigation.

This female "Jane Doe" victim was never identified and her body, like that of Mimi Boomhower and Jean Spangler, was never found.

10

17. CHERI JO BATES—ZK "By Knife"

OCTOBER 30, 1966, RIVERSIDE, California (Riverside Police Department)

The victim, age eighteen, was a student at Riverside City College, located approximately eighty miles east of Los Angeles, California.

On the evening of October 30, 1966, after conducting some research at the college library, she exited and walked to her car, a lime-green Volkswagen Bug.

She attempted to start her car, but unbeknownst to her, the suspect had opened the hood and ripped out the distributor cap and coil and wires, making the vehicle inoperable.

As she stood by her car, a male approached and offered her a ride and she apparently accepted his offer, and as Cheri Jo walked with the man to his car, he turned, viciously attacked her with a knife, and cut her throat, leaving her for dead.

A campus groundskeeper found her body on the ground the following morning.

Riverside Police responded to the crime scene and discovered that the victim had been badly beaten about the face and head, with multiple stab wounds to her chest and back. Her jugular vein had been severed so savagely she was nearly decapitated.

The victim was clutching a tuft of what is believed to be her killer's hair in her right hand.

Robbery was not a motive as her purse and contents were left at the scene. Authorities indicated she was not sexually assaulted.

One month to the day from her murder, the suspect mailed a lengthy typewritten "confession" to both the Riverside Police Department and the local newspaper.

Sadistic in the extreme, typed in all capital letters, it read:

THE CONFESSION
BY - - - - - - - - - - - -

SHE WAS YOUNG AND BEAUTIFUL. BUT NOW SHE
IS BATTERED AND DEAD. SHE IS NOT THE FIRST
AND SHE WILL NOT BE THE LAST. I LAY AWAKE
NIGHTS THINKING ABOUT MY NEXT VICTIM.
MAYBE SHE WILL BE THE BEAUTIFUL BLOND
THAT BABYSITS NEAR THE LITTLE STORE AND
WALKS DOWN THE DARK ALLEY EACH EVENING
ABOUT SEVEN. OR MAYBE SHE WILL BE THE
SHAPELY BLUE EYED BROWNETT THAT SAID
NO WHEN I ASKED HER FOR A DATE IN HIGH
SCHOOL. BUT MAYBE IT WILL NOT BE EITHER.
BUT I SHALL CUT OFF HER FEMALE PARTS AND
DEPOSIT THEM FOR THE WHOLE CITY TO SEE.
SO DON'T MAKI IT TO EASY FOR ME. KEEP YOUR
SISTERS, DAUGHTERS, AND WIVES OFF THE
STREETS AND ALLEYS. MISS BATES WAS STUPID.
SHE WENT TO THE SLAUGHTER LIKE A LAMB.SHE
DID NOT PUT UP A STRUGGLE. BUT I DID. IT WAS
A BALL. I FIRST PULLED THE MIDDLI WIRE FROM
THE DISTRIBUTOR. THEN I WAITED FOR HER IN
THE LIBRARY AND FOLLOWED HER OUT AFTER
ABOUT TWO MINUTS. THE BATTERY MUST HAVE
BEEN ABOUT DEAD BY THEN I THEN OFFERED
TO HELP. SHE WAS THEN VERY WILLING TO TALK
WITH ME. I TOLD HER THAT MY CAR WAS DOWN
THE STREET AND THAT I WOULD GIVE HER A
LIFT HOME. WHEN WE WERE AWAY FROM THE
LIBRARY WALKING. I SAID IT WAS BOUT TIME.
SHE ASKED ME, "ABOUT TIME FOR WHAT". I SAID
IT WAS ABOUT TIME FOR HER TO DIE. I GRABBED
HER AROUND THE NECK WITH MY HAND OVER
HER MOUTH AND MY OTHER HAND WITH A
SMALL KNIFE AT HER THROAT. SHE WENT VERY
WILLINGLY. HER BREAST FELT VERY WARM

AND FIRM UNDER MY HANDS. BUT ONLY ONE
THING WAS ON MY MIND. MAKING HER PAY FOR
THE BRUSH OFFS THAT SHE HAD GIVEN ME
DURING THE YEARS PRIOR. SHE DIED HARD. SHE
SQUIRMED AND SHOOK AS I CHOAKED HER. AND
HER LIPS TWICHED. SHE LET OUT A SCREAM
OXCE AND I KICKED HER HEAD TO SHUT HER UP.
I PLUNGED THE KNIFE INTO HER AND IT BROKE.
I THEN FINISHED THE JOB BY CUTTING HER
THROAT. I AM NOT SICK. I AM INSANE. BUT
THAT WILL NOT STOP THE GAME. THIS LETTER
SHOULD BE PUBLISHED FOR ALL TO READ IT.
IT JUST MIGHT SAVE THAT GIRL IN THE ALLEY.
BUT THAT'S UP TO YOU. IT WILL BE ON YOUR
CONSCIENCE. NOT MINE. YES, I DID MAXE THAT
CALL TO YOU ALSO. IT WAS JUST A WARNING.
BEWARE...I AM STALKING YOUR GIRLS NOW.
CC. CHIEF OF POLICE
ENTERPRISE

This "confession" was followed-up by the killer mailing a six-month anniversary note, on April 30, 1967, written in large block letters which the suspect sent to the police, the press, and to the victim's parents at their home address.

The note read:

BATES HAD TO DIE
THERE WILL BE MORE

Z

A third message, a poem carved into one of the library desks and discovered after the crime, pointed to the likelihood that Cheri's killer had stalked her inside the library, probably lay in wait, and watched her while she conducted her research.

The poem read:

Sick of living/unwilling to die
cut.
clean.

if **red/**
clean.
blood spurting,
dripping,
spilling;
all **over** her new
dress
oh well
it was red
anyway.
life draining into an
uncertain death.
she won't
die.
this **time**
someone ll find her.
just wait till
next time.

rh[6]

Cheri Jo Bates's killer's three separate 1966–1967 taunting messages. Upper Left is the typed "confession," Upper Right the "Bates Had To Die; There Will Be More," and Lower Left is a photograph of the poem written on the desktop inside the library while he stalked his victim immediately before the assault and murder.

6   At the time of the murder, R. H. Bradshaw was the president of Riverside City College. Police *speculated* the killer may have known this and possibly used his initials as part of a subtle taunt.

Los Angeles Times

ZODIAC LINKED TO RIVERSIDE SLAYING

Los Angeles Times, November 16, 1970, headline announcing police link Zodiac Killer to Southern California, Cheri Jo Bates murder

18. LUCILA LALU—ZK "By Knife, By Rope"

MAY 28, 1967, MANILA, Philippines (Manila Metropolitan Police Department) "THE JIGSAW MURDER," AKA "The Chop Chop Murder."

> **"I SHALL CUT OFF HER FEMALE PARTS AND DEPOSIT THEM FOR THE WHOLE CITY TO SEE."**
>
> Z (Cheri Jo Bates Confession Letter, November 30, 1966)
>
> **"BATES HAD TO DIE THERE WILL BE MORE"**
>
> Z (Cheri Jo Bates Note April 30, 1967)

Victim Lucila "Lucy" Lalu y Tolentino was an attractive twenty-nine-year old businesswoman. Lucy owned Lucy's Beauty Salon and The Pagoda Cocktail Bar in the city of Manila, Philippines. Both businesses shared the same address.

(Left) Victim, Lucila Lalu y Tolentino (Right) Lucy's House of Beauty. A crowd gathered after hearing about the "Chop Chop Murder."

On the night of May 28, 1967, the victim was assaulted in her place of business. She was beaten about the face and body, and police speculated that she was then forced into a waiting vehicle.

Miss Lalu was taken to an unknown location where after having her hands bound with a rope she was then strangled to death.

Her body was bisected as well as having her arms and legs disarticulated by what the Manila Coroner said, "Had to have been performed by a skilled surgeon."

The victim's upper torso was placed just off the street adjacent to a vacant lot.

Her disarticulated lower legs were taken to a separate section of the city where they were wrapped in newspaper and placed atop a trash can. The victim had been decapitated, and the head was never found.

The victim was initially a "Jane Doe" until her fingerprints were checked and found to be on file in the Manila Police Department from when she had previously filed to be a waitress in a restaurant.

The Manila Times

MANILA, PHILIPPINES, WEDNESDAY, MAY 31, 1967

Girl's headless body identified

Manila Times announcing body identified from fingerprints

Map of Manila, Philippines and Makati District
1) George Hodel Office 2) George Hodel Family Residence
3) Lalu body off Zodiac Street.

Makati District enlargement showing body location adjacent to "Zodiac" Street.

19-20. BETTY JENSEN AND DAVID FARADAY—ZK "By Gun"

DECEMBER 20, 1968, VALLEJO, California (Solano County Sheriffs)

Victims Betty Lou Jensen, age sixteen, and David Faraday, age seventeen, were on their "first date" after attending their Hogan High School Christmas Concert.

Both teenagers were residents of Vallejo, California.

At approximately 11:30 p.m., the young couple drove and parked in an isolated "lovers' lane" location on Herman Road, near the entrance to the Benicia Water Pumping Station.

Shortly after David parked his 1961 Rambler station wagon, a second car pulled up and parked nearby.

The suspect, armed with a .22-caliber semiautomatic handgun, approached the couple and fired a shot through the rear window of the vehicle.

Both victims attempted to exit the right front passenger door. David was shot in the head, and Betty Lou was shot five times in the back as she attempted to flee on foot and collapsed just ten feet to the rear of the vehicle.

Police determined that a total of ten shots were fired.

The cause of death to both victims was found to be "gunshot wounds."

A witness came forward who had just driven by the location and heard shots and had observed a second vehicle parked next to the Faraday station wagon, but could not describe the make or model, nor could he provide a suspect description.

The crime remained an isolated, motiveless, apparent random double-homicide with no real leads.

It would not be connected to "The Zodiac Killings" until Zodiac claimed ownership in 1969.

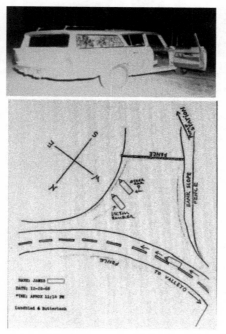

(Top) Photo of Faraday Rambler station wagon at scene.
(Bottom) Police sketch of Herman Road and vehicles per eyewitness description.

4— Santa Cruz Sentinel   Sunday, December 22, 1968

Two Vallejo Teenagers Found Slain On Road

Vallejo (AP) — Investigators quizzed friends of two Vallejo teenagers yesterday searching for clues in their double murder Friday night as they returned from a high school Christmas concert.

Bettilou Jensen, 16, and David Faraday, 17, were found sprawled on the side of a lonely road about 10 miles east of Vallejo, shot in a volley of rifle fire. Investigators described the double slaying as "exceptionally gruesome."

Mrs. Manuel Borges, who was en route to pick up her children at a movie in nearby Benicia, saw the bodies in the headlights of her car and notified police.

Faraday, a senior at Vallejo High School where he was on the wrestling team, died en route to a hospital. Miss Jensen, a junior at Vallejo's Hogan High School, was dead at the scene.

Coroner Dan Horan said investigators were looking into the possibility the young couple, who were on their first date, had been trailed from the concert at Hogan High.

Horan said the youngsters had "apparently just stopped" on the road, a favorite parking spot for young couples, when the shootings occurred. The car's heater was still running when investigators arrived.

They said: Faraday was shot in the left side of the head after getting out of his car and walking around to the passenger side.

Miss Jensen then apparently ran and was shot in the back with five .22-caliber bullets at a range of about 10 feet. Four spent 22-caliber shell casings were found at the scene. There was a bullet hole in the back window of the car.

Investigators described both victims as "good kids from nice homes." They said neither "had ever been in any kind of trouble."

Faraday, son of Mr. and Mrs. Jean L. Faraday, was an Eagle Scout and held the God and Country Award, one of scouting's highest honors. His father works for the Pacific Gas and Electric Co.

Miss Jensen was the daughter of Mr. and Mrs. Vincent M. Jensen. Her father is a programmer for the U.S. General Services Administration.

Santa Visits Fatherless Of Farmington

Farmington, W.Va. (AP).—Santa and Mrs. Claus came to this grief-stricken coal mining community yesterday and for a brief moment the children o[...]

Santa Cruz Sentinel December 22, 1968

21-22. DARLEEN FERRIN AND MICHAEL MAGEAU—ZK "By Gun"

July 4, 1969 Vallejo, California (Vallejo Police Department)

Victim Darleen Ferrin, age twenty-two, and Michael Mageau, age nineteen, were seated in Darleen's 1963 Corvair in an isolated parking lot adjacent to Blue Rock Springs Park, in Vallejo, California.

The suspect drove up and parked nearby; then approached the couple on foot holding a flashlight in hand and shined it in Mageau's face.

He then, without saying a word, fired multiple rounds at both victims while they remained seated inside the parked car.

Both victims were found fifteen minutes after the shooting by a passing motorist who summoned the police and ambulance.

Mageau survived his gunshot wounds, but Darleen Ferrin died in the ambulance while en route to the hospital.

Mageau was unable to provide any accurate description of the shooter, informing the police, "He was a white male. It was dark, and I only saw his profile. I never saw his face from the front."

On July 5, shortly after the shooting, the suspect, calling from a payphone just a few blocks from the Vallejo Police Station, called the police department and stated:

> I want to report a double murder. If you will go one mile east on Columbus Parkway to the public park, you will find the kids in a brown car. They were shot with a nine-millimeter Luger. I also killed those kids last year. Good-bye.

On July 31, 1969, the killer mailed a two-page handwritten letter to the *San Francisco Chronicle* identifying himself as the shooter in both the Jensen/Faraday and Mageau/Ferrin shootings.

On August 2, the suspect provided more information along with a three-part cryptogram and for the first time would announce himself to the public in what would become his familiar introduction, "This is the Zodiac Speaking…"

Along with providing his new "Zodiac" pseudonym, he would henceforth sign his letters with the familiar cross-and-circle zodiac symbol.

Zodiac's signature

Letter mailed to San Francisco Chronicle July 31, 1969

Zodiac's three-part cryptogram published August 3, 1969

23-24. CECELIA SHEPARD AND BRYAN HARTNELL —ZK
"By Rope, By Knife, By Gun" ZK

SEPTEMBER 27 , 1969 Napa (Napa Sheriff's Department)

Victims Cecelia Shepard, age twenty-two, and her boyfriend, Bryan Hartnell, age twenty, had driven to Lake Berryessa in Bryan's Karmann Ghia to view the sunset.

The young couple was seated on a blanket at shore side when they were approached by a man wearing an "executioner's type hood and tunic." Sewn or drawn on the tunic was a three-inch cross-and-circle, identical to the one the Ferrin/Mageau shooter had been using as his signature in his August 3, 1969 "This is the Zodiac Speaking..." mailings to the press.

The suspect, armed with a large blue-steel automatic handgun, stated to victim Hartnell, "I want your car keys and money. My car is hot... I'm going to Mexico."

Removing some precut lengths of clothesline from his pocket, the assailant told Cecelia to tie up her boyfriend. She followed his instructions. He then ordered Hartnell to get on the ground and further hogtied his hands and feet.

Without warning, the masked man began stabbing both victims with a long bayonet-type knife. Cecelia was stabbed multiple times in both the front and back of her body and Bryan was then stabbed numerous times in the back.

The suspect fled on foot, leaving both victims for dead.

A passing boat motorist heard Bryan's call for help and summoned the police.

Both victims were rushed to the hospital, and while Bryan Hartnell would survive, Cecelia would succumb to her multiple stab wounds two days later.

Hartnell was unable to provide an accurate description of the suspect as he claimed he "only saw him in profile through the eyehole in the mask."

A month later, on October 24, 1969, Hartnell was contacted by a San Francisco Police Department sketch artist and provided the below composite of how "Zodiac" appeared during the Lake Berryessa attack on himself and Cecelia Shepard.

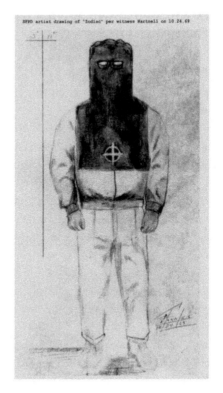

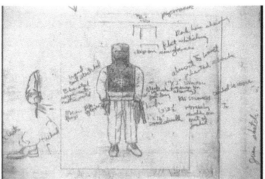

"Zodiac" police composite provided by victim/witness Bryan Hartnell

Following descriptors of the suspect provided by Hartnell were included and noted on drawing by artist:

"5' 11, Dark hair, clip on sunglasses, black gloves, Blue steel semi-automatic, foot long knife, 1"x 12" wood sheath, ½ boots pants tucked in boot, pleated slacks, 3"x 3" symbol."

The killer before leaving the crime scene took the time to write the following unique taunt on the passenger door of Bryan's Karmann Ghia, which was parked at the roadside.

His message was clear. Beginning with his Zodiac signature symbol, he was taking credit for the Jensen/Faraday attack of 12/20/68, the Ferrin/Mageau attack of 7/4/69, and now, today, "By knife" he committed the Shepard/Hartnell attack of 9/27/69.

Vallejo

12-20-68

7-4-69

Sept 27-69-6:30

By knife

Written with black felt pen on right front door panel of Hartnell's Karmann Ghia

Furthermore, to underscore his authenticity, Zodiac drove to downtown Napa to a phone booth outside of a car wash, just four blocks from the police station just as he had done in the Ferrin/Mageau crime. He then called the police dispatcher and stated:

Caller: I want to report a murder—no a double murder.
They are two miles north of Park Headquarters.
They were in a white Volkswagen Karmann Ghia.

Police: Where are you?

Caller: I'm the one who did it. (Hangs up phone)

"By Rope"

Red Lipstick Killer

Black Dahlia Avenger

Manila Jigsaw Killer

Zodiac

(Photo lower Right) Napa Sheriff's evidence photograph showing precut clothesline used by "Zodiac" to bind victims Hartnell and Shepard at Lake Berryessa. Bringing precut clothesline to a crime is a highly unusual "MO"; however, we know George Hodel did so in: 1. Chicago Lipstick Murder, 2. the Manila Jigsaw Murder and 3. the Black Dahlia Avenger/LA Lone Woman Murders.

25. PAUL STINE—ZK "By Gun"

OCTOBER 11, 1969, San Francisco, California (San Francisco Police Department)

Victim Paul Stine was a twenty-nine-year-old graduate student at San Francisco State College who was driving part-time for Yellow Cab Company.

On the evening of October 11, 1969, the victim, driving his Yellow Cab taxi, was hailed by a male passenger near Powell and Geary Streets in downtown San Francisco.

The suspect instructed him to drive to "Washington and Maple" in Presidio Heights.

As the cab approached its destination, Stine was told to drive one more block to the intersection of Washington and Cherry.

Without warning, the suspect then placed a 9mm handgun to the victim's right temple and fired one round, execution-style.

Teenagers heard the shot from their upstairs bedroom across the street and looked out their window in time to observe the suspect standing at the open right front passenger door of the yellow cab.

The shooter appeared to be rifling his clothes and robbing the cab driver, whose body was slumped over in the front seat. (It was later determined that the suspect was ripping or cutting a section of the victim's bloodied shirt which he took with him.)

The teens immediately telephoned the police and continued to watch as the man removed a white rag or handkerchief from his pocket and began wiping down the exterior doors on both the passenger and the driver's side of the cab.

Paul Stine cab at Zodiac crime scene, Washington and Cherry Streets on October 11, 1969

(Left) Stine's bloody shirt and men's leather gloves size seven booked as evidence by SFPD. (Right) George and June Hodel circa 1995, Orcas Island, Washington. GHH with his wife, June, seen putting on his leather gloves, believed to be "size seven" which was a regular part of his accoutrement.

The teens watched as the shooter walked northbound on Cherry Street, out of sight.

The following suspect description was immediately provided to the SFPD uniformed officers from these four witnesses:

> "Male, White, early forties, 5-8, crewcut hair, dark
> glasses, wearing dark brown trousers, dark shoes and a
> dark blue or black parka jacket."

During the assault, the suspect left a pair of men's gloves, size seven, inside the Stine taxi, which were blood splattered and booked into evidence.

A responding patrol unit observed a male Caucasian walking down the street just a few blocks away whom they questioned and released.

Two days after the shooting, "Zodiac" sent another taunting letter to the press and police taking credit for the Stine murder and included a piece of the victim's torn bloody shirt as proof.

SFPD Criminalist comparing section of shirt mailed to press by Zodiac to Stine evidence shirt.

Almost one month later, on November 9, 1969, "Zodiac" sent a second lengthy six-page letter to his favorite newspaper of choice, *The San Francisco Chronicle*. (George Hodel was employed as a reporter/columnist for that newspaper in the 1930s.)

In addition to a detailed description of his various crimes in a highlighted "P.S. Must Print in paper," Zodiac "called out" the uniformed officers who responded to the Stine shooting. Zodiac informed the public that the two officers stopped and talked to him, and he sent them off on a ruse telling them he "saw a man running down the street with a gun in his hand" at which point they took off in fresh pursuit, allowing him to escape into the night.

Here is the "P.S." portion of the letter mailed to the *San Francisco Chronicle* which, at Zodiac's insistence, the newspaper published three days later, on November 12, 1969.

It read:

> Ps. 2 cops pulled a goof abot 3 min after I left the cab.

> I was walking down the hill to the park when this cop car pulled up & one of them called me over & asked if I saw any one acting supicisous [sic] Or strange in the last 5 to 10 min & I said yes there was this man who was Running by waveing [sic] a gun & the cops peeled rubber & went around the corner as I directed them & I disappeared into the park a block & a half away never to be seen again. Hey pig doesn't it rile you up to have your noze rubed [sic] in your booboos?

Zodiac November 9, 1969, letter (page 3) "Must print in paper."
Printed in the newspaper on November 12, 1969

SFPD uniformed officer Donald Fouke Memo November 12, 1969

The publication of Zodiac's ridiculing SFPD patrol officers for "Question and Releasing" him and mocking them for their "booboos" forced the involved Officer Fouke to write a responding internal Department Memo explaining the hitherto unmentioned event.

In that memo, Officer Fouke denied stopping Zodiac, but provided a highly detailed description of the suspect from what he termed a "five-second drive-by." (Fouke's partner, Officer Eric Zelms tragically, was killed in the line of duty a month later, but had informed his wife that "Fouke and he had in fact stopped and talked to Zodiac." The investigating SFPD detective assigned to the Stine murder also confirmed that Fouke acknowledged stopping and talking to Zodiac, but he [detective] decided it was best to let it go and not embarrass the officer or the department.]

Fouke's description, "Male Caucasian 35 to 45 years ("closer to the high end") 5-10", 180-200, Crew cut hair, pleated baggy pants" was incorporated into the teen's description and the results circulated throughout the San Francisco Bay Area.

Additional witness composites were obtained and all are shown below.

George Hodel 1962   **George Hodel 1974**

SFPD sketch   Joe Barros SFPD sketch   Neal Adams SFPD sketch

(Top Row) Photos of GHH in 1962 and 1974. His appearance at the time of Zodiac murders would have to be merged in the viewer's mind. (Age the 1962 photo by seven years or youthen the 1974 photo by five years.)

(Bottom Row) Shows three separate witness "Zodiac" composites obtained. The "Neal Adams" sketch was drawn by Adams based on combining the two previous witness sketches. The result was used for the cover drawing for a chapter, "This is the Zodiac Speaking" written by journalist Duffy Jennings and included in a true-crime book, Great Crimes of San Francisco, *published in 1973.*

Neal Adams "Zodiac" composite was an almost picture-perfect likeness to Dr. George Hill Hodel

October 19, 1969, newspaper article (The Tennessean) describing all of the Bay Area Zodiac crimes featuring the victims. (Surviving gunshot wound victim Michael Mageau included, but no photo was shown.) The seventh known Zodiac victim, Cheri Jo Bates (Riverside, California) would not be linked to Zodiac for another year. (November 1970.)

This concludes the limited overview on all twenty-five victims that I consider "Definites" as being murdered by my father, Dr. George Hill Hodel, spanning the years 1943-1969.

These two summary chapters in no way attempt to present all of the evidence in each case. That requires a reading of the complete pentalogy. The suggested order would be *Black Dahlia Avenger* (Skyhorse/Arcade 2015), *Most Evil* (Dutton 2009), *BDA II* (2014 ed.), *Most Evil II* (Rare Bird Books 2015) and finally this updated *Black Dahlia Avenger III* (Rare Bird Books 2018).

> George Hodel was a prolific serial killer whose signature is visible not in any single method of murder, type of victim, or specific killing ground, but rather as a series of complex arrangements, installations, and obscure references to art, culture, and film that, taken together, reveal a chilling and never-before-documented variety of serial murder: murder as a fine art.
>
> Steve Hodel, *Most Evil*, 2009

I will close with this excerpted section from *Most Evil II* (Rare Bird books 2015), Chapter 1:

Black Dahlia Avenger and Zodiac MO/ Crime Signature Comparisons

THE FOLLOWING CRIME SIGNATURES were used by both the Black Dahlia Avenger and Zodiac:

- *Serial Killer.*
- *Created his own marketing/public relations campaign along with inventing and providing newspapers with a pseudonym for them to use in headlining his crimes and his "reign of terror." (Black Dahlia Avenger and Zodiac)*
- *Contacted and taunted press by telephone after crimes.*
- *Contacted and taunted police by telephone after crimes.*
- *Used press as his instrument to terrorize public, promising, "There will be more."*
- *Drew crude picture of a knife dripping blood and mailed the drawing to press.*
- *Brought precut lengths of clothesline and used them to bind and tie victims during crimes.*
- *Mailed more than a dozen notes to press and police feigning illiteracy, using misspelled words and disguised handwriting.*
- *Mailed cut-and-paste notes to press and police.*
- *Mailed typewritten letter describing his actions to police.*
- *Placed excessive postage and multiple stamps on the taunting notes he mailed to press and police.*
- *Addressed press mailings, "To the Editor."*
- *Mailings sent on particular "anniversary dates" related to crimes.*
- *Packaged and mailed personal items belonging to his murdered victims to the press to prove he was the killer.*
- *Told victims and press he was "Going to Mexico."*
- *Used both a knife and gun(s) in his separate crimes.*
- *Included puns and word games in his mailings.*
- *Continued to send in mailings to press and police months and years after original crimes.*

- *Egomaniacal personality demanded constant media publicity and front-page coverage under threat of additional killings.*
- *Identified himself as an "Avenger," claiming he was wronged by the female victim or that he was getting revenge for being spurned and ignored by the victim.*
- *Informed the public that the crime was "justified" or was "divine retribution."*
- *Stabbed several victims with a long-bladed jungle or bayonet-style knife.*
- *Wrote taunting messages at the scene either on the bedroom wall, a nearby telephone post, a door panel of victim's vehicle, or the victim's body.*
- *Manually ripped away band from a men's wristwatch and left both band and watch at separate crime scenes, on or near the victim's body.*
- *Left men's white handkerchief either at the scene near the body, or used it to wipe away fingerprints from inside the victim's vehicle or from the knife left at the crime scene.*
- *Geographically preselected crime scene locations by plotting coordinates on a map, then randomly murdered victim(s) who by happenstance entered his "killing zone," or*
- *Geographically preselected crime scene locations by plotting coordinates on a map, then had unwitting victim (taxi driver) drive him to that specific location, where victim was then shot and killed, or,*
- *Forcibly kidnapped female victim, strangled her to death, and dismembered the body with surgical skill and precision. Then posed the body parts in public view at a specific location (street name) that provided a taunting clue related to the crime or suspect.*
- *Brutal assault and overkill particularly savage with his female victims.*
- *Telephoned and/or sent sadistic note to victim's parents after brutal murder of their daughter.*

One new discovery (our thirty-first listed here) specific to both Avenger and Zodiac MOs, unrecognized by me until only recently, is that both used the same unique signature in one of their mailed taunts to the press: "a friend." (Note that both Avenger and Zodiac signed it using a small letter "a.")

Mailed to the Newspaper Editor by Black Dahlia Avenger
Black Dahlia Avenger 1947

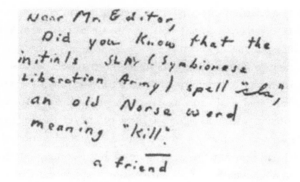

Mailed to the Newspaper Editor by Zodiac
Zodiac February 14, 1974

Procedurally, homicide detectives examining unsolved murders would become *curious* should they discover two or three matching crime signatures. Five or six would put them "on the hunt."

In these twenty-five crimes spanning thirty years, Dr. George Hill Hodel has signed his work with *thirty-one signatures, so unique that they along with the physical evidence, eyewitness descriptions, forensic analyses, and his own taped admissions and confessions leave us with no reasonable doubt.*

Black Dahlia Avenger II was originally published in 2012 then revised in 2014 and now *BDA III*, 2018.

In a sequel to the *BDA II* (2014), I published *Most Evil II* (Rare Bird Books 2015) in which I was able to further confirm George Hodel's guilt by cracking his "Zodiac Code" and literally obtained his signed confession to his crimes.

A NEW CLUE FOR CHRISTMAS 2017

It keeps happening.

I tell my publisher, "That's it, I'm done. Ready to go."

His team puts the interior design together and bingo, like clockwork, I am forced to say, "Wait a minute. Hold the presses. I've got just one more new clue, to add. It's too important not to include."

And that is precisely what happened on December 12, 2017.

This time the new clue came by way of a letter from a reader in Montgomery, Illinois.

His name is Ronald Rees.

Ron, though in the printing business, grew up in a law enforcement family.

Ron's grandfather, George H. Rees, was the Chief of Police in Aurora, Illinois in 1948, and his father Robert K. Rees was a sergeant on that same department for twenty-four years, retiring in 1971. Both were career public servants.

Ron and I had communicated several times through the years, and I knew that he had read and was familiar with most of the investigative links presented in my books as well as those posted on my blog site.

His letter was primarily a "thank you" for a signed edition of one of my books I had sent him. Also, to share with me some photographs of his father and grandfather's police badges and equipment that had been encased in an exhibit at the Aurora Police Department to honor their many years of combined service.

At the end of his handwritten letter he thanked me for my writings and investigations as follows:

> ...
>
> Once Again, Forever Affected and Inspired.
> Ronald Rees
> P.S. I've never seen mention quite like this:

P.S. I'VE NEVER SEEN MENTION QUITE LIKE THIS:

TURN 90° TO THE RIGHT FOR A "G,"
& BACK UPRIGHT FOR THE 2 "H's"
SIDE BY SIDE.

Scan of Ron Rees Zodiac 1970 Halloween Card sketch, "By Fire, By Gun, By Knife, By Rope." Ron's notation reads: "Turn 90 degrees to the right for a "G" & back upright for the 2 "H's" side by side."

In *Black Dahlia Avenger II* (2014) page 340 I had referenced the following:

…

Law enforcement, noting the strange way Zodiac wrote the message, theorized that the "clue" he was sending might be the fact the letters, as written, formed the letter "H" which they suggested could be a monogram clue to the killer's name.

Back and front of Zodiac's 1970 Halloween card sent to San Francisco Chronicle *Back: Letter H?*

I and some of the original detectives assigned to Zodiac through the years believed we were possibly seeing Zodiac providing a clue, on the "You Ache to Know My Name" card as the letter "H."

But Ron, with the eyes of a printer, accustomed to viewing the shape of letters and fonts, took a new look and what he observed is to my mind—astonishing.

He saw not one, but three letters—**G H H.**

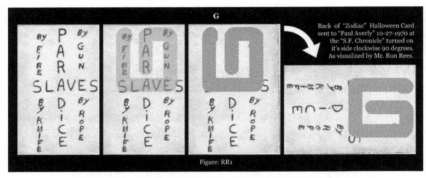

Graphic prepared by Robert "Dr. Watson" Sadler

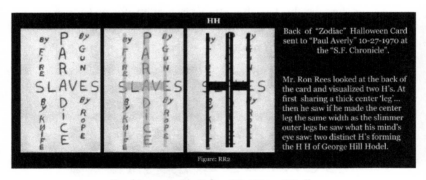

Graphic prepared by Robert "Dr. Watson" Sadler

My father Dr. George Hill Hodel always used all three of his initials in his signing of documents.

He either signed his name G. Hill Hodel MD or George Hill Hodel MD or Dr. George Hill Hodel.

Below graphic shows Zodiac's cryptogram GHH letters as well as a sampling of George Hill Hodel's signatures over the years demonstrating his repeated use of GHH.

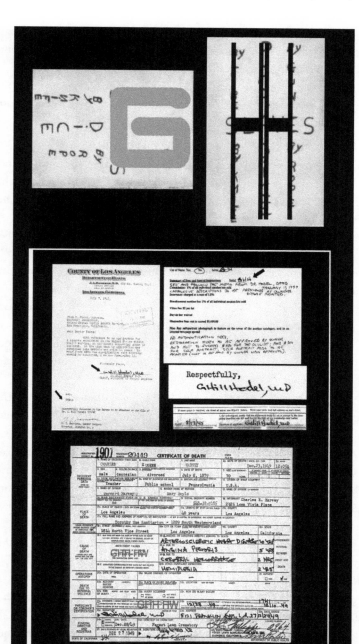

Thank you, Ron, for your keen observations, as one of the many "armchair detectives" that continue to contribute compelling circumstantial evidence to our ongoing investigation.

Obviously, there are equal parts of printer and detective pumping through your bloodstream. Your father and grandfather would **be proud**.

New Ogham Reflections

ON JULY 12, 2017, I received the below letter, emailed to me from Paris, France.

It was from my good friend, Mssr. Yves Person, the high school teacher who had cracked the original Zodiac cipher code, which the killer had mailed to the *San Francisco Chronicle* on Halloween, 1970.

Yves, after studying and "cracking the code," discovered that Zodiac, in sending the card which read, "…you ache to know my name, And so I'll clue you in…" had in fact done just that. Zodiac created a mysterious clue-symbol and placed it at the bottom of the card as his signature.

In this "clue" he had concealed five letters from the ancient and obscure fourth-century Celtic alphabet known as Ogham.

The five letters when deciphered from Ogham to English spelled out: H O D E L. (See *Most Evil II* (Rare Bird Books 2015) Chapter 10 for full details and analysis.)

Yves deciphering of the Ogham letters naturally led me to another question: How or where did my father come into contact with the Ogham alphabet?

Fortunately, I was able to link the probable connections once again to surrealism and to another modern artist, Brian O'Doherty, aka Patrick Ireland, who had displayed the Ogham letters in his artwork. (O'Doherty had previously met and published articles on both Man Ray and Marcel Duchamp.)

The show closed on October 10, 1970 (ironically, George Hodel's birthday) and just *a few days before George Hodel's mailing of the Ogham cipher to the* San Francisco Chronicle.

The Ogham/O'Doherty exhibit was on display for a full month at the Betty Parson's art gallery, located just a few city blocks from George Hodel's then INRA-New York (*International Research Associates*) business office, at 1270 Avenue of the Americas, New York.

In the following letter, Yves Person provides us with additional information which could very well corroborate and provide additional linkage and potentials of how George Hodel may have come to know and adapted the ancient Ogham alphabet as his "name clue."

I here present his letter in full, as received. One would never know from his articulate and exceptionally well-ordered writing that English is Yves' second language.

Merci Yves!

12, July 2017

Steve,

Some three months ago, I read a very interesting comment on your blog. The author was Mr. Jullian Scannell, and he pointed out a major difficulty dealing with our interpretation of the Hallowe'en cryptogram as an Ogham encoding. In order to make it short, I will rephrase Mr. Jullian Scannell's objection: How could GHH possibly find a precise reference to the encoding system of Ogham? Where could he read a complete description of that system of writing? In which public library around SF Bay area could he find a book, or a document, dealing with that very peculiar topic?

You remember that such questions were discussed by both of us with a deep perplexity at the beginning of our correspondence; they remained unsolved until you made us aware of Patrick Ireland's paintings. However, in those paintings, Ogham "letters" are drawn on the canvas as mere design patterns: none of a cryptogram. So, for some part, Mr. Scannell's question remains valid: back to 1969, which were the books someone could read in order to learn a bit about Ogham?

Moreover, a great difficulty lies in the strange pattern the author of the cryptogram gave to his Ogham signature.

I must make this point clear: a message in Ogham consists of a stem on which some series of strokes or dots are drawn from bottom to top. We can see plainly the whole and basic system in the picture you sent me at the beginning of our correspondence:

As we can see on your picture, some strokes are drawn at the left side of the stem ("H," "D") and a third kind of strokes at the right side of it ("L"). The strokes standing for the vowels ("O," "E") stretch away on both sides of the stem. In some manuscripts written in Ogham, the vowels are figured by series of dots, as it appears in the following picture:

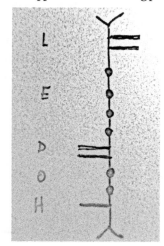

All that remains classic Ogham... Now, Zodiac's signature provides us with a new kind of system, based on two major variations of the average scripture :

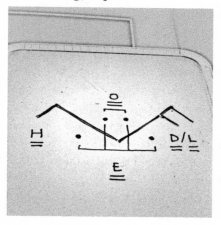

Variation n^r 1: the general scheme or shape is no longer a stem but *a broken line*, which looks like a "V."

Variation n^r 2: the dots (the vowels) are drawn *beside* the line (instead of: *"on the line"*).

Well, we are confronted with two problems:

A) Where, in what book, GHH could have learned so much about Ogham?

B) How could he make himself able to create a new kind of Ogham letterings?

There is a single solution for both of those problems.

First of all: what kind of books on Ogham were available (and/or popular) back to the fall of the 60s?

The answer is not uneasy to make: *The White Goddess* by Robert Graves, *The Codebreakers* by David Kahn. However, none of those two books give a plain and accurate *exposé* of an Ogham encoding.

Shortly before the puzzling question was asked by Mr. Scannell, I happened to read a wonderful book: *The*

Secret Languages of Ireland by R. A. Stewart Macalister (Cambridge, 1937). I call it "a wonderful book" because the scholar seems to feel a huge enthusiasm for the topic he is studying: he cares for it.

So, what is this topic? The title of the book is perfectly clear: the ways of encoding a message such as they were invented, created, during the Middle-Ages in Ireland. The first chapter ("Ogham") and the second chapter ("Cryptology") consist of a description of Ogham system and a commentary on a treatise dealing with Ogham encoding. This treatise, known as *The Book of Ballymote*, is a XIIth century manuscript in which an ancient master of Ogham cryptography delivers his teaching about some 93 ways of encoding a message. Mr. Alistair's comments are substantial, albeit, in his text, he gives very few illustrations taken from the manuscript itself. Fortunately, in 1887, *The Book of Ballymote* was published, as a facsimile, by a great Irish scholar, Robert Atkinson (1839–1908). Incidentally, a new publication was made in 1975, six years after the Hallowe'en card had been sent to Paul Avery, by Mr. Barry Feld (in The Epigraphic Society Occasional Papers).

Now: what can we see in that old manuscript?

A complete set of variations on Ogham lettering.

Let's see, for instance, n^r 90 :

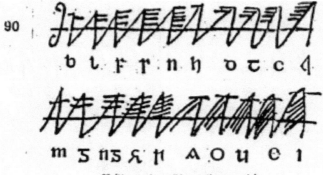

90 (Unnamed, possibly mantic or magic)

Let's describe this code: "Strokes drawn on a broken line which looks like a V." Now, look at the second letter ("L"), then at the sixth letter ("H") and think of the Hallowe'en card cryptogram: did Zodiac make a great expense of imagination, or was he a mere copyist?

Now, let's look carefully at the following codes (n[r] 40 and n[r] 49) :

40. Brec mor. - Great dotting.

49. Brecor beo.- Lively dotting.

As we can notice it in Zodiac's Ogham signature, the dots are freely drawn between the strokes or on each side of the stem.

We understand now why our twofold enigma is solved by a unique solution: the author of the Hallowe'en card cryptogram was aware of *The Book of Ballymote*. He could have read Alistair's beautiful book (1937) or could have seen the *fac-simile* edited by Atkinson in 1887. Those two potential sources were enough to provide him with the rules of Ogham cryptography.

Now, how did GHH come to ancient Ireland? He could have walked various paths: for instance, in my edition of Graves' *The White Goddess* (Faber & Faber, 1997) the bibliography mention twelve references to Macalistair. We may imagine two counterfactual hypothesis :

1. GHH at Patrick Ireland's exhibition // which makes him aware of Ogham // makes researches upon the topic // finds *The Book of Ballymote* // writes the cryptogram.

2. GHH at Patrick Ireland's exhibition // which reminds him of what he has learned about Ogham // he's got his knowledge after reading Macalister's or Atkinson's works years back // writes the cryptogram.

Now, a new Sphinx raises with a new riddle: as to GHH, which were his connections with Ireland? Were his wife and father-in-law (both of them of Irish descent) part of this game?

Please forgive a too long a letter. I hope I made the Ogham problem clearer...

Best,

Yves.

Author Note:

IT IS MY PERSONAL belief that George Hodel most likely saw the below Ogham Transcription, created by the artist O'Doherty in 1969, as one of the pieces on exhibit at the Betty Parson's Gallery 1970 showing.

He may have photographed it, purchased a print of it, or possibly it was reproduced in the artist's brochure and made available at the gallery.

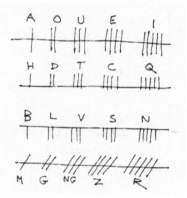

The Ogham Alphabet transcribed by Brian O'Doherty (1969)

That said, let's assume that I am mistaken, and George Hodel's attendance at the showing was not "the source" of his discovering the Ogham alphabet.

Rather, let's say Yves' speculation is correct and George had seen the Ogham alphabet previous in one of the several print sources Yves referenced. Where would my father have seen such a book?

Recall in *BDA II*, Chapter 16, "Grandfather Harvey" where we learn that my paternal grandfather, Charles Harvey, taught printing classes at Hollywood High School.

Grandfather loved printing, but he also loved BOOKS. He was an intellectual and a bibliophile with his own private library. I again quote from the Hollywood High 1939 yearbook.

"Mr. Harvey, printing instructor collects rare books and fine printing.

In his collection, he has a page from an original Gutenberg Bible."

Based on the fact that grandfather was a proud Irish intellectual, it would not be any stretch of the imagination, were we to examine his rare book collection, that we would find (perhaps right next to his page from the Gutenberg Bible) an original copy of *The Book of Ballymote*.

Or if not that then certainly a new edition of the just-published, *The Secret Languages of Ireland* by R. A. Stewart Macalister (Cambridge, 1937).

Grandfather lived and taught in Hollywood as did his daughter and son-in-law who had just returned from the Hopi and Navaho Reservations and opened up his own medical practice in Los Angeles in the summer of 1938.

Charles Harvey's first grandson, my older brother Michael Paul Hodel, would be born in July 1939, and I am quite certain that both my parents, being voracious readers themselves, would have had carte blanche access to his extensive private library.

Author's Note, 2018

It is early May 2018 and once again, as I prepare to "go to press," some dramatic and highly relevant new developments are headlining national newspapers.

A6 THURSDAY, APRIL 26, 2018   **NATION**   www.enterprise-journal.com   ENTERPRISE-JOURNAL, McCOMB, MISSISSIPPI

Former cop unmasked as Golden State Killer

SACRAMENTO, Calif. (AP) — Joseph DeAngelo's six-year career as a cop came swiftly to an end after being busted for shoplifting a can of dog repellant and a hammer from a Pay N' Save store in a Sacramento suburb in 1979.

Authorities are now wondering if the items he snatched were intended as tools for the sinister rash of crimes he's suspected of carrying out.

DeAngelo, 72, was accused Wednesday of being the Golden State Killer who terrorized suburban neighborhoods in a spate of brutal rapes and slayings in the 1970s and '80s before leaving a cold trail that baffled investigators for decades.

He was charged with eight counts of murder in three counties after being linked to the crimes through his DNA. Authorities said he was responsible for a dozen slayings and some 50 rapes and that

JOSEPH JAMES

ASSOCIATED PRESS

Sacramento County Sheriff Scott Jones, left, talks to reporters about the arrest of **Joesph James DeAngelo, seen in photo,** on suspicion of committing a string of violent crimes in the 1970s and '80s.

Jackson withdraws from consideration for VA chief

WASHINGTON (AP) — President Donald Trump's pick to lead Veterans Affairs, Ronny Jackson, withdrew today in the wake of late-surfacing allegations about overprescribing drugs and poor leadership while serving as a top White House doctor, saying the "false allegations" against him have become a distraction.

In a statement the White House issued from Jackson, he said he "did not expect to have to dignify baseless and anonymous attacks on my character and integrity."

Shortly after Jackson dropped out, President Donald Trump called into the Fox & Friends morning show to praise Jackson as an "incredible man" who "runs a fantastic operation."

Trump said Jackson had

Jackson also faced a series of accusations about his workplace conduct. The latest blow to his nomination to lead the government's second-largest Cabinet agency came Wednesday with a set of accusations compiled by Sen. Jon Tester's Democratic staff on the committee considering his nomination.

In a statement, Tester called on Congress to continue its investigation of Jackson.

The committee's Republican chairman, Sen. Johnny Isakson, said he respected Jackson's decision and "will work with the administration to see to it we get a VA secretary for our veterans and their families."

In just a matter of days, the allegations transformed Jackson's reputation as a celebrated doctor attending the president to an embattled nominee accused of

Enterprise-Journal headline announcing the Sacramento, California, arrest of ex-cop Joseph DeAngelo Jr. for eight serial murders that occurred in the 1970s and 80s.

After more than four decades of eluding police, DeAngelo was identified and arrested after police were able to trace DNA to some of his relatives, which then led to the former cop.

The DNA links were not done using the FBI's CODIS (Combined DNA Index System) database.

Rather, LE utilized civilian DNA databank open to the public known as GEDmatch.

Here is an excerpt from a 4/27/18 article from the online magazine, *arsTECHNICA* describing the DNA "hit" and arrest of ex-cop, Joseph James DeAngelo:

...

According to the *East Bay Times*, which first reported the connection to GEDmatch late Thursday evening, California investigators caught a huge break in the case when they matched DNA from some of the original crime scenes with genetic data that had already been uploaded to GEDmatch. This familial link eventually led authorities to Joseph James DeAngelo, the man authorities have named the chief suspect in the case. To confirm the genetic match, Citrus Heights police physically surveilled him and captured DNA off of something that he had discarded.

The former police officer was arrested Tuesday at his home in suburban Sacramento, having eluded law enforcement for decades. DeAngelo is expected to be arraigned Friday in Sacramento County Superior Court.

The Yolo County District Attorney said Thursday that DeAngelo "is suspected of committing over 50 rapes and a dozen murders across 10 different Northern, Central, and Southern California counties between 1976 and 1986.

Can Familial Genetic DNA Lead to the Identification of Zodiac?

THE BELOW ARTICLE IN the *Huffington Post* indicates that Bay Area detectives are going to attempt to springboard off the success of the capture of DeAngelo and at least one San Francisco Bay Area Department (Vallejo PD) is attempting to retest and obtain confirmed Zodiac DNA, with the hopes of then searching civilian genetic databases.

Here is an excerpt from a May 7, 2018 article in the *Huffington Post*, "Police Hope To Use DNA To Catch The Zodiac Killer" by David Lohr.

"We could finally have answers to one of the greatest whodunits of all time," a criminologist said.

...

Now, with advancements in DNA testing and a multitude of databases available, police might have a chance of determining the identity of Zodiac. While it's unlikely he's still alive, a positive identification would allow authorities to close the book on an infamous serial killer who once terrorized citizens of California.

"And regardless of the outcome, in this case, these new avenues of investigation have great potential," Bonn said. "Think of how useful these ancestry DNA databases could be in solving other unsolved cases."

For the past nine years, I have been calling for LE to attempt to obtain "confirmed DNA" and have written extensively in *Most Evil, BDA II,* and *Most Evil II* on their need to "pool their evidence."

My fear is that the separate agencies desire to independently "crack the case" may prevent them from joining forces to enhance the chances of obtaining Zodiac DNA.

By example, I would bet you money that the legitimate Zodiac envelope mailed to KHJ TV Studios and booked in evidence by the Los Angeles Police Department on 5/4/78 is long forgotten and has never been tested. (Note to LAPD Cold Case detectives—want to solve the Zodiac serial crimes? TEST IT.)

This letter contains a stamp and the inside of the envelope flap that could well contain Zodiac's DNA and could be the very evidence, currently in police custody, that when analyzed could yield the suspect's DNA.

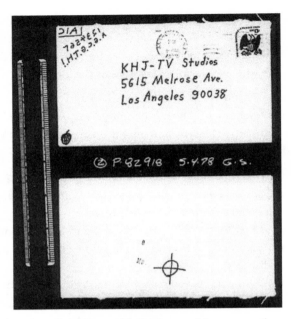

*Photo of 1978 Untested Zodiac Letter and Stamp currently
booked in Evidence at LAPD Property*

Ms. Pam Hofsass and Stine Gloves Stranger DNA

Pam Hofsass, Director of Forensic Services Division, Contra Costa County

FINALLY, THERE IS THE Stine gloves, which I have always asserted were likely
the "best evidence" potential for obtaining Zodiac DNA.

In 2009 after I met with two California DOJ agents and provided the details, their follow-up to me was, "Apparently the gloves are lost but we will keep searching for them and would get back to me."

Crickets for nine years.

Consequently, I assumed the Stine gloves were lost.

However, with the airing in 2017 of the History Channel's *The Hunt for the Zodiac Killer* a surprise witness provided some startling and hitherto unknown information.

Ms. Pam Hofsass, currently Contra Costa County's director of Forensic Services Division, was interviewed on the show and revealed that she "had formerly worked for San Francisco Police Department and had been assigned to the Zodiac case from 1989–2015."

Ms. Hofsass, speaking for the first time publicly about the Zodiac case, informed the listening audience that "in 2002 saliva from a stamp was found on one of the Zodiac letters, but it showed weak and incomplete DNA."

Ms. Hofsass went on to say that **"in a subsequent attempt by me to obtain additional DNA, I tested the size seven gloves found in the rear seat of the Stine cab."**

The results of her testing: **"Paul Stine's blood was found on the <u>outside</u> of the gloves, and there is an unknown male profile on the <u>inside</u>."**

This is truly encouraging information and dramatically advances the possibility that the size seven gloves were owned and worn by Zodiac and when he executed Paul Stine, likely from the rear seat of the cab, he was wearing the gloves (Stine's blood on the outside) and left them in the cab upon fleeing.

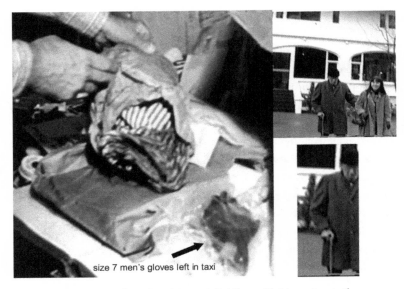

size 7 men's gloves left in taxi

(Lt) Size seven gloves from Stine taxi (Rt) George Hodel wearing similar
probable size seven gloves circa 1996

Note to SFPD: Compare Stine "Stranger DNA" to other agencies' analysis and to civilian DNA databanks such as GEDmatch and Ancestry.com.

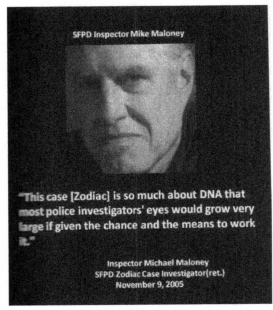

SFPD Inspector Mike Maloney

"This case [Zodiac] is so much about DNA that most police investigators' eyes would grow very large if given the chance and the means to work it."

Inspector Michael Maloney
SFPD Zodiac Case Investigator(ret.)
November 9, 2005

Afterword
OUT OF THE PAST—
1949 "In Case of Death Letter" Identifies
Black Dahlia Killer

IN THE PREVIOUS CHAPTERS, I mentioned several "Stop the Press" moments, which have delayed my publisher and editor from trying to meet their launch date for this book.

Finally, by mid-July 2018 BDA III the final draft was completed and sent off to the printer. My publisher, Tyson Cornell, my editor, Hailie Johnson, and I were happy.

One week later, on July 21, 2018, I received the following email from a woman in Indianapolis, Indiana. It read:

> Dear Steve:
>
> I am closing my parent's Estate and yesterday, I came across a hand-written statement (buried in a box for the past 69+ years), drafted in October 1949 by my Grandfather who was a resident of Los Angeles and affiliated with the Los Angeles Police Department. The statement concerns the Elizabeth Short murder and possibly offers some insightful discernment as to the case investigation during the time up to and surrounding the date of the statement.
>
> So now that I've found this statement...what do I do with it? I started researching Black Dahlia files on the web and ran across an article and a YouTube video of yourself and your connection to this case. While most of America has heard of and/or watched documentaries of this case, not all of us find a hand-written statement composed by their Grandfather, regarding it.

I would like for you to read this letter. It may (or may not) be of interest to you.

Sincerely,

Sandi Nichols

Here was my immediate response to Sandi:

Hi Sandi:

Thanks for the email information.

I would be happy to take a look at your grandfather's letter.

Can you scan and email it to me? Or, if you don't have a scanner, maybe make a copy and snail mail it to me at the below address:

Steve Hodel
12400 Ventura Blvd Box 378
Studio City, California 91604

You say your grandfather was "affiliated with LAPD." What was his affiliation?

Best Regards,

Steve Hodel
Los Angeles, California

Five days later on July 27, 2018, I received the scanned copies of the letter which had been handwritten by her grandfather on October 25, 1949.

He had sealed it in an envelope with instructions that it should be opened in case of the death of either one of his two daughters. (Margaret Ellen or Glenna Jeans) The envelope read:

"In case of Margaret Ellen's or Glenna Jeans Death."

"WGM"

*William Glenn Martin envelope was written on October 25, 1949,
in Los Angeles, California*

Enclosed in the sealed letter were the following three pages written by
W. Glenn Martin on October 25, 1949.

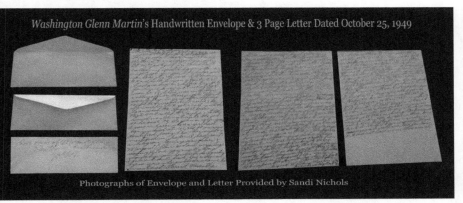

*W. Glenn Martin envelope and three pages written on 10.25.49 (Graphic
prepared by my sometimes long-distance partner and fulltime friend, retired
Dallas PD Officer, R. J. "Dr. Watson" Sadler*

I Believe Choate framed this Oct 25-1949 Black Dahlia Killer.
with McCawley to let G.H. get out of it on the kingon

This is what happened. I. or we
Mother, G.H. & me were eating supper.
St. McCawley of L.G. Police Dept
called me said I have another one
night job for you, like before. will
you take it? I said I'll be down in
AM and talk to you about it. I
had worked on 2 different nights
for him. I knew not what job
was to be till I was with him
& other officers those nights. Then it
was to try to see if other officers
could be inveigled into crime.) So,
after supper G.H. got a call in which
he answered OK. Kay, I'll be down.
Next AM I called McCawley & told
him I would not take the job.
so he said "OK. the job was over anyway.
I saw in paper where a girl had
been murdered at 116 E 3d St. an unidentified body plus other conditions
mentioned in paper. I had sent
a telegram to my daughter, 18,
Margaret Ellen, who is very large
reading "I Love you & will always
stand by you", her birthday greeting
I believe it sent, back here & received
by someone who grabbed a chance to
misinterpret the card. Recently

Martin Letter Page 1

G.H. was grilled by police on
Louise Springer death; he + I both
knew her. The investigating officers
became G.H. friend soon after dropped
He threatened to get even with me.
I had nothing to do with it. He
bragged while drunk in a salloon (the charge) I believe
Joe Choate who Margaret Ellen feard
took her to the Hotel (where the
police especially McCawley tried
to make her admit that I, her
father had committed the
much famous Black Dalia. Of course
she would not do that; as God + she
knows I did not; her face was
beaten so badly, hardly recognizable
I have friends in Coroners office who
in talking next AM. let me see the
body, also do a lot of those known on
jury, there, see. I near came sick at
sight. It now developes G.H. got credit
at "Stark" 949 S Brdway. On it he says
his wife's name is Ellen. The papers
in Coroners office name police officers
present. in case. Of course people from
Okl. were sent word of a Luigll Bowen.
(Hodges) death I believe that a phoney
made by G.H. as he knew all Okla City
neighborhood. they would think it Luelle
but where is Margaret Ellen Martin or
Glenna Jean. G.H. was with Joe when he took
her to hotel.
Signed W. Glenn Martin.
knew he would get out

Martin Letter Page 2

I believe Choate Framed this
with McCawley to make M.E.
mistake or accuse another, so the
real killer would continue free.
Choate always knew and was paid
off as att. first and then blackmail.
Now $$ have stopped + Grand Jury is
pressing. Not Grand Jury bribe, but
Choate to a Police Officer, ether
Jack Donohue or McCawley. Remember
the other murdered girls at time
of Dalia, were all (2 or 3) dumped near
City Hall. They were all friends.
perhaps knew too much. Why
just Mirror call on M.E. murder?
All friends of "Nell Vaughn" alias, 519
S. GRANDVIEW. whod believe is very an-
xious also, with Joe to convict some-one
else on all these including Oakes; and
man found in Mts. San Ber. + others. Same,
as Eva Krone. Guilty person murder in
Crestline + this by newspaper. These
crowd knew I worked for Saw
and did not have me in there crowd.

1

Martin Letter Page 3

To WHOM IT MAY CONCERN:

I, SANDi NiCHOLS, AM THE GRANDDAUGHTER
OF THE LETTER WRITER, W. GLENN MARTIN
AND DO HEREBY CERTIFY THAT THIS LETTER
WAS FOUND IN MY MOTHER'S PERSONAL EFFECTS
AND HAS REMAINED IN THE CUSTODY OF OUR
FAMILY SINCE MY GRANDFATHER WROTE IT
BACK IN 1949. I HAVE PERSONALLY PLACED
MY INITIALS ON EACH PAGE OF THE ORIGINAL
LETTER FOR IDENTIFICATION PURPOSES.

SIGNED: *Sandi Nichols*
DATE : AUGUST 30, 2018
LOCATION: ███████████████
INDIANAPOLIS, INDIANA

INITIALS S/N

*Signed Declaration of Sandi Nichols identifying handwriting and establishing
the provenance of her grandfather W. Glenn Martin's letter as being in the
family possession since 1949*

Typed SKH transcription of Washington Glenn Martin Letter (Verbatim)

Oct 25, 1949

Page 1

I believe Choate framed this with McCawley to let G.H. get out of it or (as?) Black dalia killer.

This is what happened. I or we Mother, G.H. & me were eating supper.

ST. McCawley [Sgt. McCauley?] of LA Police Dept called me & said I have another one night job for you, like before. Will you take it? I said "I'll be down in AM and talk to you about it." (I had worked on 2 different nights for him. I knew not what job was to be till I was with him & other officers those nights. Then it was to try to see if other officers could be inveigled into crime.) So after supper G.H. got a call in which he answered OK Ray, I'll be down. Next A.M. I called McCawley & told him I would not take the job so he said, "OK, the job was over anyway." I saw in paper where a girl had been murdered at 116 E 3rd St. an unidentified body, plus other conditions mentioned in paper. I had sent a telegram to my daughter, 18, Margaret Ellen who is very large reading, "I love you & will always stand by you," her birthday greeting I believe it sent back here & received by someone who grabbed a chance to misinterpret the card. Recently,

Page 2

G.H. was grilled by police on Louise Springer death; he and I both knew her: The investigation officers became G.H. friend so matter dropped. He threatened to get even with me. I had nothing to do with it. He bragged while drunk in a salloon [sic] (the charge). I believe Joe Choate who Margaret Ellen feared took her to the hotel where the police especially McCawley tried to make her admit that I, her father had committed the much famous Black Dalia. [sic] Of course she would not do that, as God & she knows I did not; her [assume Dahlia or possibly Springer?] face was beaten so badly, hardly recognizable. I have friends in Coroners Office who in talking next AM let me see the body, as do a lot of those known on jury [?] there see. I near came sick at sight. It now developes G.H. got credit at "Starr" 949 S. Brdway [Broadway]. On it he says his wife's name is Ellen. The papers in Coroner's Office name police officers present in case. Of course people from Okl. [Oklahoma? Oakland?] were sent word of a Lucille Bowen (Hodges) death I believe that a phoney made by G.H. as he knew all Okla City neighborhood. They would think it Lucille but where is Margaret Ellen Martin & Glenna Jean. G.H. was with Joe when he took her to hotel & knew he would get out of it.

Signed W. Glenn Martin

Page 3

I believe Choate Framed this with McCawley to make M.E. (Margaret Ellen?) mistake (misstate?) or accuse another, so the real killer would continue free. Choate always knew and was paid off as att. (attorney?) first and then blackmail.

Now $$ have stopped & Grand Jury is pressing, not Grand Jury bribe, but Choate to a police officer, either Jack Donahue or McCawley. Remember the other murdered girls at time of Dalia (sic) were all (2 or 3) dumped near City Hall. They were all friends. Perhaps knew too much. Why just Mirror call on M.E. murder?

All friends of "Nell Vaughn" alias, 519 S. GRANDVIEW who I believe is very anxious also, with Joe to convict someone else on all these including Oakes; and man found in Mts. San Ber. (mountains, San Bernardino?) & others. Same as Eva Krone Guilty arson & murder in Crestline this by newspaper. These crowd knew I worked for Law and did not have me in there (sic) crowd.

END Of TRANSCRIPTION

Analysis of the W. Glenn Martin Letter

To BEGIN WITH, IT becomes obvious that the Martin Letter was not intended for public consumption. It was written to be read by law enforcement only if either of his daughters came to foul play.

It was written in fear that "GH" might harm one or both to gain revenge against Martin for his statements to LAPD in connection with the Louise Springer Murder, and possibly the Dahlia?

The letter effectually is a first cousin to what we call a "dying declaration."

Secret statements naming names and stating truths that were meant only to be read "In Case of Death."

Absent that the letter was intended to remain a family secret taken to the grave.

The timing of when the letter was written, October 25, 1949, is also a critical factor to our further understanding.

Here is a short timeline of related and relevant events from June to October 1949:

June 13, 1949—9:05 p.m.

Louise Margaret Springer, age twenty-eight, was kidnapped while sitting inside her brand new 1949 Studebaker convertible in front of her beauty salon at Santa Barbara Avenue and Crenshaw Boulevard, just three blocks south from where the Black Dahlia's body had been posed two years earlier.

(Detailed summary of the Louise Springer investigation to follow)

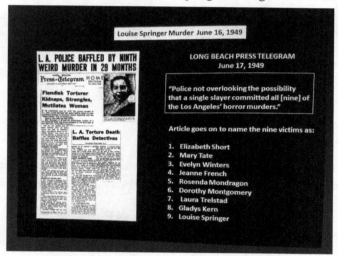

Long Beach Press-Telegram *6/17/49 indicating police suspect that at least nine of the Lone Woman Murders were committed by the same suspect including the Elizabeth Short "Black Dahlia" and Louise Springer crimes.*

August 18, 1949

Socialite Mimi Boomhower kidnapped from her Bel Air residence. Suspect leaves her purse at a phone booth in Beverly Hills with a message to the police. (In 2000, Hanna McFarland a court certified handwriting expert identifies writing on the purse as being written by George Hodel.)

LA POLICE DEPT
1949 UNSOLVED

Wealthy Widow Feared Victim of Knife Slayer

Police Recall
Still Unsolved
Kern Killing

Fear gripped police yesterday that Mrs. Mimi Boomhower, 48, wealthy Bel-Air widow who disappeared last Thursday in the midst of a series of real estate appointments, may have suffered the fate of another woman killed last year with a hunting knife while showing homes to prospects.

An all-points bulletin reporting the stocky Frenchwoman's disappearance and asking for clues to her whereabouts was issued by Wes, Los Angeles police as the sixth day passed without a hard to her possible fate.

At first, Capt. Emmett E. Jones, head of the West Los Angeles detective bureau, lent credence to theories the gay, socially prominent and popular widow may have eloped with one of several of her recent escorts.

Kern Records Studied

But, with no hint of her existence forthcoming despite her prominence, he grimly turned to records of the hunting-knife murder Feb. 23, 1948, of Mrs. Gladys Kern, 43, real estate woman robbed and murdered while showing a house at 4217 Cromwell Ave. to a prospective male buyer.

MYSTERY—Fate of Mrs. Mimi Boomhower, wealthy Bel-Air widow, remained a mystery yesterday as the sixth day passed without a definite lead to her disappearance

Truman Name Used to Aid 5%-ers

THE **MIRROR**

Note Hints Foul Play

PURSE CLOUDS WIDOW'S FATE

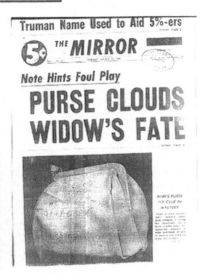

October 6, 1949

Dr. George Hodel arrested by LAPD Juvenile detectives for Incest and Child Molestation and booked. Hodel posts bail and is released from custody.

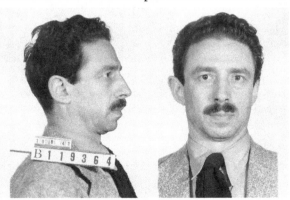

George Hodel October 6, 1949 booking photo for incest/child molestation.

October 7, 1949

Actress Jean Spangler goes on a date with a man fitting George Hodel's description and is seen at several Hollywood locations with him late that same night and into the early morning hours of October 8.

The last sighting was at a Hollywood gas station in the early mornings hours of October 8, where a terrified Spangler yells out to the attendant, "Get our license plate and call the police."

Spangler is never seen again. Her purse is found two days later discarded in Fern Dell Park, just a half-mile from George Hodel's residence.

A handwritten note by Spangler is found in her purse suggesting she may have had or intended to obtain an abortion.

1949 Jean Spangler murder

October 14, 1949

A preliminary hearing was held in Municipal Court and Dr. George Hodel is charged with two felony counts. (Incest and child molestation.) Witnesses provide testimony at that hearing, and George Hodel is "held to answer" and bound over to Superior Court where his full trial is set for December 8, 1949.

Mid-October 1949

LADA Lt. Frank Jemison, DA-Bureau of Investigation is assigned by 1949 Grand Jury to take over the Black Dahlia and other unsolved Lone Woman Murders from LAPD, and he begins his DA investigation forming an eighteen-man Task Force. (LAPD insists some of their detectives be included to "assist" as they want to have their own eyes and ears monitoring the DA investigation.)

October 25, 1949

LAPD Confidential Informant W. Glenn Martin writes his three-page letter, providing information on "GH" as being the actual killer of Elizabeth "Black Dahlia" Short as well as "GH" personally being acquainted (along with himself) with the murder victim, Louise Springer before her death.

Martin writes that GH is the likely killer of Springer who was sadistically murdered just four months earlier.

Martin seals and secrets the letter in his personal effects, and it is not found for another sixty-nine years—some forty-two years after his own death in 1976.

October 28, 1949

Just three days after Martin writes his letter, and completely independent of his naming GH as the Dahlia / Springer killer, DA Lt. Frank Jemison provides his first preliminary written report to the 1949 Grand Jury. (This report was confidential and remained so until being discovered locked in the DA vault along with the other Hodel / Black Dahlia Files in 2003 where they were first revealed in the updated paperback edition of *Black Dahlia Avenger* in 2004.)

I quote directly from page three of that typewritten report by Lt. Jemison where he makes the following recommendation in secret to the 1949 Grand Jury:

> "On the date of this report, [October 28, 1949] there are
> one hundred and seven remaining possible suspects after
> a definite elimination of two hundred and nine suspects.
> There have been nineteen suspects who have confessed
> to the murder of Elizabeth Short.

After examination of the files and evidence it appears that the investigative effort should be continued and concentrated on the following suspects:

Leslie Dillon—Mark Hanson[sic]—Carl Balsiger—Glen Wolfe—Henry Hubert Hoffman—Dr. *George Hodel*— [emphasis mine]

[SKH Note: George Hodel is named here even prior to his trial, which will not begin until mid-December 1949 –some six-weeks before the forty-two-day electronic stakeout of Hodel's residence (Feb 15-March 27, 1950).]

In that future stakeout Lt. Jemison will obtain George Hodel's recorded admissions to" killing both the Black Dahlia, and his personal secretary, Ruth Spaulding and to other crimes, and police payoffs."

In his October 28, 1949 report to the Grand Jury Lt. Jemison advises that Hodel should be placed at the top of their suspect list. Also, of the other four named suspects *Dr. Hodel is the only one capable of the skilled surgical bisection (hemicorpectomy) that was performed on Elizabeth Short's body.]*

Lt. Jemison at the close of this written report to the 1949 Grand Jury also mentions a possible sixth suspect as "Elizabeth Short's unidentified doctor." Jemison writes:

"Also, the victim's doctor, as he is a suspect and he is unknown. Victim has stated to several persons that she was taking treatments from a Los Angeles Doctor for female trouble and asthma just prior to her death."

As I previously observed in *BDA* (2004), it is my opinion that Elizabeth Short's "unidentified downtown doctor" and my father *were one and the same.*

We know that Lieutenant Jemison's euphemistic term, "female trouble" refers to her Bartholin's gland cyst. This could have originated as a sexually transmitted disease. The logical location for her to seek treatment? My father's First Street VD Clinic in DTLA.

Independent of Lt. Jemison's report to the Grand Jury we will also learn (as will Lt. Jemison three months hence, in late January 1950) that George Hodel "knew and was acquainted with Elizabeth Short" which he documents in his later investigative findings and the transcribed interview he conducts with my mother, Dorothy Hodel in March of 1950.

Additional information developed in BDA II [published in 2012] established that George Hodel likely originally met Elizabeth Short in Los Angeles as early as 1943 when she posed for paintings for his close personal friend, surrealist artist, Man Ray. (Posed for his *L'Equivoque* painting in 1943)

Based on the fact that George and Elizabeth were personally acquainted and dated before her murder, vastly increases the likelihood that George Hodel was Lt. Jemison's "unknown downtown doctor/suspect" who would have been providing her gratis medical treatment out of his First Street Clinic, or his private Franklin Avenue residence in Hollywood.

At the close of his report to the 1949 grand jury, Lt. Jemison makes the following remarkably candid observations

> ...

> These records and reports which were obtained from the officers of the police department and the Chief of Police indicated to the undersigned that the present administrators of the police department are of the opinion that there was an error made on the part of the preceding administrators when they assigned the Gangster Squad and Dr. Paul De River [sic] as psychiatrist to investigate the Short murder. They appear to be of the opinion that the Homicide Division officers should have had control over it at all times.

> The LAPD records and reports indicate some stupidity and carelessness on the part of some of the more inexperienced officers who were working on the case from time to time, but as of this report dated October 28, 1949† there has not been found any indication of payoff, misconduct or concealment of facts on the part of any officers.

> It is the consensus of Officers Ed Barrett, Jack Smyre, F.A. Brown, and the undersigned that there is insufficient evidence as of this date, October 28, 1949, upon which any suspect could now be brought to trial for the murder of Elizabeth Short.

> Respectfully submitted,
> Frank B. Jemison
> [Presented to Grand Jury on October 28, 1949]

...

On the date of this report there are one hundred and seven
remaining possible suspects after a definite elimination of
two hundred and nine suspects. There have been nineteen suspects
who have confessed to the murder of Elizabeth Short.

AFter examination of the files and evidence it appears that
the investigative effort should be continued and concentrated on
the following suspects:

      Leslie Dillon -- Mark Hanson -- Carl Balsiger -- Glen
      Wolfe -- Henry Hubert Hoffman -- Dr. George Hodel --

-4-

      Also the victim's doctor, as he is a suspect and he is
unknown. (Victim has stated to several persons that she
was taking treatments from a Los Angeles Doctor for female
trouble and asthma just prior to her death.)

...

*A scan of original October 28, 1949, DA Lt. Jemison's typed report to 1949
Grand Jury naming Dr. George Hodel as prime suspect in Black Dahlia murder.*

Examining the W. Glenn Martin Letter's Contents

GLENN MARTIN HANDWROTE HIS letter just three weeks after my father's
arrest for the Incest and Child Molestation (October 6) and prior to his
actual trial.

Clearly, Martin is terrified that "GH," who knows and is associated
with one or both of his daughters, will harm one or both of them.

He writes and seals the letter "In Case of Their Deaths." While Martin
only refers to him as "GH," it is clear he knows LAPD knows who he
is referring to and claims they are working to protect "GH" from being
connected to both the Black Dahlia and Louise Springer murders.

Here are some bullet points on the contents of the letter:

- Glenn Martin is personally acquainted with, and he and his mother are
having dinner with "GH" when LAPD calls his home.
- On the call, LAPD detective McCawley asks Martin if he wants to work
a job for them? Probably undercover as a CI (Confidential Informant).

- An individual calls back the same night and asks to speak with "GH" who indicates he will meet with him, "Ray" the following morning. [I believe this is a separate caller and probably totally unrelated to the earlier Martin call from "McCawley."]
- Martin writes that his daughter, Margaret Ellen was taken to a hotel and met with an attorney Joe Choate and Sgt. McCawley who try to get her to fabricate a lie that her father killed "The Black Dahlia." He writes, "GH was with Joe when he took her to hotel & knew he would get out of it."
- Martin goes on to write that these officers are friendly with GH and that GH was the actual killer of the Dahlia.
- Martin acknowledges in the letter that both he and GH knew the victim Louise Springer and that GH "was grilled by detectives who believe GH killed Springer," but because he was friends with LAPD, they covered it up."
- Martin claims GH was upset with Martin because he believed he (Martin) turned the police onto him on the Springer Murder and speculates that GH may seek "revenge" on him by harming one or both of Martin's daughters, which is the reason he writes the letter, "In Case of their Death."
- Martin goes on to implicate attorney Joe Choate in the corruption and cover-up by LAPD detectives who were attempting to transfer the guilt from GH to Martin and or? [In 1949 Choate was a private attorney and had been a former LA Deputy DA for six years in the late twenties and early thirties, a very corrupt time in LA which continued through the early Fifties. In 1948 Choate was Gen. MacArthur's California for America campaign manager.]
- It is obvious that the "GH" referenced by Martin is known to law enforcement (LAPD) and is friends with attorney Joe Choate.
- Knowing this, Martin did not need to provide GH's full name, since GH was directly involved with Choate and McCawley and was in effect an "accomplice."
- On page two of the Martin letter he writes, "It now developes G.H. got credit at "Starr" 949 S. Brdway. On it he says his wife's name is Ellen." At the time this letter was written by Glenn Martin, George Hodel was known to be actively engaged in a relationship with his housemaid,

"Ellen," and numerous sexual encounters between them ("Sounds like George got another blowjob from Ellen") were tape-recorded and later documented by the stakeout detectives in the Hodel DA transcripts., just three months after Martin made his "Ellen" mention in this letter.

Absent additional information, we may never be able to prove that the "GH" mentioned in the Martin letter was in fact, George Hodel.

However, what are the odds that another "GH" was also known and was actively being investigated by LAPD and the DA?

George Hodel was named not only in confidential LAPD reports but also as the top suspect identified and *named by Lt. Jemison in his report to the Grand Jury just three days after this letter was written.*(None of these written police reports would have been known or accessible to Glenn Martin.)

Martin in this letter in real time, just months after the Springer murder, confirms what LAPD homicide detectives Harry Hansen and Finis Brown suspected back in 1949, that the Dahlia and Springer murders were likely committed by the same suspect.

Further, he states boldly that both he and GH knew the Springer victim and that GH "was grilled by LAPD detectives for that reason." (*To this day, to my knowledge, current Cold Case LAPD detectives have never even looked at the Springer case, as being serially related, though as previously stated, the original detectives believed it and other "Lone Woman Murders" were connected to the Dahlia murder.)*

While speculative only at this point, Glenn Martin's connection to my father may have been through my grandfather.

Why?

According to Martin's granddaughter, Sandi Nichols, her grandfather worked as an insurance agent for Occidental and or Prudential Insurance in downtown LA in the thirties and forties.

My own paternal grandfather (George Hodel Sr.) was a senior insurance agent for *Equitable Life Insurance*, and in October 1949 he was just months away from retiring after being employed with the company for thirty-five years. (1915-1950) His office was located at 607 S. Hill St. in downtown Los Angeles.

My guess is that my father, George Hodel was somehow acquainted with Martin's daughter, Margaret Ellen back in 1949, even though she was just eighteen.

Alternatively, she could have been a patient at his First Street Clinic, and just temporarily in Los Angeles visiting her father and grandmother at their home?

According to Sandi Nichols, her grandfather, Glenn Martin divorced their mother in LA in 1944, and the ex-wife and two daughters relocated to Indianapolis, Indiana. Sandi also indicated that her mother, Margaret Ellen did not want to leave LA in 1944 stating, "I know she wanted to stay and break into Hollywood."

The fact that Margaret Ellen was "taken to a hotel and grilled by attorney Choate and Sgt. McCawley" in the presence of GH, in an apparent attempt to get her to claim her father, Glenn Martin, "killed the Black Dahlia" indicates something extremely nefarious was underway. This action by itself suggests that Glenn Martin's relationship with LAPD must have been that of a confidential informant and suggests that he was serving as their conduit to the criminal underworld in Los Angeles.

From Martin's wording in the letter, perhaps my use of "confidential informant" might be a bit high class for him. Glenn Martin comes off sounding more like a cheap hood and a "snitch," a "stool pigeon," or in the colloquialism of that day just, "a stoolie."

My basis for this includes: 1) His close personal association to George Hodel, 2) the fact that according to his granddaughter, "none of our relatives wanted anything to do with him" and after the 1944 divorce he became persona non grata, 3) his statement revealing that LAPD detectives attempted to coerce his daughter into accusing him of being "the Black Dahlia suspect," and finally, 4) the tone and verbiage used in his letter which, at least to my ear, sounds much more like a street-thug than an "insurance agent."

The Named "Players" in W. Glenn Martin's Letter

THE FOLLOWING INDIVIDUALS ARE named and referenced in the Martin Letter:

1. Attorney Joe Choate
2. LAPD Sgt. McCawley
3. Margaret Ellen (daughter)
4. Glenna Jean (daughter)
5. Lucille Bowen Hodges (possible murder victim?)

6. LAPD Jack Donahue (Donahoe)
7. "Ray"?
8. "Nell Vaughn" (519 S. Grandview)
9. "Oakes"
10. Eva Krone (guilty arson/murder in Crestline)
11. Louise Springer

JOE CHOATE

Attorney Joseph Choate Los Angeles Times *September 15, 1946*

The following is from the *Los Angeles Times* October 18, 1997 (Some thirty-seven-years after Joe Choate is mentioned in the Martin Letter.)

Joseph Choate—Longtime Lawyer Wrote About Gen. MacArthur

October 18, 1997

Joseph Choate Sr., 97, believed to be the second oldest attorney in California. A graduate of UC Berkeley, he studied international law at Harvard and Oxford universities. *Choate was a deputy district attorney in Los Angeles from 1927 to 1934 before opening a general practice law firm.* [Emphasis mine] Choate was a friend of Gen. Douglas MacArthur and was head of the California committee to nominate the World War II hero for president in 1948. He later wrote the book, "Douglas MacArthur, As I Knew Him."

JOSEPH CHOATE WAS BORN on January 14, 1900 [ironically, the same day that Elizabeth "Black Dahlia Short" was abducted and murdered.] Choate died on October 14, 1997. [Ironically, the same day that Dr. George Hodel was "held to answer" in Superior Court on two felony counts: Incest and Child Molestation.]

At age eighteen, he shows a draft registration (WWI) under the name of Walter Joseph Choate with a residence address of 610 E. Shorb Ave, Los Angeles. (Alhambra)

February 28, 1931, he is now employed by the LADA's office as a criminal prosecutor and DDA's Joseph Choate, and Gene Blalock win a murder conviction on the Eberly/Hatch murder which occurred three years prior.

May 4, 1939, Joseph Choate marries Miss Dorothy Drew of Boston at Scotty's Castle in Redlands. (See article below From Santa Ana Register)

Married In Scotty's Castle

Joseph Choate, now an international attorney at Los Angeles, and native son of Santa Ana, and Dorothy Drew, writer and musician, were married yesterday at Death Valley Scotty's huge castle in the middle of the desert, United Press wire. dispatches said today. The ceremony was the first of its kind ever held at the castle.

Scotty and his partner, A. M. Johnson, participated in the ceremony, Scotty acting as best man, while Johnson, a retired banker, gave away the bride.

The wedding was permitted at the castle only because Choate is counsel for Scotty, it was said. Scene of the marriage was the luxurious music room of the castle. Choate is a direct descendant of the original Joseph Choate, noted New York attorney and orator who once fought Tammany Hall, while Miss Drew is a member of a prominent Boston family.

During the 1940s Joseph Choate maintains his law office at 530 West Sixth Street, just two blocks from George Hodel's medical office at Seventh and Flower Street.

LAPD CAPTAIN JACK DONAHOE

LAPD Captain Jack Donahoe

THE LEGENDARY POLICE CAPTAIN who reportedly "knew where all the bodies were buried."

In 1947 Captain Donahoe was in charge of LAPD Homicide at the time of the Elizabeth Short, "Black Dahlia" murder.

He assigned detectives, Harry Hansen, and Finis Brown, to be the lead detectives on the case.

Three weeks after the Elizabeth Short murder, a Mrs. Jeanne French was savagely beaten and stomped to death, and her nude body was posed on a vacant lot some seven miles directly west of the Dahlia's body.

The killer used lipstick to write on her body "Fuck You B.D." (Black Dahlia) Captain Donahoe in charge of both investigations publicly confirmed that "the French and Dahlia murders were connected."

> "Choate always knew and was paid off as att. First and then blackmail. Now $$ have stopped & Grand Jury is pressing. Not Grand Jury bribe, but Choate to a Police Officer, ether Jack Donohue or McCawley."
>
> W. Glenn Martin Letter, October 25, 1949

Below is an excerpt from *BDA* written back in 2002 related to Captain Jack Donahoe. [Of course, at that time I never suspected that his name might surface some sixteen-years later in a letter from an LAPD confidential informant accusing him of "receiving bribes and or payoffs."]

Captain Jack Donahoe

LAPD's Captain Jack Donahoe and the very real part he played in the Dahlia investigation has, for me, become one of the most enigmatic questions of my own investigation. We may never discover his true role. Was he hero or villain? There is no simple answer, and probably like Chief Parker, he was both.

It's clear from the outset that he controlled the Dahlia investigation because it was his administrative responsibility as the captain of Homicide Division. In the early weeks, he fully cooperated with the press and provided them with ongoing updates about where the investigation was heading. In my estimation, and certainly by today's standards, he was overly candid and released far too many investigative details that should have been kept secret. The press's ability to stroke one's ego on page one each morning can be a not-so-subtle seduction, and Captain Jack may have simply enjoyed and succumbed to the notoriety. But Donahoe didn't last too long as the supervisor of the Dahlia investigation, because once he went public with his belief that the Elizabeth Short and Jeanne French murders were connected, Chief of Detectives Thad Brown promptly removed him.

It is obvious to me that, at least initially, Donahoe didn't know who committed the murder of Elizabeth Short and was actively and energetically chasing every lead. Had he possessed knowledge of the suspect or been involved in the cover-up, he would not have pursued the investigation so aggressively or released vital information to the press and public in the hope of developing new leads. Donahoe was taken off both investigations by his superiors, presumably by Chief of Detectives Thad Brown, in mid-February 1947.

His years inside the detective bureau and his promotions during the 1930s and '40s would have assured Donahoe of being in the loop within the department. While no one knows what he did or didn't do, whether he was on the take or not, we certainly can be confident that having survived the corrupt years of Mayor Frank Shaw and Chief James Davis and "the Purge," he knew who was dirty and who was not. He was Chief Thad Brown's right-hand man, and in this case, the right hand had to know what the left hand was doing.

If Donahoe was not actively involved in corruption, he certainly knew of its existence. His position as captain in charge of the Homicide Division would have placed him in direct supervision of Charles Stoker's "Bill Ball and Joe Small." It is difficult to believe that Donahoe could or would have turned a deaf ear to this large-scale operation without either taking his share of the profits or taking action to eliminate the corruption, which was an immediate threat to his power and authority as Homicide commander. If he did know of the Dahlia-French-Spangler cover-ups, it would make Captain Jack as dark and as sinister a police captain as his fictional counterpart, Captain Dudley Smith, in James Ellroy's novel *L.A. Confidential*.

Donahoe retired fifteen years after the murder of Elizabeth Short and, like the fictional Captain Smith, died a hero to the department and the world. Here are extracts from what the *Los Angeles Herald Examiner* had to say about the man and his career in his obituary of June 20, 1966:[7]

37-YEAR L.A. POLICE VETERAN
CAPT. JACK DONAHOE DIES

Capt. Jack Donahoe, sixty-four, was mourned today by law enforcement officers everywhere.

One of the most noted detectives in the country Donahoe died yester-day at his Hollywood home after a lengthy illness…

After thirty-seven years on the Los Angeles Police Department, the detective better known as "Captain Jack" retired four years ago. He was honored by more

---

7   Three weeks later, Chief Parker would suffer a massive heart attack while giving a public speech and die. Thad Brown would then assume command.

than seven hundred men and women from every walk of life at an official banquet at the Police Academy...

The six foot one, more than two-hundred-pound enemy of crime, had been suffering for the past three years from a back injury, and was found dead in his living room chair by his wife, Ann...

On Donahoe's retirement, Chief of Detectives Thad Brown said: "I have lost my right hand."

What I, then only a three-year rookie out of the Hollywood Division, and most of the rest of LAPD were never told was that Captain Jack, at 11:21 on the morning of June 18, 1966, while seated in his living room chair, had removed his service revolver, placed it over his heart, and pulled the trigger. His death report, a public record, reads not "after a lengthy illness" but "John Arthur Donahoe, Suicide, Cause of Death—Gunshot Wound of Chest Perforating Heart and Aorta with Massive Hemorrhage."

It is almost certain that we will never know why this senior command officer, the highest-ranking detective assigned to the Black Dahlia murder investigation, took his own life. Was it illness? Depression? Or was it guilt? If he left a suicide note or explanation of any kind, it has long since been destroyed.

Even though we may never discover the entire truth about what actually took place inside the LAPD during the years from 1947 to 1950, it's possible to speculate with confidence about what probably happened as the two candidates for chief, Brown, and Parker vied for power. I firmly believe that both men, possibly thinking they were acting in the department's best interests, actively covered up not only the abortion ring investigation, but the Dahlia, French, Spangler, and other sexual homicides as well. Even the grand jury investigation of 1949 could not pry the full story loose.

LAPD SGT. MCCAWLEY

INFORMATION IS PENDING FURTHER investigation on my attempts to confirm the actual identity of Glenn Martin's "St. McCawley."

With the caveat that without a first name or additional information, I cannot be certain, still, I believe and have high confidence that I know the identity of the officer named in Glenn Martin's letter.

I believe that officer referenced in Martin's letter was not "McCawley," but rather was—KENNETH J. MCCAULEY.

Here is what my research has revealed.

K. J. MCCAULEY BACKGROUND

KENNETH J. MCCAULEY was born on April 18, 1910, in California.

He married Carmen M. Conly on January 23, 1933. Carmen, just eighteen, had graduated from Los Angeles' Lincoln High School in 1932. They had two daughters.

McCauley joined LAPD in 1937. He took a leave of absence from the police force to serve in World War II, and records show he "returned to LAPD from war service on October 25, 1945."

Kenneth McCauley's rise on the Department was meteoric. Promoted to Sergeant in the mid-forties, Police Lieutenant in 1949, Captain in 1950, and to Police Inspector in 1955.

When I joined LAPD in 1963 Inspector McCauley was a highly respected "old school" veteran command officer. When I promoted to Homicide Detective and was assigned to the Hollywood Homicide Unit in the early 1970s, McCauley was still on the job with 34-years' service and had a sterling reputation.

Let's focus now on what was publicly known about then Sgt. Kenneth McCauley back in the late forties, which is the time (October 25, 1949) that the Martin Letter was written.

Here is why I believe K. J. McCauley and Glenn Martin's "Sgt. McCawley" are the same individual.

Kenneth McCauley was one of then Inspector William H. Parker's "Golden Boys."

Like Parker, McCauley was a WWII veteran with twelve years on the job.

Sgt. McCauley in 1948 was initially assigned to the LAPD Personnel Division.

His duties consisted of investigating police corruption complaints and prosecuting bad cops for their misconduct and exonerating the good ones. Personnel Division was the precursor to what a year later would become the newly established "Internal Affairs Division."

From 1948–1950 Sgt. McCauley's name appeared as one of the investigators and or the LAPD spokesman in almost every major police corruption scandal of that day.

These included most of the *LA Times* headlined cases occurring in 1948–1950: The Madam Brenda Allen Scandal, Mobster Mickey Cohen, Whistleblower Sgt. Charles Stoker Investigation, Chief Horrall's Perjury Trial, Sgt. Jackson/Brenda Allen Police Payoff Scandal, the Dr. Kirk Police Payoff Abortion Ring investigation, etc.

In 1949 Inspector Parker promoted McCauley to Lieutenant and chose him to be his right-hand man in his newly established Internal Affairs Division.

The *Los Angeles Times* headline for July 23, 1949, read:

NEW POLICE BUREAU TO HANDLE
COMPLAINTS AGAINST OFFICERS

LAPD Internal Affairs Division established July 23, 1949
Lt. Kenneth McCauley appointed as Insp. Parker's Executive Officer

Excerpts from the July 23, 1949 article:

> ...
>
> Chief of Police Worton took another step in Police
> Department reorganization yesterday when he created
> a new Bureau of Internal Affairs which he charged with
> the duty of dealing with complaints against officers and
> department employees.
>
> William H. Parker, who was recently named staff
> inspector, was placed in command of the new bureau.
>
> ...
>
> **Staff of 12**
>
> The staff under Inspector Parker will consist of Capt.
> Cecil Wisdom, who was one of the witnesses before the
> county grand jury as to the Brenda Allen recordings, Lt.
> Kenneth J. McCauley, eight sergeants and two women
> shorthand reporters.

*July 13, 1949 photo of Lt. Kenneth McCauley (standing) with Capt. W. H.
Wingard (seated) interviewing two witnesses ("party girls") related to the
Sgt. Stoker/Brenda Allen arrest and investigation.*

MOVES — Police Inspector
William H. Parker takes
quarters of deputy chief.

Los Angeles Times *photo of Inspector Parker in 1949*

Lt. McCauley—Black Hat, White Hat, or Gray?

INSPECTOR WILLIAM H. PARKER known to the rank and file as "Whisky Bill" in 1949 was exactly where he wanted to be.

As Commander of the newly established Internal Affairs Division, he would use his position to first, "Clean Up Dodge" and rid the Department of its long-entrenched "bad apples."

With twenty-years plus on the Department, Parker knew most of the corrupt officers' names and how their gambling and prostitution fiefdoms were being operated.

Parker appointed Lt. Kenneth J. McCauley to be his right-hand man, his Sword of Damocles with which Parker would root out the Department's Evil Doers and make them an offer they couldn't refuse—"Retire or be fired, prosecuted, and go to prison."

Parker with the aid of Lt. McCauley and a handful of other loyal Internal Affairs detectives, played hardball in this house of cards for just over a year.

272 | Steve Hodel

His reward?

In August 1950. William H. Parker was appointed chief of police and would remain in power ruling the LAPD with an iron "proactive" fist for the next sixteen years, until his death from a stroke in 1966, just a year after the Watts Riots.

Based on the timeline of events and his position as an attack dog in Internal Affairs during the exact time Glenn Martin wrote his letter, I am confident that Kenneth McCauley was in fact, Martin's, "St. McCawley."

Let's review Martin's Letter and his statements that relate specifically to "Sgt. McCawley."

Martin writes:

> ...
>
> "This is what happened. I or we Mother, G.H. & me were eating supper. St. McCawley of LA Police Dept called me & said I have another one night job for you like before. Well you take it"? I said I'll be down in AM and talk to you about it." (I had worked on 2 different nights for him. I knew not what job was to be till I was with him & others officers those night. Then it was to try to see if other officers could be inveigled into crime.
>
> ...
>
> I believe Joe Choate who Margaret Ellen feared took her to the Hotel where the police especially McCawley tried to make her admit that I, her father had committed the much famous Black Dalia.
>
> ...
>
> I believe Chaote Framed this with McCawley to make M.E. mistake or accuse another so the real killer would continue free. Choate always knew and was paid off at att. First and then blackmail. Now $$ have stopped & Grand Jury is pressing. Not Grand Jury bribe, but Choate to a Police Officer, ether Jack Donohue or McCawley.

These "McCawley" accusations of corruption, bribes, and heavy-handedness sound more like a snitch's speculations, Martin's, "I believe," rather than actual hardcore facts.

Little is known about W. Glenn Martin other than what he tells us in the letter, which is that he had worked undercover for McCauley on two prior occasions. Those jobs involved what sounds like "a sting operation" where he was attempting, at their direction, to see if specific LAPD officers would be willing to involve themselves in, or be, in Martin's words "inveigled into committing crimes."

Add to this the fact that apparently because of Martin's admitted association and friendship with "GH" the officers transported his eighteen-year-old, daughter, Mary Ellen, to a hotel, where they reportedly interrogated and pressured her in an attempt to connect her father as a possible accomplice in the then two-year-old murder of Elizabeth "Black Dahlia" Short. (Recall, that at this time, though unbeknownst to Martin, DA Lt. Frank Jemison was just one month away from declaring in secret to the 1949 Grand Jury that Dr. George Hodel was the top suspect in the Black Dahlia murder.)

Finally, and separate from these facts, we have Martin informing McCauley that "Both he and GH personally knew and were acquainted with victim Louise Springer" prior to her sadistic murder, which occurred just months (June 1949) before his writing the letter.

This information of course, resulted in GH being "grilled by LAPD" on the Springer murder (and possibly on the Dahlia?) and became the impetus for Martin documenting the information out of fear that GH would seek revenge on Martin for "snitching him out" by possibly harming one or both of his daughters.

Though at this stage of the investigation, we are getting only a "soft focus" picture of W. Glenn Martin, still it is one of a man apparently steeped in LA crime. A man seemingly well-connected to the underworld, who could, for the most part, walk amongst them freely, but also a man who some suspected of being an informant and a snitch, because in Martin's words referring to those connected to specific crimes in the San Bernardino area:

"These crowd knew I worked for Law and did not have me in there crowd."

Washington Glenn Martin

BORN AUGUST 4, 1893, in Indianapolis, Indiana. Registered for the draft in WWI on June 5, 1917, at age 18. Residence address at that time was, 949 Sanders St., Indianapolis Indiana. He gave his profession as "Chauffeur."

Married Mary M. Taylor (date of birth, April 8, 1906) in Marion, Indiana on June 24, 1925. Daughter, Glenna Jean Martin, born in Indianapolis, Indiana, in 1926,

Shortly after their marriage, circa 1931, the family moved to Los Angeles, California.

In advance of the families relocation, Glenn Martin came west to look for employment and in a letter home dated June 12, 1931, he wrote that he was attempting to obtain employment with the Los Angeles District Attorney's Office. I quote from a section of that letter provided me by his granddaughter, Sandi Nichols.

> …You cannot imagine the vastness of this place. Beautiful and otherwise;. I was out to Long Beach. It is the same way. Have not seen Venice & Ocean Park. Went thro (sic) the boulevard. *Have been trying to get a Good Job, first With Fitts, office District Attorney. Don't know yet.* [Emphasis mine.]

A scan of W. Glenn Martin's 1931 letter indicating
he is seeking employment with LADA.

This information is of interest for the following reasons.

While Glenn Martin did not get the job with the LADA's Office then headed by legendary DA Buron Fitts, we know that, as mentioned previously, Joe Choate in 1931 was employed as a deputy district attorney working for Fitts on active criminal prosecutions.

Also of interest is the fact that in 1934, LADA Buron Fitts would be indicted for perjury and hired top criminal defense attorneys Jerry Giesler and William E. Simpson to defend him.

Fifteen years later, in 1949, at the same time Glenn Martin wrote his "In Case of Death" letter, Giesler would be hired by my father, Dr. George Hill Hodel to defend him in trial for the incest and child molestation charges. (October to December 1949)

Giesler's ex-defense partner, William Simpson had by then become Los Angeles's district attorney and would have been aware that Dr. Hodel was his investigator, Lt. Frank Jemison's "prime Black Dahlia suspect."

Four months later, William Simpson still in charge of the DA's Office, would also have been the one to order the return of all the evidence, witness statements and taped confessions made by Dr. Hodel to the custody of the LAPD, and give the order to Lt. Jemison to "back off and shut it down."

November 1934 Buron Fitts indicted in LA for perjury

*Attorney Jerry Giesler (lt) DA Buron Fitts (middle) and William Simpson (rt)
in court in 1934 preparing Fitts defense on perjury charges.*

A second daughter, Margaret Ellen was born to Glenn and Mary Martin in Los Angeles on November 12, 1931.

Glenn and Mary divorced in 1944, and his wife and two daughters moved back to Indianapolis, Indiana.

According to Martin's letter, his younger daughter, Margaret Ellen, returned to Los Angeles [possibly only for a short visit?] and became involved with LAPD who interrogated her at a hotel. It is believed this occurred in 1949, but Glenn Martin provided no exact date of the police contact, so could have been earlier?

In my interview with Martin's granddaughter, Sandi, though she had minimal information on her grandfather, she did state that during his time in Los Angeles "he was employed as an insurance agent with the Prudential Insurance Company."

W. Glenn Martin died in North Hollywood, California, on July 3, 1976, at age eighty-three.

In early September, Sandi Nichols mailed me a second packet containing some of her grandfather's additional personal effects. Included were some family photographs along with a hardbound "Desk Private" book for the year 1947.

Inside the book, Glenn Martin had written:

> "This Belongs to W. Glenn Martin, 1806 5th AVE, Los Angeles 6, California."

Within the pages of this book, Martin had secreted an original newspaper article from the *Los Angeles Herald-Express* dated Wednesday, March 17, 1948, headlined, "Missing- Have You Seen Any of These Girls?

The article displayed the names and photographs of four Missing Girls and requested the public's help in locating them. (See below photograph).

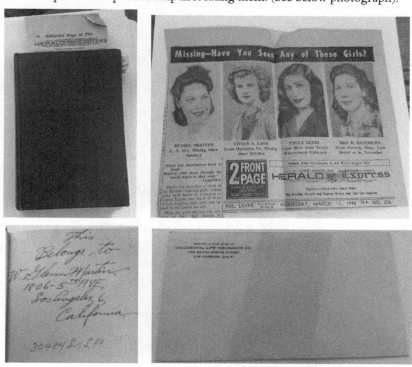

1948 LA "Missing Girls" Muriel Shaffer, Vivian A. Lash, Paula Rubio, Mrs. R. Matthews

Also found inside Martin's "1947 Private Desk Calendar" was an unaddressed blank envelope with a return address that read, "Return in five days to OCCIDENTAL LIFE INSURANCE CO. 756 South Spring Street Los Angeles." (This may have been a second employer of Glenn Martin?)

W. Glenn Martin in 1928(top left), 1953 (top right), and 1954 (bottom).

Margaret Ellen Martin

THE YOUNGEST DAUGHTER OF W. Glenn Martin. Born in Los Angeles in 1931.

After her mother, Mary M. Martin (Taylor) divorced her father in 1944; she returned with her mother and older sister, Glenna Jean, to Indianapolis, Indiana.

Margaret Ellen married in 1951 in Indianapolis, had a daughter in 1958, and passed away on October 4, 2015.

Margaret Ellen Martin 1949

Glenna Jean Martin

ELDEST DAUGHTER OF W. Glenn Martin. Born in Indianapolis, Indiana, in 1926. Lived with parents in Los Angeles until their divorce in 1944, when she returned to Indianapolis, with her mother and sister, Margaret Ellen.

Glenna Jean died in Tempe, Arizona, in 1997.

Glenna Jean Martin, 1943, age seventeen (Los Angeles)

Aurilla Bland Polen Martin

BORN ON APRIL 15, 1870, in Indiana. Mother of Washington Glenn Martin.

According to her son's letter, she was acquainted with "GH" and had dinner with him and her son at their residence, sometime in 1949.

The 1940 US Federal Census shows that Aurilla (age seventy), Glenn (age forty-seven), Mary (age thirty-four), Glenna Jean (age thirteen), and Margaret Ellen (age nine) were all living together in the same residence in Los Angeles, California.

Aurilla Martin died in Los Angeles on October 19, 1956.

Aurilla and Glenn Martin 1920 (Tijuana, Mexico)

Louise Springer

THE LOUISE SPRINGER MURDER
JUNE 13, 1949

THIS MURDER OCCURRED JUST four months before Glenn Martin wrote his letter.

Like the Elizabeth Short crime, it was also a kidnap/murder and occurred just *three city blocks* from the Dahlia vacant lot crime scene.

I identified and summarized the Springer murder in both BDA I and II, however; it has been mostly ignored by today's LAPD. (This even though their own, on-scene investigator, and lead Dahlia detective, *Harry Hansen was actively assigned to the case from the onset, and publicly stated his belief that the crime was very likely, "Dahlia connected."*)

"The Black Dahlia and the Louise Springer murders
might be linked. Both crimes could have been committed
by the same man."

Detective Harry Hansen, LAPD Homicide
Los Angeles Times, June 17, 1949

Harry Hansen circa 1949

LAPD Detective Harry Hansen was assigned to investigate both the
1947 Elizabeth Short and the 1949 Louise Springer Murders. Five days
into the Springer investigation he publicly informed the press that the two
crimes were possibly connected.

WHY?

LOUISE SPRINGER CRIME SUMMARY:

AT APPROXIMATELY 9:15 P.M. on the evening of June 13, 1949, Laurence
Springer, drove his new Studebaker convertible to pick-up his wife.

Louise Springer met him in the parking lot of the shopping mall on
Crenshaw Blvd, near Santa Barbara Avenue, where she worked as a beautician.

As she entered their car, Louise noticed she had left her eyeglasses
inside the beauty parlor.

Her husband offered to get them for her as he wanted to pick up the day's newspaper and cigarettes at an adjacent drugstore. He was absent less than ten minutes.

Upon his return, both his car and Louise were gone.

The husband immediately contacted LAPD who referred him to the University Division Police Station, where the desk officer advised Mr. Springer, "They could not take a formal Missing Person Report, for twenty-four hours."

The husband attempted to convince the officers that his wife would not simply drive away and that she had to have been the victim of a kidnapping, or foul play. Sadly, his pleas fell upon deaf ears.

Frustrated and angry, the husband returned to his Hollywood home to be with their three-year-old son and could only hope his wife would call.

Three days later, Laurence Springer's suspicions were confirmed. Louise Springer's body was found in the back seat of the car, which the suspect, by circumstance, had been forced to park on a quiet residential street just an hour after the abduction and murder.

Here are the investigative highlights and findings:

June 13, 1949—9:15 p.m.

The victim was kidnapped (highjacked) in her car while waiting for her husband to return to the vehicle.

The victim was sexually assaulted by a suspect who used a 14" long tree limb to sodomize victim in her vehicle.

The suspect then strangled her using a clothesline rope which he had brought with him and then moved her body to the rear seat of her car and covered her with a beautician's tarp belonging to the victim.

The kidnap location of Louise Springer (shown below) was on Crenshaw Blvd. just north of Santa Barbara. (Now renamed Martin Luther King Blvd.) This location is just five hundred yards south of where Elizabeth "Black Dahlia" Short's body parts were found at the vacant lot, at 3815 South Norton Avenue.

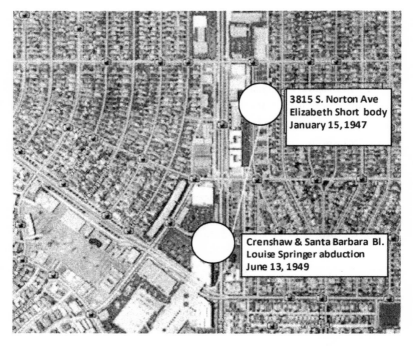

Posing of Black Dahlia in 1947 and the 1949 kidnap-murder of Louise Springer
occurred just five hundred yards apart.

June 13, 1949—10:30 p.m.

NEIGHBORHOOD WITNESSES OBSERVED SPRINGER'S vehicle being driven eastbound on Thirty-Eighth St. and saw the driver quickly swerve the car to the south curb and park in front of 126 W. Thirty-Eighth St., Los Angeles.

The driver turned off the headlights and immediately slumped down behind the driver's wheel.

Seconds later, an LAPD uniformed patrol car with its emergency lights blinking pulled over a teenage driver for a traffic violation. The driver pulled his car into a driveway immediately across the street, and the police car stopped in the street just a few feet away from the parked Springer Studebaker.

As the witnesses watched from their residence, the man in the Studebaker sat motionless and slumped down while the officers exited their patrol car and wrote a ticket to the teenager, standing directly across the street.

The officers after citing the teen then reentered their police car and drove off.

The witnesses continued looking out their window and saw the man reach toward the back seat, then after a few minutes he was seen to exit the Studebaker and walk away.

Due to the darkness, the only description they could provide was "a male with black curly hair."

These actions occurred just one-hour after the abduction, but because the witnesses were unaware that any crime had occurred, nothing was reported for three days.

On June 16, a separate neighbor became suspicious about the abandoned vehicle and called the police.

Officers in checking the license plate determined it was the missing Springer vehicle and responded to find the victim strangled to death under a tarp in the back seat.

A neighborhood check by homicide detectives for witnesses resulted in the three coming forward to describe what they saw on the night of June 13.

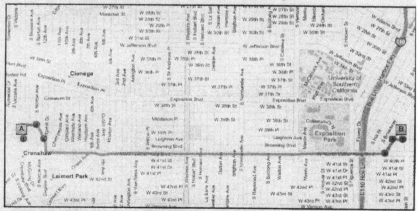

126 West Thirty-Eighth Street. Four miles (ten minutes) from abduction location.

Louise Springer Murder Headline June 17, 1949
Los Angeles Examiner—*June 18, 1949*
"Police Missed Mad Killer in Auto with Slain Victim, Parked Near Squad Car"

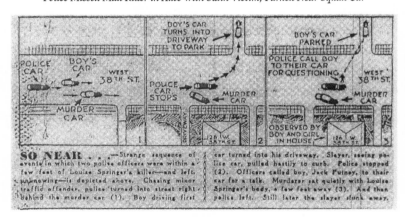

The Examiner *printed a diagram showing the relative positions of the police,
the teenage traffic offender and the murder suspect on Thirty-Eighth Street.
The article reads, "Murderer sat quietly with Louise Springer's body, a few feet
away (3). And then police left. Still later the slayer slunk away."*

1949 photo of George Hodel showing his "Black Curly Hair."
1949 Studebaker Convertible <u>similar</u> *to Springer model.*

Los Angeles Examiner of June 17, read:

> ...
>
> BODY VIOLATED
>
> "And with a 14-inch length of a finger-thick tree branch, ripped from some small tree, the killer had violated her body in such manner as to stamp this crime at once and indelibly in the same category as the killing of Elizabeth Short, "the Black Dahlia."

LAPD Criminalist Ray Pinker called in a botanist expert on the Louise Springer case who identified the tree branch as coming from a "Bottlebrush Tree."

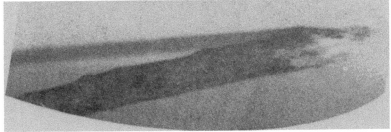

(Top) Photograph of a Bottlebrush Tree, which is indigenous to all areas of Los Angeles County. (Bottom) Photograph of the actual tree branch used in the sexual assault (sodomy) of victim Springer. As can be seen, the sadistic and enraged killer took time to sharpen one end of the tree branch before using it to assault the victim anally.
(Photo edited and cropped from original autopsy photo by author.)

In 1949, police procedures and crime-scene investigation were light years behind today's standards.

In what today's forensic and CSI would consider being an absolute "no-no," LAPD Homicide Detective Capt. Francis Kearney, accompanied by Coroner's Deputy Victor Mallage, actually drove the vehicle, *with the victim's dead body in the back seat,* from Thirty-Eighth Street to the LA County Morgue, at the Hall of Justice where Dr. Frederick Newbarr performed the autopsy. (Newbarr also performed the autopsy two years earlier on victim Elizabeth Short.)

Chief LAPD criminalist Ray Pinker took charge of the forensic investigation at the scene.

Some additional Springer investigative findings:

- Police suspected the killer might have known Louise Springer prior and theorized that her killer could have been a jealous ex-boyfriend?

  Detective Harry Hansen and his partner traveled to San Francisco for a full week of investigation into the victim's background and attempted to check out potential suspect links to her from the Bay Area.

  Newspapers of the day hinted at a "possible romantic affair and questionable paternity of her young son, Laurence Springer, twenty-one months of age, however, no hard evidence, was ever publicly released.

- Detectives determined that immediately before the murder a male called Laurence Springer's work telephone (six times) over six days and kept hanging up. He also called Springer's home residence.

Los Angeles Times
June 17, 1949

1. *Photo of Louise Springer circa 1949*

2. *Springer 1949 Studebaker convertible at the crime scene, 126 West 38th St., Los Angeles*

3. *Laurence Springer Jr., twenty-one-month-old son. [In the remote chance that the crime was one of jealousy and passion and that her suspected killer,*

Dr. George Hodel was the father of the child, even today a DNA comparison could be conducted with either Laurence Springer Jr., or one of his living relatives to that of the full DNA of my father, and or to my own. If GHH was the father, then I would be Laurence Springer Jr.'s half-brother.]

4. *Witnesses that saw the suspect in the Springer car and described his "Black Curly Hair."*

5. *LAPD Printman Keith Woodward attempting to lift fingerprints at the crime scene.*

6. *Springer residence in Hollywood at 8029 Hemet Place.*

7. *Victim's husband, Laurence Springer.*

In 1949 at the time of Louise Springer's murder both the Springer's and Hodel resided in the Hollywood Hills. The distance between their privates residences was four miles. Glenn Martin in his letter stated that both he and GH knew Lousie Springer before she was abducted and slain and that LAPD detectives "grilled GH as a suspect in her murder."

- Though LAPD continued to suspect the Springer and Elizabeth Short and other lone woman crimes were connected, Louise Springer's sadistic killer, like the others- was never publicly identified.
- The 1949 Grand Jury demanded a reinvestigation of the Elizabeth Short and other unsolved murders as is evidenced by the below 1949 headlines, where we see Louise Springer's photo added to the long list of unsolved *Lone Woman Murders.*
- For the first time in Los Angeles history, the 1949 Grand Jury ordered that these active murder investigations be taken away from LAPD and reassigned to the LADA Bureau of Investigation.

January 1947

January 12, 1950

Additionally, the following named individuals, Lucille Bowen (Hodges), "Ray," Nell Vaughn (519 S. Grandview) and "Oakes" are also pending further investigation as to their identities and potential connections as referenced in the 1949 Martin Letter.

Some Closing Thoughts

THE NEWLY DISCOVERED W. Glenn Martin Letter is important new evidence in the corroboration that Dr. George Hill Hodel was an active serial killer in 1940s Los Angeles.

Some readers will question letter writer Glenn Martin's motives and truthfulness and suggest that perhaps he was seeking "fifteen minutes of fame" or "accusing LAPD because of some perceived wronged act committed by them on or against him?"

Others will say, "Martin was a lowlife and a police snitch, and anything he says is not to be believed."

Not so.

The most convincing evidence that his letter speaks the truth is *the fact that he never intended it to become public.*

His letter was a police informant's last words, his last "snitch" to law enforcement, meant to survive beyond his death, but *never to be revealed* except in the untimely death of one or both of his daughters.

His fears of GH "seeking revenge" and harming his children never occurred, hence the letter, as intended, remained secret and unopened for sixty-nine years.

It was only by happenstance that it was discovered by his granddaughter, Sandi Nichols in July 2018.

Found in a box as she was inventorying her mother, Mary Ellen's estate.

Sandi, after reading the letter, then researched the "Black Dahlia" and as described at the outset of this chapter, contacted me and forwarded the documents, photographs, and related material.

Her actions are identical and reminiscent of Judy May's, the granddaughter of LAPD detective Harry Hansen, who also found evidence (original never before seen Black Dahlia crime scene photographs) and contacted and provided them to me to help further my investigation.

Even against some of her relative's wishes, Sandi "did the right thing" and came forward to provide critical truths that shed much light on both the Dahlia and Springer murders from seventy-years past.

The Glenn Martin letter presents readers with a never-before-seen handwritten letter of the greatest historical import.

His letter was never intended to become public, but, happenstance and the courage of a lone family member saw to it that seventy-years later—"Murder Will Out."

My sincere thanks to Sandi Nichols of Indianapolis, Indiana, for helping to advance the investigation by providing one of the most dramatic historical documents ever connected to the Black Dahlia investigation.

Steve Hodel
September 2018

Acknowledgments

A BIG THANK YOU to my good friend, Robert Sadler, the retired Dallas police officer and mystery writer for his ongoing assistance as my "partner" in helping me examine the evidence and designing the graphics. Also, Yves Person, the Paris high school teacher and my "French Connection" who not only contributed a scholarly essay expanding his thoughts on the Ogham cipher, which he originally cracked in 2015, but also volunteered his artistic skills in providing the beautiful *Through the Willows* sketches of Elizabeth Short. To all the staff at Rare Bird Books including my publisher, Tyson Cornell, my editor and designer, Hailie Johnson, a big THANK YOU AND WELL DONE. I seriously doubt any other publisher on the planet would put up with my last-minute requests to, "Hold the presses, I've got another five pages of new evidence to add."

Bibliography

Anger, Kenneth. *Hollywood Babylon*. San Francisco: Stonehill Publishing, 1975.

Anger, Kenneth. *Hollywood Babylon II*. New York: NAL Penguin, 1984.

Bonelli, William G. *Billion Dollar Blackjack*. Beverly Hills: Civic Research Press, 1954.

Blanche, Tony, and Brad Schreiber. *Death in Paradise: An Illustrated History of the Los Angeles County Department of Coroner*. Los Angeles: General Publishing Group, 1998.

Breton, Andre. *Manifestoes of Surrealism*. Ann Arbor: University of Michigan Press, Ann Arbor Paperbacks, 1972.

Bruccoli, Matthew J., and Richard Layman. *A Matter of Crime, Vol. I*. San Diego: Harcourt Brace Jovanovich, 1987.

Carter, Vincent A. *LAPD's Rogue Cops*. Lucerne Valley, Calif.: Desert View Books, 1993.

Chandler, Raymond. *The Blue Dahlia: A Screenplay. Chicago*: Southern Illinois University Press, 1976.

Cohen, Mickey. *In My Own Words*. Englewood Cliffs, NJ: Prentice-Hall, 1975.

Cox, Julian. *Spirit into Matter*. J. Paul Getty Trust. Los Angeles, 2004

Demaris, Ovid. *The Last Mafioso*. New York: Times Books, 1981.

De Rivers, J. Paul, MD. *The Sexual Criminal: A Psychoanalytical Study*. Burbank, Calif.: Bloat, 1949; rev. ed. 2000.

Domanick, Joe. *To Protect and to Serve: The L.A.P.D.'s Century of War in the City of Dreams*. New York: Pocket Books, 1994.

Douglas, John, and Mark Olshaker. *The Cases That Haunt Us*. New York: Lisa Drew Books/Scribner, 2000.

Douglas, John. *Mind Hunter*. New York: Lisa Drew Books/Scribner, 1995.

Ellroy, James. *The Black Dahlia*. New York: Mysterious Press, 1987.

Ellroy, James. *My Dark Places*. New York: Alfred A. Knopf, 1996.

Ellroy, James. *Crime Wave*. New York: Vintage Crime/Black Lizard Vintage Books, 1999.

Fetherling, Doug. *The Five Lives of Ben Hecht*. Toronto: Lester & Orpen, 1977.

Finney, Guy W. *Angel City in Turmoil*. Los Angeles: Amer Press, 1945.

Fowler, Will. *The Young Man from Denver*. Garden City, N.Y.: Doubleday & Company, 1962.

Fowler, Will *Reporters: Memoirs of a Young Newspaperman*. Malibu, Calf.: Roundtable, 1991.

Giesler, Jerry, and Pete Martin. *The Jerry Giesler Story*. New York: Simon & Schuster, 1960.

Gilmore, John. *Severed: The True Story of the Black Dahlia Murder*. San Francisco: Zanja Press, 1994.

Goodman, Jonathan. *Acts of Murder*. New York: Lyle Stuart Books, Carol Publishing Group, 1986.

Granlund, Nils T. *Blondes, Brunettes, and Bullets*. New York: David McKay, 1957.

Gribble, Leonard. *They Had a Way with Women*. London: Arrow Books, 1967.

Grobel, Lawrence. *The Hustons*. New York: Charles Scribners's Sons, 1989.

Halberstam, David. *The Powers That Be*. New York: Alfred A. Knopf, 1979.

Hall, Angus, ed. *Crimes of Horror*. New York: Phoebus, 1976.

Halleck, Seymour L., MD. *Psychiatry and the Dilemmas of Crime*. New York: Harper & Row, 1967.

Harris, Martha. *Angelica Huston: The Lady and the Legacy*. New York: St. Martin's Press, 1989.

Henderson, Bruce and Sam Summerlin. *The Super Sleuths*. New York: Macmillan, 1976.

Hecht, Ben. *Fantazius Mallare: A Mysterious Oath*. Chicago: Pascal Covici, 1922.

Hecht, Ben. *The Kingdom of Evil: A Continuation of the Journal of Fantazius Mallare*. Chicago: Pascal Covici, 1924.

Heimann, Jim. *Sins of the City: The Real L.A. Noir*. San Francisco: Chronicle Books, 1999.

Hodel, George Hill. *The New Far East: Seven Nations of Asia*. Hong Kong: Reader's Digest Far East, 1966.

Hodel, Steve, *Black Dahlia Avenger: A Genius for Murder*, Harper, New York, 2006.

Hodel, Steve, with Pezzullo, Ralph, *Most Evil: Avenger, Zodiac, and the Further Serial Murders of Dr. George Hill Hodel*, Dutton, New York, 2009.

Hodel, Steve, *Black Dahlia Avenger II*, Thoughtprint Press 2014

Hodel, Steve, *Most Evil II*, Rare Bird Books 2015

Huston, John. *An Open Book*. New York: Alfred A. Knopf, 1980.

Huston, John. *Frankie and Johnny*. New York: Albert and Charles Boni, 1930.

Jeffers, Robinson. *Roan Stallion, Tamar, and Other Poems*. New York: Boni & Liveright, 1925.

Jennings, Dean. *We Only Kill Each Other: The Life and Bad Times of Bugsy Siegel*. Englewood Cliffs, NJ: Prentice-Hall, 1967.

Kennedy, Ludovic. *The Airman and the Carpenter*. New York: Viking Penguin, 1985.

Keppel, Robert D. *Signature Killers*. New York: Pocket Books, 1997.

Klein, Norman M., and Martin J. Schiesl. *20th Century Los Angeles: Power, Promotion, and Social Conflict*. Claremont, Calif.: Regina Books, 1990.

Knowlton, Janice, and Michael Newton. *Daddy Was the Black Dahlia Killer*. New York: Pocket Books, 1995.

Lane, Brian, and Wilfred Gregg. *The Encyclopedia of Serial Killers*. New York: Diamond Books, 1992.

Martinez, Al. *Jigsaw John*. Los Angeles: J. P. Tarcher, 1975.

Morton, James. *Gangland International: An Informal History of the Mafia and Other Mobs in the Twentieth Century*. London: Little, Brown & Company, 1998.

Mayo, Morrow, *Los Angeles*, Alfred A. Knopf, New York, 1933.

Nelson, Mark and Bayliss, Sarah Hudson. *Exquisite Corpse,: Surrealism and the Black Dahlia Murder*, New York, Bulfinch Press, 2006.

Nickel, Steven. *Torso: The Story of Eliot Ness and the Search for a Psychopathic Killer*. Winston-Salem, N.C.: John F. Blair, 1989.

Pacios, Mary. *Childhood Shadows: The Hidden Story of the Black Dahlia Murder*. Downloaded and printed via electronic distribution from the World Wide Web. ISBN 1-58500-484-7, 1999.

Parker, William H. *Parker on Police*, Charles C. Thomas Publisher, Springfield, Illinois, 1957.

Parrish, Michael. *For the People*. Los Angeles: Angel City Press, 2001.

Phillips, Michelle. *California Dreamin': The True Story of the Mamas and Papas*. New York: Warner, 1986.

Rappleye, Charles, and Ed Becker. *All American Mafioso: The Johnny Rosselli Story*. New York: Doubleday, 1991.

Reid, David. *Sex, Death and Gods in L.A.* New York: Random House, 1992.

Reid, Ed. *The Grim Reapers: The Anatomy of Organized Crime in America*. Chicago: Henry Regnery, 1969.

Richardson, James H. *For the Life of Me: Memoirs of a City Editor*. New York: G. P. Putnam's Sons, 1954.

Roeburt, John. *Get Me Giesler*. New York: Belmont Books, 1962.

Rothmiller, Mike, and Ivan G. Goldman. *L.A. Secret Police: Inside the L.A.P.D. Elite Spy Network*. New York: Pocket Books, 1992.

Rowan, David. *Famous American Crimes*. London: Frederick Muller, 1957.

Sade, Donatien-Alphonse-François de. *Selected Writings of de Sade*. New York: British Book Centre, 1954.

Sade, Donatien-Alphonse-François de. *The Complete Justine, Philosophy in the Bedroom and Other Writings*. New York: Grove Press, 1965.

Sade, Donatien-Alphonse-François de. *The 120 Days of Sodom and Other Writings*. New York: Grove Press, 1966.

Sade, Donatien-Alphonse-François de. *120 Days of Sodom, or the School for Libertinage*. New York: Falstaff Press, 1934.

Sakol, Jeannie. *The Birth of Marilyn: The Lost Photographs of Norma Jean by Joseph Jasgur*. New York: St. Martin's Press, 1991.

Seaver, Richard, Terry Southern, and Alexander Trocchi, eds. *Writers in Revolt: An Anthology*. New York: Frederick Fell, 1963.

Sjoquist, Arthur W. *Captain: Los Angeles Police Department 1869–1984*. Dallas: Taylor, 1984.

Smith, Jack. *Jack Smith's L.A.* New York: McGraw-Hill, 1980.

Starr, Kevin. *Inventing the Dream: California through the Progressive Era*. New York: Oxford University Press, 1985.

Starr, Kevin. *The Dream Endures: California Enters the 1940s*. New York: Oxford University Press, 1997.

Stevenson, Robert Louis. *The Strange Case of Dr. Jekyll and Mr. Hyde and Other Stories*. New York: Barnes & Noble, 1995.

Sterling, Hank. *Ten Perfect Crimes*. New York: Stravon, 1954.

Stoker, Charles. *Thicker'n Thieves*. Santa Monica: Sidereal, 1951.

Stoker, Charles. *Thickern'n Thieves,* Los Angeles: Thoughtprint Press, 2011.

Tejaratchi, Sean, ed. *Death Scenes: A Homicide Detective's Scrapbook*. Portland: Feral House, 1996.

Terman, Lewis M. *Genetic Studies of Genius*. Vol. 1. Stanford: Stanford University Press, 1925.

Terman, Lewis M., and Melita H. Oden. *The Gifted Group at Mid-Life: Thirty-Five Years' Follow-Up of the Superior Child*. Stanford: Stanford University Press, 1959.

True Crime—Unsolved Crimes. Alexandria, Va.: Time-Life Books, 1993.

Tygiel, Jules. *The Great Los Angeles Swindle*. New York: Oxford University Press, 1994.

Viertel, Peter. *Dangerous Friends: At Large with Huston and Hemingway in the Fifties*. New York: Nan A. Talese/Bantam Doubleday Dell, 1992.

Viertel, Peter. *White Hunter Black Heart*. New York. Doubleday, 1953.

Underwood, Agness. *Newspaperwoman*. New York: Harper & Brothers, 1949.

Waldberg, Patrick. *Surrealism*. New York: Thames & Hudson, 1997.

Walker, Clifford James. *One Eye Closed the Other Red: The California Bootlegging Years*. Barstow, Calif.: Back Door Publishing, 1999.

Webb, Jack. *The Badge*. Greenwich, Conn.: Fawcett, 1958.

White, Leslie T. *Me, Detective.* New York: Harcourt, Brace & Company, 1936.

Wilson, Colin. *Murder in the 1940s.* New York: Carroll & Graf, 1993.

Woods, Gerald, *The Police in Los Angeles,* Garland Publishing Inc. New York, 1993.

Wolf, Marvin J., and Katherine Mader. *Fallen Angels: Chronicles of L.A. Crime and Mystery.* New York: Facts on File, 1986.

Weintraub, Alan. *Lloyd Wright: The Architecture of Frank Lloyd Wright Jr.* New York: Harry N. Abrams, 1998.

Work Projects Administration. *Los Angeles: A Guide to the City and its Environs.* Hastings House. New York, 1941.

MAN RAY RESEARCH–RELATED BOOKS

Foresta, Merry. *Perpetual Motif: The Art of Man Ray.* New York: Abbeville Press and the National Museum of American Art, 1988.

Man Ray. *Self Portrait.* Boston: Little, Brown & Company, 1963.

Man Ray. *Man Ray Photographs.* New York: Thames & Hudson, 1991.

Penrose, Roland. *Man Ray.* New York: Thames & Hudson, 1975.

Robert Berman Gallery. *Man Ray: Paris–L.A.* New York: Smart Art Press Art Catalog, 1996.

Butterfield and Dunning. *Fine Photographs.* Catalog, November 17, 1999.

Butterfield and Dunning. *Fine Photographs.* Catalog, May 27, 1999.

NEWSPAPER SOURCES

San Francisco Chronicle, 1969-1978; *San Francisco Examiner,* 1969-1970; *Vallejo-Times Herald,* 1969; *Los Angeles Record,* 1925; *Riverside Press Enterprise,* 1966-1971; *Los Angeles Times,* 1941-1972; *Los Angeles Mirror,* 1947; *Los Angeles Herald Express,* 1945-1951; *Los Angeles Examiner,* 1947-1950; *Chicago Daily Tribune,* 1945-1950; *The Manila Times,* 1967.

MISCELLANEOUS

FBI, FOIA Files on Elizabeth Short.

Los Angeles District Attorney, Bureau of Investigation, "Black Dahlia and Dr. George Hill Hodel Files"; Electronic Surveillance Files on George Hodel, and Investigative summaries on Black Dahlia by DA Lt. Frank B. Jemison; 146-page Hodel-Black Dahlia transcripts; Frank Jemison/Dorothy Hodel 6-page interview transcripts.

Sowden House, Historic American Survey, National Park Service, Department of Interior 1969.

WEBSITES:

Stevehodel.com

Zodiackiller.com

Lapl.org

Lmharnisch.com

BLACK DAHLIA AVENGER TELEVISION DOCUMENTARIES & SHOWS

Dateline NBC, "Black Dahlia" Josh Mankiewicz (2003, twenty-minute segment)

Court TV, "Who Killed the Black Dahlia?" Josh Mankiewicz (2003, one hour)

CBS *48-Hours Special,* "Black Dahlia Confidential" (2004, one hour)

A&E *Bill Kurtis Cold Case Files,* "Black Dahlia" (2006, one hour)

NBC Universal (France), "'The Truth about the Black Dahlia" (2006, one hour)

CNN *Anderson Cooper 360,* "Black Dahlia" (2006, eight-minute author interview)

Discovery Channel, *Most Evil* (2007, one hour)

Cadaver Dog Buster and the Black Dahlia, NBC News, Los Angeles

Pompidou Centre Author/Audience Interview (2006, ninety minutes)

Through the Decades, Author interview (2018), KCBS and Charter/Spectrum television channel

Buzzfeed, "Chilling Mystery of the Black Dahlia (2016)

CPSIA information can be obtained
at www.ICGtesting.com
Printed in the USA
LVHW040228280219
608985LV00003B/4